Contents

GIRLS PRIMARY EDUCATION

GIRLS PRIMARY EDUCATION

V.C. Pandey

ISHA BOOKS
DELHI-110 033

Girls Primary Education

ISBN: 81-8205-082-0

Published in 2007 in India by
Isha Books,
B-63, Ist Floor, New Gupta Colony,
Near DDA Market, Delhi-110 009
Phone : 9212142040
Email : ishabooks@hotmail.com

Laser Typesetting at : Shree Vaishnavi Creations, Delhi

Printed at :
Rajdhani Printers, Delhi

Preface

Girls are often treated as inferior and are socialized to put themselves last, thus undermining their self-esteem. Discrimination and neglect in childhood can initiate a lifelong downward spiral of deprivation and exclusion from the social mainstream. Existing discrimination against the girl child in her access to education, health services endangers her current and future life.

Encouraging girls to remain in school until they complete primary education has increasingly become a priority of national and international communities. With increases in the educational participation of girls, the main national development indicators improve. Some important ones are lowered infant and maternal mortality, longer life expectancy, lower fertility rates, and improvements in health, nutrition, literary, and economic growth.

Initiatives should be taken to prepare girls to participate actively, effectively and equally with boys at all levels of social, economic, political and cultural leadership. Gender-biased educational processes, including curricula, educational materials and practices, teachers' attitudes and classroom interaction, reinforce existing gender inequalities. Change can result from deliberate actions of state and civil society groups, leading to reforms in the legislative and institutional framework of society. In these ways, changes in the expectations and incentives that govern human behaviour – including those that affect educational participation and performance – can be achieved.

This book describes the importance of educating girls for social, economic, political and cultural development. It will serve as a dependable reference tool to educators, policy-makers, students, teachers, social welfare agencies and other administrative bodies concerned with women's development.

Editor

1

Girls Education

Encouraging girls to remain in school until they complete primary education has increasingly become a priority of national and international communities. With increases in the educational participation of girls, the main national development indicators improve. Some important ones are lowered infant and maternal mortality, longer life expectancy, lower fertility rates, and improvements in health, nutrition, literary, and economic growth. In addition there are advantages passed on by educated women to their families-better health, nutrition, higher income,; and the increased educational attainment of younger generations.

Domestic, industrial, and agricultural productivity improves, and there is often greater participation in civil society. Overall, countries with the highest educational participation of females evidence the highest levels of economic development. The greater investment returns realized from educating girls has caused many national officials and international donors to focus scarce resources on girls' participation, rationalizing that since girls normally make up a larger proportion of non-enrolled children than do boys, steps to improve girls' participation will increase boys' participation as well.

In developing countries, although the greatest investment returns are derived from primary education, there are also returns for secondary' and higher education, and these averages are higher across the board for the lowest income countries. Strangely, the improvements in development indicators occur even when education programs are weak and specific information-on health, nutrition and other topics that would appear necessary to those improvements-is absent from the content of education programs.' The mechanisms that link education and development indicators until now are not entirely clear.

Some suggest they result from important, if not widely recognized, increases in self-esteem that women gain from becoming "educated people." Perhaps it is because school settings provide girls' with role models for new behaviours. Or maybe girl-students are permitted relative independence of action and come to know how to access services. Maybe it is the consequence of having to meet responsibilities and maintain a more organized lifestyle, or because they are involved in networks of informed people who serve as knowledge communicators.

Studies have shown that adolescence is a time when critical decisions are made that affect adult lives. Understanding better the mechanisms whereby education is converted into improved development indicators could make it possible to enhance the already known positive effects of retaining girls longer in school. Some have claimed that in almost every education measure available, boys are more disadvantaged than girls in the United States.

According to Barbara Herz, in USAID's Symposium on Girls' Education, it appears that secondary education may have much larger returns-as much as 30 percent. Therefore, ensuring that girls reach this stage may produce even larger benefits. Colclough notes, "even if resources are scarce, and if the affordable quality of schooling is low, a further extension of the coverage of primary education can still be expected to bring benefits." In support of this contention that increasing access is important anyway, he says, "individual behavioural changes that result from schooling are stronger when the schooling is widely spread than when it is more concentrated".

Hamamsy also says "Education separates women in to two distinct categories from whom different behaviour patterns are expected." As example, an educated woman can wait to marry while an uneducated woman is pressured to marry early. Perhaps it is even more important to encourage girls to stay in school longer for equity and personal reasons. If, on the whole, more girls than boys drop out of school sooner and are therefore less likely to complete essential stages of education, they will also be less equipped with the skills to live fully productive adult lives, whether in domestic or public roles. It is difficult to know how a decision today not to enrol or to retain children may affect their lives 20 years from now.

What is clear is that the private rates of return for educating girls lags behind the social benefits to society. Were these returns to increase-if they were to develop better skills and improve their employability-it is possible they would be willing to invest more time and resources in schooling. Overall, while the social returns of investing in girls have been high, the private returns have not been commensurate; consequently, it has sometimes been difficult for girls and their parents to see the benefits of extended education. The logic of this evidence suggests that the objectives of girls' educational participation need to be expanded from the aim of simply enrolling girls, to retaining them as long as possible, and of providing them better and more relevant programs.

As Fuller notes, "The economic returns from improvements in school quality are comparable to those from school expansion". School venues are important but school buildings are not. Schooling can take place almost anywhere-in a home, community hall, or under a tree. Removing the cost of construction would provide major relief to school budgets of many developing countries. Girls cannot attain higher levels of schooling without mastering the basic academic skills required to enrol in them. With each increase in level she completes, we are assured, the benefits for national development increase. Logic also tells that improving academic programs to include better skill development and more program content related to health, nutrition, and other desired outcomes is likely to improve further the impact on development indicators" and possibly increase the private benefits" girls receive from education.

That in turn may increase the motivation of parents to keep their girls in school and of girls to stay in school. Improving program quality is likely to have the additional benefit to the nation of reducing the inequities of wealth, region, and ethnicity where the educational disadvantage of girls is usually more severe. Of the 960 million illiterates in the world two-thirds are female. Figure 1 shows the adult literacy rates in 1995 for five regions of the world. Since 1980, the gender gap has narrowed in four regions while increasing slightly in the fifth, South Asia.

Nearly a quarter of the world's population of 6- to 11-year-old girls-85 million-remain out of school, constituting roughly 60 percent of all out-of-school children in the age group. The total number of out-of-school girls is projected to double by the year 2015 compared witty 1990 rates. There is a basic minimum of schooling necessary if improvements in some indicators are to be realized. By the end of primary education, for example, the rise in fertility that peaks in women with three or four years of schooling begins a substantial decline.

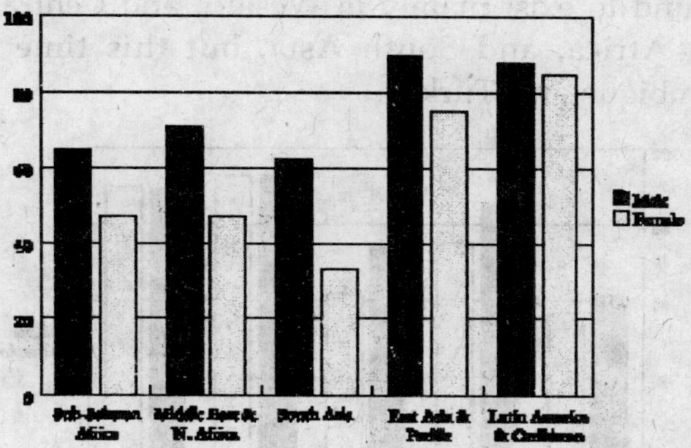

Figure 1. Adult Literacy Rate (%) 1995

Figure 2 shows that primary participation varies by region. The "primary school attendance ratios" used to calculate the bar graphs in this figure are based on

Demographic Health Surveys (DHS) data that may be more accurate than official gross or net primary participation ratios. The figures show the lowest rate of participation in sub-Saharan Africa and the largest gender gap in South Asia. East Asia and Latin America have high rates of participation for both boys and girls, and in the latter there is even a small gender gap favouring girls. To focus the problem further, the largest disadvantage for females is found mainly in Western and Central Africa, North Africa and South Asia.'

Girls have higher participation rates than boys in Latin America. Rates of completion also vary from region to region. South Asia has the lowest rates and the Middle East and North Africa and East Asia have the highest rates of completion. The patterns of regional disadvantage in higher stages generally follow the patterns of enrolment above. When broken down they are found to exist mainly in Western and Central Africa, North Africa, and South Asia, but this time include Mozambique and Turkey.

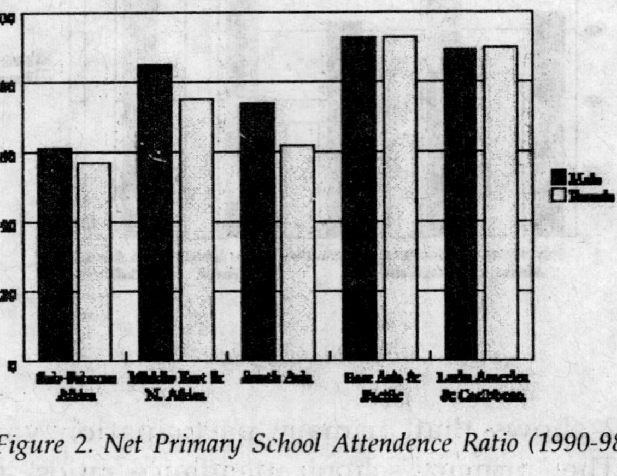

Figure 2. Net Primary School Attendence Ratio (1990-98)

In countries such as Brazil almost all children complete grade 1 while considerably fewer complete grade 6. In others such as India, considerably fewer complete grade 1, but once they do Filmer 1999 ranks 38 developing countries by region into eight categories from the lowest to highest enrollments of girls ages 6 to 14: 1) Western and Central Africa, 2) North Africa, 3) South Asia, 4) Eastern and Southern Africa, 5) Central America and the Caribbean, 6) East Asia and the Pacific, 7) South America, and 8) Middle East and Central Asia.

The length of primary education may vary from as little as five years in some countries to as much as eight or nine years in others under the broader rubric of "basic education." Certain statistical documents use the term primary level as a contrast to secondary level education, and consequently it is difficult to find either a single internationally accepted definition of the length of primary education or statistics that can be reliably compared across countries.

Primary education also varies from country to country in the way it is presented. In some cases it may be divided into distinct lower and upper elementary stages, or into elementary and middle (intermediate) stages. Alternatively it may appear as a seamless stage that reaches from first (or preprimary) to sixth or eighth grade. The length of primary education and whether it is divided into discrete stages has important implications for girls' retention.

Parents may remove their children from school during the transition between two distinct stages, especially if those stages are located in physically separated spaces, or if they are marked with other hurdles such as major promotional exams. For the most part, primary education is assumed here to comprise six years, although when useful for illustrative reasons, other definitions may be used to show how completion can be affected by the different arrangements of stages.

Primary education should not be confused with two other similar terms, basic education or compulsory education. Basic education, a term used first by the United Nations, originally referred to the basic or essential educational needs of children rather than a period of time, and included functional literacy and numeracy, practical skills such as basic woodworking, agriculture, electrical repair, or plumbing that children could use in daily living.

Compulsory education usually refers to the period of education that a nation determines all children must attend. Governments usually take responsibility for providing sufficient schooling opportunities for compulsory education, whether or not its duration is considered adequate to develop the skills citizens need for national development.

Persistence implies a sense of volition or desire on the part of individuals to continue. Attainment implies arriving at a given schooling grade or level, or in the case of learning, achieving some expected mastery of skill. Completion, unless otherwise noted, implies finishing a particular grade or stage. Access is the most difficult term to define because of its multiple usages. Here it means the ability of a child to enter and continue in the schooling system, i.e., there are no obstacles, physical, psychological, parental, or institutional that would prevent her from doing so.

The crucial points of access are the entry years into each educational level. But there are other times when access remains an important concept. A child who completes three years of a local school, for example, may not be able to continue to grade 4 if it exists in a far away community. For this reason, access here includes the looser definition of an absence of barriers to a child's participation at any grade or level. In its narrowest meaning, retention is measured by enrolment at different grade or program levels.

Improvements and deterioration in the rates of retention are assessed over time by examining the relative rises and declines in the measures of a target group at different levels of an education system or, alternatively, through comparisons with the measures of a normative or optimum population. A comparative approach might determine, for example, whether girls continue their schooling at the same rate as boys or to the same educational level as boys.

The larger aim of retaining girls in school implies broader expectations about results than simply that girls have completed specified stages. One such expectation is that girls will have the same opportunity as boys to acquire basic learning skills. Research has shown that girls often experience a different teaching-learning environment than boys in the same classrooms. To determine whether they have acquired the expected skills, the most easily available proxy measure of learning is achievement data, e.g., test scores, pass rates, or promotional statistics.

A second expectation of retaining girls is that they, like boys, would be eligible for and have access to higher levels of education. These outcomes can be tested through transition rates from the completed level to a higher level of' education and by enrolment rates at the higher level. Other education measures with direct or indirect implications for girls' retention are data on age-related enrolment, attendance, grade repetition, drop out, and promotional standards.

Girls who start at an older age may also have fewer years of enrolment if their dropout is related to puberty. Older children, on the other hand, may be able to learn more quickly if flexible programming is provided. Underage children by contrast may become discouraged and drop out, or may not attend regularly and end up repeating early grades. Poor attendance may lead to poor achievement, which in turn may lead to grade repetition and eventually dropout.

In March 1990, 1,500 participants from 155 governments, 20 intergovernmental bodies and 140 non-governmental organizations met at the World Conference on Education for All (WCEFA) in Jomtien, Thailand, moved by a common concern for the global condition of education. They were seized by the imperative to make a fresh start and a new commitment to fulfilling the goal of education for all - especially for girls. Three ground-breaking emphases in the drive for universal access to quality education emerged from the conference:

1) adult literacy as a key in extending efforts to provide educational for children;

2) the recognition that girls and women constituted the majority of the unschooled in almost every region of the world, particularly in sub-Saharan Africa and South-East Asia; and

3) an expanded vision of education as a lifelong process of learning that includes, but is not limited to, schooling.

Participants made a global commitment at Jomtien to 'ensure access to, and improve the quality of, education for girls and women, and to remove every obstacle that hampers their active participation'. Every country, organization and agency dedicated itself to achieving this goal. Getting girls into school and ensuring that they benefited from the experience in a supportive, enabling environment was identified as critical to achieving education for all. This decade has seen some of the greatest strides ever for women and children. The Convention on the Rights of the Child, formulated in 1989, claimed the right to a quality education for all girls and boys.

From a human rights perspective, girls' education must remain a top priority, since girls still constitute almost two-thirds of the children excluded from a basic education. Education for girls means that as women they will be able to exercise their rights to participate in political and economic decision-making in the community as well as in the household; that they will be able to participate in development efforts in both the household and the community.

Educating girls has benefits at the personal, community and social levels that make it one of the most important investments that any developing country can make. Several decades of research have demonstrated that educated girls become more effective mothers who have higher survival rates among their children because they have better nutrition and health practices. Educated women are more likely to enter the formal labour market, earn higher wages and thus contribute more directly to a nation's economic productivity. There is also an intergenerational impact in that the daughters and sons of educated women are more likely to be educated and thus carry the benefits into succeeding generations. A recent review and analysis that aimed to 'identify the main elements of successful country performance in human development' concluded that the one 'seemingly necessary condition is a high female (primary) enrolment ratio'.

Since many countries dedicate significant proportions of their national budgets to supporting their education systems, stakeholders at all levels should work to ensure that education systems are effective and efficient. Education systems should provide quality education to both boys and girls, teaching them in a cost-effective manner what they need to know for life in the twenty-first century. When a significant proportion of the population is not obtaining these benefits—as is the case in most regions of the world - all stakeholders need to review the system's functioning to ensure that the funding dedicated to this sector is being well spent.

Targeting girls' and women's education is a key strategy for increasing the efficiency and effectiveness of school systems. Not only girls benefit from this focus. One of the clearest lessons from activities of the past decade is that boys also benefit from efforts to promote the participation of girls, in enrolment and even in achievement.

The participants at the Jomtien conference faced the reality that the gender gap in primary school enrolment ratios had not diminished despite a significant expansion of education in the least developed countries. After girls entered school, they often dropped out earlier than boys. Circumstances needed to be more favourable to permit girls' retention within the system. Schools had to be cheaper, better and closer to home to attain universal access for girls, especially in the poorest countries and the regions of Southern Asia and sub-Saharan Africa. While other regions had reached universal access or were close to it at the primary level, in many countries differentials between girls and boys still persisted at the secondary and tertiary levels in many countries. Further, the data from higher educational levels in almost all regions revealed that girls studied mathematics and science and entered the more technological careers at far lower rates than boys.

Beyond issues of access and subject choice, the school experience itself was significantly different for girls than for boys. The hidden curriculum in teaching materials, notably textbooks, and the attitudes of teachers, administrators, and other pupils conveyed the message to girls that they were inferior to boys and should have lower aspirations for themselves. There was a strong suspicion that these negative attitudes and experiences were being reflected in the generally low attainment and achievement levels for girls as compared to boys. These and other factors led participants to the conclusion that many education systems are systematically biased against girls. Some populations were more likely to have low schooling rates.

For example, poorer communities, those isolated by geographic or cultural barriers, or those belonging to religious or ethnic minorities, were much more likely to enrol fewer children, especially girls. Governments and societies were excluding significant portions of their population. Participants at Jomtien adopted a Framework for Action as the guiding document to achieve education for girls and all excluded populations by the end of the decade.

The WCEFA Framework for Action designed the following targets and objectives for girls' education:

1) universal access to and completion of basic education by the year 2000, keeping in mind that basic education refers to primary education or whatever higher level of education is considered in a given country as 'basic'; and

2) reduction of the adult literacy rate to one-half of the 1990 level by the year 2000, with sufficient emphasis on female literacy to significantly reduce the current disparity between male and female illiteracy rates.

Ten years later, the convening partners commissioned a series of thematic studies to examine the progress that has been made in reaching those goals. Female literacy rates are addressed in places where they emphasize the critical need for girls' education. The parameters for analysing girls' education may be listed as follows.

— *Access:* Are girls and women physically, culturally and legally able to access educational services? How are the needs of the excluded addressed?

— *Achievement:* Do girls and women within educational institutions learn as much as boys and do they demonstrate similar achievement patterns in their learning through standard assessment measures?

— *Attainment:* To what extent do girls and women progress toward secondary, technical and tertiary levels?

— *Completion:* Having attained a certain level of education, what percentage of girls and women are able to complete it?

— *Dropping out of school:* At what stage and in what proportion do girls and women drop out of educational systems?

Teaching practices, curriculum, teacher and community attitudes, cultural practices, and state policies help to explain the parameters in their contextual perspective. Lessons learned from the 1990s offer insights into the challenges to be addressed in this new century.

STATUS OF GIRLS' EDUCATION

The information presented here is gleaned from country Education For All (EFA) assessments as they became available. Because assessments were by necessity not carried out identically, comparable information was often not available across countries. Net enrolment ratios (NER) have risen in some countries in all regions of the world. While in developed countries net enrolment rates were already universal or close to it in 1990, the average level of NER in the developing countries was 85.6 per cent for boys and 77.2 per cent for girls. The levels were projected to be 87.9 per cent for boys and 81.5 per cent for girls in 2000. Primary net enrolment ratios for primary school girls have risen in all regions since 1990 and are projected to increase further up to 2010. This also means that the absolute number of girls in school has risen in all regions since 1990 and is projected to increase further up to 2010. However, because of population growth and the tendency for less progress to have been made in the areas with higher growth, the absolute number of girls of primary age (worldwide) out of school has risen since 1990 and is expected to continue rising up to 2005.

ENROLMENT GROWTH

Net enrolment ratios have grown overall, and girls' enrolment ratios have grown substantially over the past decade. As Table 1 indicates, girls' enrolment has grown more than boys' in all regions of the developing world, particularly in East Asia and the Arab States. However, the growth has not been 'accelerated' and girls are still less likely to be in school than boys.

In the Arab States, there appears to have been a contraction in the net enrolment rates of boys at the primary level at the same time that there has been an increase at the secondary level. The reasons for this are unknown and have caused some concern. Girls' enrolment levels at primary level have increased at above average rates and there has been significant growth for females at secondary level within the region.

In all regions, the ratios for the secondary level have increased more than the ratios for the primary level. Without a more indepth analysis, it is impossible to state precisely the reasons for this. The expansion of the more expensive secondary level may indicate that the more affluent members of society are disproportionately enrolling their children in secondary school. Another explanation could be that the different starting levels explain the higher growth rates at secondary level; the primary level would be more constrained by ceiling effects. Since the primary level enrolment is higher to start with, an increase of a given size would form a smaller proportion of the enrolment.

GENDER GAP

It is sometimes argued that if the general trend to get more girls into school is succeeding, then one should not worry unduly about whether the gender gap is narrowing or widening. However, it matters because its presence reflects why the differentials exist in the first place. A persistent gender gap strongly suggests that the underlying causes of disadvantage and discrimination against women and girls are not being meaningfully addressed.

Worldwide, the gender gap in enrolment ratios is closing. However, this overall figure masks considerable regional variation in both the starting level and the degree of improvement. As can be seen in Table 2, in 1990 Southern Asia and the Arab States had the highest gender differentials. Both regions have narrowed this differential by approximately 5 percentage points. Sub-Saharan Africa was the third highest in terms of gender gap, but despite the fact that net enrolment ratios for both boys and girls have risen, the gender gap has widened by 0.7 percentage points in this part of the world.

Table 1

Percentage growth in net enrolment ratios, 1990-2000, by gender

Region	*Primary*		*Secondary*	
	M	*F*	*M*	*F*
Developing Countries	2.7	5.6	13.4	24.3
Sub-Saharan Africa	6.2	5.9	13.9	16.8
Arab States	-1.1	6.0	10.2	24.8
Latin America/Caribbean	7.5	7.0	16.6	16.8
East Asia	0.9	3.4	12.4	38.9
Southern Asia	4.8	13.4	7.4	18.5

Table 2
Primary net adjusted enrolment ratios

Region	1990			2000		
	M	*F*	*Gap*	*M*	*F*	*Gap*
Developing countries	85.6	77.2	8.4	87.9	81.5	6.4
Sub-Saharan Africa	62.7	54.1	8.6	66.6	57.3	9.3
Arab States	84.7	72.8	11.9	83.8	77.2	6.6
Latin America/Caribbean	88.4	87.1	1.3	95.0	93.2	1.8
East Asia/Oceania	98.2	95.4	2.8	99.1	99.0	0.9
Southern Asia	81.5	64.3	17.2	85.4	72.9	12.5

In Latin America and the Caribbean, net enrolment ratios in 1990 were high, and these have improved for both genders. However, the gender gap in Latin America, which was the smallest in 1990, has widened by 0.5 percentage points and is now greater than that of East Asia/Oceania. Such a small increase is probably not statistically significant, but it should be a reminder that it is possible to move backwards in the struggle for gender equity in education.

The East Asia/Oceania region is notable not only for reaching near universality between boys and girls at the primary level, but also for reducing its gender differential to less than 1 per cent at the same time.

Table 3. Secondary net adjusted enrolment ratio

Region	1990			2000		
	M	*F*	*Gap*	*M*	*F*	*Gap*
Developing countries	58.3	43.7	14.6	66.1	54.3	11.8
Sub-Saharan Africa	45.1	33.3	11.8	51.4	38.9	12.5
Arab States	60.6	46.8	13.8	66.8	58.4	8.4
Latin America/Caribbean	59.1	58.9	0.2	68.9	68.8	0.1

East Asia/Oceania	58.5	47.6	10.9	70.9	66.1	4.8
Southern Asia	61.0	38.4	22.6	65.5	45.5	20

There have been similar overall improvements in the gender gap at the secondary level (Table 3). East Asia/ Oceania has succeeded in reducing the size of the gender gap by six percentage points, more than half of the original difference. The Arab States have also made good progress with a reduction of more than 5 percentage points in their gender gap.

Although secondary net enrolment ratios have increased in sub-Saharan Africa, there has been little change in the gender gap in this region. The increase in the gender gap in sub-Saharan Africa has even caused a change in its relative position. In 1990, sub-Saharan Africa had the third highest gender gap, behind Southern Asia and the Arab states, but in the year 2000 only Southern Asia will have a higher gender gap at the secondary level.

Gender parity at all levels and in all types of education is a goal for universal basic education. However, if countries are characterized by gender parity this does not necessarily mean that equitable conditions exist for girls and boys in school; neither does gender bias in favour of girls (as in Botswana, the Philippines, Lesotho and countries in the Caribbean) indicate that conditions have become inequitable for boys. The qualitative aspects of schooling are important factors: these may include leadership opportunities for girls in the classroom and school; equal access to resources, including the teacher's time and attention; parents' and teachers' attitudes toward girls' aspirations and education; and the respect teachers and other students accord to girls (and boys).

All of these elements affect the quality and equity of pupils' school experiences. Indicators of these qualitative factors have yet to be consistently developed, but descriptive information (less easily quantified) is also needed to point to gender equity in a school or an education system. These kinds of data are valuable and necessary, and need to be considered in future assessments.

Due to economic constraints, the data presented above, in general, have been geographically aggregated. Urban and rural populations, as well as populations reflecting different traditions or religions, those living in remote mountain villages as well as those living in exclusive urban suburbs, have all been summed together. This aggregation frequently obscures radical differences, not only in actual levels of educational participation, but also in the constraints to participation and the kinds of strategies that can be used to address them.

This is true for small countries, but is even more acute in large countries where remote and/or minority populations may have rates of female and male educational participation that are strikingly different from the norm. Muslim populations in countries where Christian populations are in the majority (or vice versa), nomadic groups, or other minority groups might just as well, for all intents and purposes, be living in a completely different country.

The growth of the urban under-class living in slums and squatter settlements on the fringes of large urban areas in most developing countries is a notable development of the 1990s. Girls and boys in these communities are very unlikely to attend school. Some of the variations within regions and within countries are discussed below. Closing the gender gap must remain an important objective within the Education for All movement, in light of regional variation, and the fact that some regions and nations are not making any progress in this area.

REGIONAL PROFILES

The disadvantaged position of girls within the education sector is revealed through limited access; lower rates of representation at particular levels; rates of completion; and rates of achievement. In addition, girls' representation in 'higher status' areas of study, the kinds of careers that they are able to enter, and in which careers they can advance are other indicators of the relative position of girls within the system.

The supportive factors that encourage girls to succeed include, inter alia, literate women and the presence and number of women in the teaching force. The profiles presented below take these factors into account as they reveal trends across the geographical regions of the world. Eastern Asia and Oceania. Primary net enrolment rates have been increasing in all countries, although much variation exists in this broad region. The Democratic People's Republic of Korea and the Cook Islands have achieved universal access to primary education. China, Indonesia, Fiji, Samoa, Thailand, and Malaysia are close to that goal. Other countries such as Cambodia and Viet Nam are making steady progress.

Countries such as Malaysia, the Philippines, and the Democratic People's Republic of Korea show gender parity in achievement as well as in access. In China, absolute gender disparity in net enrolment ratios narrowed from 1.80 per cent to 0.14 per cent, indicating that disparity in access between girls and boys has basically been eliminated.

On the other hand, there is a large gender imbalance in schools in Papua New Guinea. Cultural attitudes militate in a very significant way against girls' education; approximately 10-15 per cent more boys than girls entered first grade between 1992 and 1997. If young women do complete an education, the labour market provides few opportunities for them to be employed in supervisory and management positions.

In some of the countries where important gains have been made, there are still pockets of marginalized children that are hard to reach—those belonging to ethnic or religious minorities or living in geographically remote regions. In these communities girls are particularly vulnerable to being left out of school. For example, in Lao People's Democratic Republic, the gender balance of student enrolment nationally is 45 per cent girls and 55 per cent boys, but gender differences in primary school are even more prevalent in provinces with a high ethnic minority population. In one region, boys have a 114.7 per cent gross enrolment ratio, compared with 76.2 per cent for females; in another, 75 per cent of the non-enrolled children are girls.

The economic slump in this part of the world, and the growing tendency for the state to partially or completely withdraw even primary education from funding is forcing parents to decide whether or not to send their daughters to school for financial reasons, and the result does not generally favour girls. The situation for the region at the secondary level is less positive than for the large numbers of primary school children in the East Asia/Oceania region.

Not only are overall rates of participation lower, but the gender gap is also wider - 13 percentage points in favour of boys in Cambodia, 12 in Lao People's Democratic Republic, and 9 in China and Indonesia. Mongolia is an exception with a 20 percentage point gap in favour of girls. In Indonesia the transition rate for boys is increasing, but the girls' transition rate has dropped dramatically from 74 per cent to an expected 56 per cent in 2000—below the 1990 rate of 57.7 per cent.

Literacy rates vary widely between and within countries as well. Gender disparity in illiteracy rates in China has narrowed by 6.3 per cent, yet regional disparities remain significant. Relative gender gaps in illiteracy rates have increased in 17 provinces and autonomous regions. Adult illiteracy rates in Qinghai and Tibet are as high as 43.6 per cent and 54.1 per cent respectively; gender disparities in these areas are even more striking.

In Vietnam, there is an 8 percentage point gender gap in literacy rates for the 15-35-year-old age group, but in the main labour force, literacy rates have increased from 86 per cent in 1990 to 95.6 per cent in 1998, with no gender gap registered. Papua New Guinea reports a low literacy rate for females at 38 per cent. There are more qualified women teachers than men in such countries as the Philippines, Kiribati, and the Cook Islands.

In Southern Asia more than one-third of girls are unlikely to ever receive a formal education, and adult women have the lowest literacy rate in the world. There have been some signs of improvement, however, with girls' enrolment at the primary and secondary levels growing more rapidly than boys'.

Variations within and between countries are particularly obvious in this region. In 1999, all countries were still classified in the World Bank low-income group with GNP per capita income of less than US$675 per year. In Maldives, access to schooling is no longer an issue, but the quality of education is, especially for schools on the outer islands.

Primary enrolment rates in Bangladesh have climbed to 75 per cent for both boys and girls. The total enrolment level for all children of school-going age in Bhutan is 95 per cent. Schooling rates for girls in Afghanistan have plummeted, however, following the closing of girls' schools.

Within India, the state of Kerala has an enrolment rate of 90 per cent, while the rate for Bihar is approximately 50 per cent. Innovations to address these dramatic differences and low rates include a multi-sector partnership in the Indian city of Mumbai and the Intensive District Approach to Education for All (IDEAL) programme in Bangladesh. The Pratham Mumbai Education Initiative has set up 1,600 pre-schools and renovated 1,200 primary schools in Mumbai.

IDEAL promotes more childfriendly classrooms by training teachers about children's individual learning patterns. Also in India, the state of Andhra Pradesh conducted a 'Back-to-School' programme; that is, transition classes for working children and 16,000 summer schools for 360,000 children in Grade One.

Nepal and Bangladesh have designed policies and programmes to bring more women teachers into schools as a means of providing security, safety and role models for their girl students. Nepal's 1991 census showed a literacy rate of 25 per cent for girls aged six and over.

The literacy rate for women of the 18 years and older age group was 18 percent. Most of the illiteracy in Nepal is found in the rural population, and includes both adults and school-age children who can not attend school. In Bhutan, female literacy issues have not been sufficiently studied, but over 10,000 adults have been enrolled in nonformal education programmes, 70 per cent of whom are women. Attention to girls' education in Southern Asia is an urgent priority. This region has the largest number of out-of-school children in the world, two thirds of whom are girls. Without concerted action in this region, EFA will never be achieved.

Central Asia and Eastern Europe: A tradition of generally equal access to education exists in all of the post-socialist countries of Central Asia and Eastern Europe. In many countries, gender equality is written into fundamental laws or the national constitution. Women made significant advances in education under socialist forms of government, and current statistics on gender parity in education in most of the region reflect this progress. Some nations in the region, such as Georgia and Kyrgyzstan, say universal primary education along with gender parity on indicators such as persistence and literacy. The educational systems of most of the countries in this area are undergoing major changes, however. Most have suffered serious economic and social destabilization during the present transitional period.

In the education sector, this has led to reduction in the availability of teaching materials, diminished purchasing power for teachers, and increased numbers of drop-outs. In Tajikistan, the number of drop-outs is increasing at all levels of education. Approximately 20 per cent of boys and 25 per cent of girls between 7 and 17 years old in rural areas did not attend school in 1996. The percentage of female students has fallen to almost one-third of the high school population and it is decreasing annually, as a result of material difficulties within the family, shrinking job opportunities for women, and educational priority being given to young men. Despite these grim statistics, the transition period in Central Asia has also allowed for some positive developments, such as policy reform and the introduction of new curricula and instruction methods.

Turkey's countrywide NER is 87.5 per cent total, but the rate for girls lags behind boys by 10.3 percentage points. In Romania, a 1994 study of the Institute for Sciences of Education on functional illiteracy showed that 11 per cent of the total functional illiterate group among graduates of compulsory education were girls, while boys represented only 8.9 percent. Girls in this group are at a particular disadvantage, since non-formal education is more available to the male population.

In some of the countries struggling the most to develop a new economic and social environment, the introduction of higher education fees has coincided with lower family incomes and sharp reductions in state support for education generally. In Bulgaria, for example, state funding fell by three quarters. In Kyrgyzstan, the Republic of Moldova and the former Republic of Macedonia, heating schools in winter has now become a problem.

UNICEF's International Child Development Centre suggests that not only are the standards of education and the enrolment levels falling, but that the egalitarian feature of the former system is also rapidly eroding. Ethnic and religious minorities and rural populations are being disproportionately affected, as are girls.

Western Europe: Nearly universal access to education has been achieved in Western Europe, with boys and girls equally represented in early childhood and primary education. Indeed, girls often achieve higher levels of education than boys. Persistent rates of high unemployment have plagued many parts of this region, however, so the focus of educational reform has centred on education for employment in information-based economies. In many Western European countries, including Norway, high rates of illiteracy among minority and immigrant populations are of special concern. In Cyprus, overall illiteracy dropped from 6 per cent in 1991 to 4 per cent in 1997, and the women's illiteracy rate dropped from 10 per cent to 6 percent. In spite of the decrease in illiteracy in the female population, the percentage remains relatively high. This may be attributable to the fact that social conventions kept many older women, especially those in rural areas, from attending school. One half of Ireland's population aged 25-64 years had not completed upper secondary education in 1996 compared to 62 per cent in 1989. The low relative ranking in this indicator reflects the low level of educational investment in Ireland up to thirty years ago. Women in this age group have more average years of schooling than men. However, the position improves for the younger age groups. One-third (34 percent) of Ireland's population aged 25-34 years had not completed upper secondary education in 1996, and among young people aged 20-24, the percentage declined by the equivalent of 12 percentage points (from 38 per cent to 26 percent) between 1989 to 1995.

In Finland, as in several other Western European countries, women have surpassed men in both enrolment and graduation rates, especially in tertiary education.

Both education and employment continue to be divided into men's and women's fields, however, and have not become substantially less segregated over the past 20 years. In another example, vocational education in the Netherlands, only 11.5 per cent of girls were enrolled in technical courses in 1997/98, while 86.8 per cent were enrolled in non-technical fields of preparation. This represents only a slight change from 1990, when the figures were 10 per cent and 90 per cent respectively. Women in adult education, however, represented 63 per cent of all participants in 1997/98.

Women's participation in the work force has contributed to the growth of early childhood education in a number of countries. In Sweden, for example, the majority of children between 1 and 12 years old now have a place in publicly funded child-care centres. In Ireland, by contrast, education for children under 4 years old is not well developed, but nearly all 5-year-olds and more than half of 4-year-olds attend primary school. The participation rate among 4-yearold girls is four to five percentage points higher than that for boys. In France, as in many other countries in Europe, the majority of teachers are women. In 1998, about 77 per cent of French teachers were women. In the Netherlands, the percentage of female teachers in primary education rose from 64 per cent in 1991 to 76.8 per cent in 1997, although at secondary level women accounted for only 25 per cent in 1993 and 28 per cent in 1997.

Arab States and North Africa: Early childhood care and development is receiving greater attention in this region, especially in Tunisia, Egypt, Jordan and Iraq. Other countries like Palestine, Lebanon, Syria, Iran and Djibouti are moving in the same direction. Iran has made great strides in rural areas, and girls' attendance is now over 90 percent. In both Bahrain and Syria the gender parity index for early childhood care in pre-schools favours males, although the index for Syria has increased from .89 to .91. Female primary net enrolments have improved except in Yemen, Djibouti and Mauritania, but girls in the 6-10 age group still have lower rates than boys (except in Jordan and Lebanon).

The gap is widest in Yemen and Morocco. For the 11 to 15 year age group in the region, there has been an increase in the gender gap at primary level since 1995. Egypt's primary education enrolment represents an increase in basic education of 12 per cent over a five-year period. With 55.4 per cent males and 44.6 per cent females, this also represents a slight increase in gender parity. Girls are still more likely to drop out or repeat in this region, although there are exceptions. In Iraq, repetition rates among males were higher than for females, but grade 4 achievement rates favoured males (57 percent) over females (43 percent). At the secondary level, male enrolment ratios still exceed that of females everywhere except Jordan. Based on achievement data from nine countries, girls scored higher than boys in the area of life skills and Arabic language. The results for mathematics were mixed, with girls outscoring boys in Oman, Palestine, United Arab Emirates, Jordan and Kuwait.

The literacy rates are increasing in Bahrain but there is still a marked gender difference in the rates of 80.4 per cent for men and 73 per cent for women. Iraq's literacy rate is 27.4 per cent for males and females ages 10 and older, 20 per cent for males and 34.5 per cent for females. In Syria, females' ability to read and write has risen strikingly from 60 per cent to 73 per cent over the past five years, an increase averaging 2.5 per cent per year. Regional efforts are being undertaken to make the promotion of girls' education a regional imperative with the creation of the Regional Task Force on Girls' and Women's Education, made up of women leaders from Jordan, Morocco, Egypt, Syria, Sudan, Yemen and Iran. However, the persistent conflicts in some countries (Algeria, Sudan, the West Bank) and the sanctions against Iraq have disrupted schooling, particularly for girls.

Sub-Saharan Africa: Despite notable gains by African countries to ensure that every African child has access to quality basic education, only about 10 countries have achieved universal primary education. An estimated 41 million school age children are out of school, and 56 per cent of them are girls. Approximately 20 to 29 per cent repeat a grade or more, and the number of students dropping out of school is increasing. Most sub-Saharan African countries have a gender gap that disadvantages girls. Chad's general enrolment increased by 14 per cent from 1996 to 1998 but the gender gap widened by six per cent from 1997 to 1998, after narrowing by two per cent in 1997. The gender gap remains at 26 per cent in both Chad and Benin. Some countries in East and Central Africa experienced declining enrolments in the early- and mid-1990s (Kenya and Tanzania) but appear to be reversing this trend in the latter part of the decade. Swaziland had a large drop in net enrolment, decreasing from 93 to 80 per cent between 1993 and 1996, due in part to the serious impact of HIV/AIDS on Swaziland. The pandemic costs Swaziland's educational system an estimated three to four teachers each week. Adolescent girls are increasingly being seen as a group vulnerable to educational disruption—there is a high demand for their labour in the household, and many girls are still being married in their mid-teens. For those outside marriage, their age and gender make them easy targets for sexual exploitation, and consequently they generally record the highest rates of HIV/AIDS infection.

All of these factors: household labour, early marriage, unwanted pregnancy and sexually transmitted diseases—threaten their schooling and will make them a priority target group for increased education over the next 10-15 years. Sub-Saharan Africa had the second highest gender gap in 1990. Since then several regional initiatives have emerged; the Forum of African Women Educationalists (FAWE), the Female Education in Mathematics and Science in Africa (FEMSA), the NGO Alliance, the African Girls' Education Initiative (AGEI), and others. Advocacy and awareness-raising activities have brought about remarkable progress, and girls' enrolment has risen markedly in sub-Saharan Africa. Nevertheless, despite excellent progress in some countries (Guinea, Benin and Senegal) there has been a slight overall widening of the gender gap. Adult illiteracy, particularly among females, continues to grow, fuelled by high population growth and inadequate supply of educational services.

Latin America & Caribbean: Latin America has the highest literacy rates in the developing world - 87 per cent, with women's literacy at 85 per cent. Enrolment rates for girls and boys at primary and secondary levels are high throughout the region. Quality is an important issue, however. Gross enrolment rates are usually over 100, implying a large percentage of overage students as well as high levels of repetition. In nearly half of the 21 countries for which data is available, at least 10 per cent of the children are repeating grades. In Brazil the rate of repetition exceeds 15 percent. The rates are slightly higher for boys than for girls. Dropout rates are also high. One quarter of children entering primary school drop out before reaching the fifth grade. In Colombia, the Dominican Republic, El Salvador, Haiti and Nicaragua, the dropout rate is at least 40 per cent. In Bolivia, primary enrolment slightly favours girls, but only 42-54 per cent of girls or boys finish fifth grade. Girls' rate of promotion in primary is slightly higher and the dropout rate is slightly lower for girls than for boys. More significantly, 42 per cent of girls finish school, compared to a mere 35 per cent for boys. Throughout Latin America, the enrolment levels are relatively lower and the gender gaps higher among certain parts of the population, particularly the indigenous Indians.

Rural girls' dropout and repetition rates are twice as high as those of boys and the gender gap in primary completion is widest in rural areas. Over the last two decades Brazil has experienced a rapid increase in the schooling of the female population. Net enrolment rates in primary education are high, graduation rates in primary education are going up, and more Brazilian females are also enrolled in secondary education. More important is the rapid decline of illiteracy rates among younger women. The proportion of illiterates is significantly lower now among women than among men in all population groups up to the age of 39. Among the reasons given for this situation are the entry of women into the labour market and the increasing professionalization of the female work force, associated with higher aspirations for girls; and the reality that male children and adolescents are more often forced to leave school and work to increase the family income.

Latin America is also home to some of the most innovative educational initiatives, including community schools in Colombia (Escuela Nueva) and Guatemala (Nueva Escuela Unitaria) where girls actively participate in learning and have increased opportunities for leadership throughout primary school. New kinds of business and community partnerships support education in Brazil. And as Honduras recovers from the devastation of Hurricane Mitch, it has elected to restructure its education system, engaging in yet another innovation. Middle school education is being provided by radio to citizens throughout the country through partnerships with churches, private enterprise, donor partners, and NGOs.

The United States has achieved education for all at the primary level and virtually all adults now have at least a primary education. However, not all students obtain a high school diploma. Among persons 25 to 34 years old, 87.9 per cent of females, but only 85.9 per cent of males, have completed secondary education. As in most industrial countries, men and women in the United States persist in school at similar rates, though in recent years females have had a slight and growing edge. The event dropout rate for males in grades 10 to 12 rose from 4.0 to 5.0 between 1990 and 1997 and the rate for females rose from 3.9 to 4.1 during the same period.

Achievement presents a somewhat more complex picture, with girls doing better in reading and boys in mathematics and science, especially at advanced levels. Male students usually outscore female students in mathematics and science; in reading and writing female students tend to outperform males. In science, mathematics and reading, the gender gaps in 1996 were not significantly different from those in early 1970s. As in almost every other country, academic achievement in the United States correlates closely with socio-economic status, that is, children from higher socio-economic backgrounds score higher on measures of achievement. Other inequities relate to the racial and ethnic background of students, gender, geography, mother tongue, and immigrant status. For children with disabilities, legislation has required since the early 1970s they be provided with the sort of education that will enable them to develop their skills and knowledge to the fullest extent possible. Programmes at the national, state, and local levels support this policy for girls and for boys.

After Jomtien, the United States set a goal of reducing the adult illiteracy rate, especially the disparity between male and female rates. In the International Adult Literacy Survey initiated in 1994 by nine countries, approximately one-fifth of American adults scored at or above level 4 on all three scales (only Sweden scored higher). However, a disproportionate number of adults scored at level 1 (only Poland had a greater percentage of adults scoring at this lowest literacy level). Further analysis of the American data showed a strong correlation between parental education and the literacy levels of youth.

In addition to changes in enrolment trends and dropout rates, gender parity indices, and other indicators of quantitative change over the past decade, key aspects of the discourse on girls' education have also shifted. International awareness of girls' education as an issue has increased significantly. Educators, politicians, donors, and others— especially from countries with significant gender differentials—are now much more likely to cite gender-specific data on enrolment, dropout, and achievement. Some countries have only recently begun to disaggregate data by gender and only a small minority of countries submitting EFA reports did not mention some aspect(s) of gender and education (e.g. gender parity in early childhood development, enrolment, repetition, completion, women teachers, women's literacy rates, gender-sensitive curriculum development). Emphasis has also shifted from documenting barriers to engaging in advocacy and action. Practical aspects of girls' education issues have evolved from problem identification to moving into action. As a basis for advocacy and as a means of documenting girls' education issues early in the decade, it was often important for actors to 'discover' barriers and constraints to girls' education and to present the information to national or regional workshops of policy makers.

The formation of networks and partnerships developed widely over the decade, as awareness has grown of the complexity of the issues and the importance of networks for women's empowerment and for basic questions of democracy and freedom. Partnerships between organizations promoting girls' schooling and those promoting literacy for adult women, education on legal rights, economic empowerment, environmental protection and democracy are critical to those networks.

Educators now have a deeper understanding of the barriers to girls' education. Earlier conventional wisdom assumed that parents did not send daughters to school because parents felt girls were not worth educating. It is now obvious that relatively modest incentives have been sufficient to transform girls' enrolment rates. Tuition waivers in Malawi and organizing community schools with respected women teachers for girls in Balochistan (Pakistan) are examples of this. We now know that if parents believe that schools are appropriate, safe, and of good quality, they usually will send girls to schools willingly.

Through the preparation that took place before, during and after international conferences and other efforts, a key understanding was reinforced: girls' equal access to quality schooling is their fundamental right and is necessary for national and human development.

INTERNATIONAL CONFERENCES PROMOTING GIRLS' EDUCATION

A series of international conferences since Jomtien has prompted countries and agencies around the world to implement new policies, programmes, and projects that have resulted in reducing the gender gap. These international meetings have highlighted the importance of educating girls in order to achieve social and development goals and have mobilized governments, NGOs, and other organizations for change in several ways: symbolically, as members of the world community rally around issues of girls' and women's education; through their substance and through networks constructed at the conference; and through their subsequent plans for action that nations consult in developing national and local action plans. In 1993, representatives from the world's nine most populous countries (Bangladesh, Brazil, China, Egypt, India, Indonesia, Mexico, Nigeria and Pakistan) came together at the E-9 Education Summit. These countries, which account for more than half of the world's population and 70 per cent of its illiterates, pledged to achieve universal primary education by 2000.

The International Conference on Population and Development in Cairo (ICPD), underscored the importance of human rights, female empowerment, autonomy and education and linked these to the development of society as a whole. Participants from 179 countries re-examined the role of population in development and adopted a programme of action calling for the gender gap in primary and secondary education to be closed by 2005.

Participating states in the World Summit for Social Development in Copenhagen pledged to advance universal, equitable access to quality education to help eradicate poverty, promote employment and foster social integration, with a particular emphasis on girls' education. Attention to education runs throughout the entire platform of the Fourth World Conference on Women in Beijing and occupies a prominent position within the separate critical area of concern on the girl-child. Strategic objectives include the following:

— Equal access to education including 80 per cent completion rates and closing the gender gap by 2005;

— Reducing female illiteracy to half its 1990 level, focusing on disadvantaged women and expanding the definition of literacy;

— Promoting women's roles in vocational and technical training for income-generating opportunities, particularly in food and agricultural research and extension;

— Advancing non-discriminatory education through gender awareness training for teachers, leadership training, the use of gender studies and research to improve education, and the development of multicultural, multilingual curricula for indigenous women and girls;

— Allocating sufficient resources for educational reforms and monitoring;

— Promoting lifelong learning for girls.

Participants in the Mid-Decade Meeting of the International Consultative Forum on Education for All in Amman candidly reported that progress in girls' and women's education since Jomtien had been very slow. The gender gap in net enrolment rates (NER) had worsened everywhere except in the Arab states. The agenda for the last half of the decade called for legislation for compulsory education; social mobilization to persuade families of the benefits of educating girls; enhanced gender sensitivity in curricula and throughout education systems; safe, girl-friendly schools; awareness of cultural and religious needs; and the need for incentives. It also called for the media to communicate positive images of educated girls and women.

The International Conference on Child Labour in Oslo focused on the detrimental impact of children's work on their opportunities for education. Participating governments agreed to create time-bound programmes for universal and compulsory education with a particular emphasis on girls' education.

Conferences have contributed to new initiatives for girls' education. Particularly in the second part of the decade, a number of international agencies increased their support for girls' education. While some viewed this as particularly aggressive advocacy, others saw it as a critical strategy to assist countries to achieve EFA. This section highlights a few of the programmes that have promoted various aspects of girls' and women's education. Within international agencies and governments a number of factors also militate against success in promoting girls' education. An important one is the limited state of knowledge about the complexity of girls' education issues. Since advocacy is frequently the first step in promoting girls' education, agencies must take this complexity into account and ensure that initiatives in this area receive the careful study, design, implementation and monitoring that they require. Merely formulating the objective of improving girls' enrolment, attendance or achievement is not sufficient. Logical links between the activities or strategies and the objective must be clear. When they are not, it is not uncommon that so-called girls' education projects benefit boys more than girls, and result in little discernible impact on girls.

This preparatory phase that focuses on understanding complexity is as crucial to eventual success as is the implementation phase itself. Analysis and planning need to be factored into the design phase and supported with adequate time and resources. To facilitate this, appropriate criteria for tasks and for job performance need to be developed. Similarly, the knowledge gained through research, programming and implementation need to be widely disseminated—both the successes and failures.

Each of the following international agencies (and others) have sponsored studies, evaluations, and reviews that have played a major role in documenting the experience in girls' education. Information about innovative programmes, what works, and lessons learned have often emanated from or been supported by these agencies. In addition, most of them maintain web sites that make such information available via the Internet.

The Canadian International Development Agency (CIDA), in partnership with UNICEF, provided $10 million between 1994 and 1996 to 15 countries in sub-Saharan Africa and the Middle East and North Africa to support girls' education. The purpose of the CIDA investment was threefold:

1) to assure girls' access to equitable, quality and relevant primary education so that they would have equal opportunity in participating in their community and society;
2) to develop a long-term plan and strategy for continued CIDA-UNICEF partnership in advancing girls' education; and
3) to contribute to implementation of the UNICEF Global Girls' Education Programme.

The development of a multi-country girls' education programme helped to identify common programmatic categories requiring attention in each participating country. It became clear that additional attention was needed for policy development; capacity building of the teaching staff, managers, planners, administrators, and institutions; raising awareness of girls' education and gender issues through advocacy and social mobilization efforts; and improving monitoring systems.

The United Nations Development Programme (UNDP) is a broad based, multi-sectoral agency. It does not identify specific target groups. However, within its general mandate of poverty eradication, the agency has invested several hundred million dollars in basic education and adult learning.

The United Nations Educational, Scientific and Cultural Organization (UNESCO) programme to promote girls' education has focused on Africa, principally through two projects. The first, a six-year Special Project on Scientific, Technical and Vocational Education of Girls in Africa, was launched during the biennium 1996/97, with the aim of reducing gender disparities in these areas. Support is provided for such activities as science camps for girls (Ghana and Botswana). An ongoing collaboration with FEMSA has worked to identify science topics of greater interest to girls (e.g. on environmental issues or solar energy). The second project is Guidance and counselling for school-age girls in Africa, a programme that trains trainers to help girls (and boys) deal with issues such as HIV/AIDS infection, drug abuse, and pregnancy. The Guidance, Counselling and Youth Development Centre for Africa (giving special attention to the needs of girls) has been established in Malawi since 1997.

The United Nations Food and Population Agency (UNFPA) promotes basic education, particularly the education of girls, within the overall context and goals of the ICPD Programme of Action. It recognizes the need for improvements in basic education as an important prerequisite to sustainable development and as a factor in the development of well-being through its links with demographic as well as economic and social factors. As stated in the ICPD Programme of Action, reduction of fertility, morbidity and mortality rates and the empowerment of women are largely assisted by progress in education. Specifically, the Programme of Action aims to:

a) achieve universal access to quality education, with particular priority being given to primary and technical education and job training, to combat illiteracy and to eliminate gender disparities in access to, retention in, and support, for education;

b) promote non-formal education for young people, guaranteeing equal access for women and men to literacy centres; and introduce and improve the content of the curriculum so as to promote greater responsibility and awareness on the interrelationships between population and sustainable development, health issues, including reproductive health and gender equity'.

Through the education activities it supports, UNFPA aims to contribute to improvements in the quality of basic education through the introduction of more relevant (population and development related) curricula, promoting curricular reforms and more effective teaching techniques; and to keep the education of girls and women high on national and international agendas. Implementation of this strategy requires comprehensive and sustained advocacy efforts at global, regional and national levels to get the full commitment and support of gov-ernments, as well as those of relevant international agencies and non-government organizations. At the country level, advocacy has been directed at encouraging community participation in support of education, both in terms of parents' support to girls' access and parent/ community support for population education activities.

The United Nations Children's Fund (UNICEF) Global Girls' Education Programme is a multi-country programme that supports girls' education and aims for equitable and quality education for all in more than 60 countries. UNICEF's rationale was that by targeting girls, UNICEF would be reaching a large proportion of the educationally disadvantaged, and doing so in a way that would benefit the entire educational system. Using a set of seven broad strategies - support to ongoing country programmes of co-operation, advocacy, partnership, communication, knowledge building, support to NGOs and resource mobilization - UNICEF is supporting education opportunities in countries such as Viet Nam, Bangladesh, Pakistan, Mali, Senegal, Uganda, Guinea and Egypt.

The Sara and Meena Initiatives in Africa and Asia, respectively, have produced a series of comic books, videos and posters in support of girls' education. Advocacy for girls' education continues with UNICEF support in places such as Djibouti, Bhutan, Central and Eastern Europe and the Commonwealth of Independent States. Building on UNICEF's work with CIDA, a partnership between Norway's Royal Ministry of Foreign Affairs and UNICEF has increased girls' access to education in most of the 18 countries and targeted zones served by the African Girls Education Initiative (AGEI) being carried out in sub-Saharan Africa. AGEI emphasizes regional capacity building and nation state's attention to girls' education at all levels, from national education plans and policies to classroom instruction and interaction. Noteworthy experiments with alternative and non-formal education (NFE) include Guinea's Nafa Centres, Satellite Schools and NFE centres in Burkina Faso, and schools in remote areas of Namibia, Zimbabwe, and Botswana.

The US Agency for International Development (USAID) has supported girls education programmes in 17 countries in Africa, South-East Asia, and South and Central America since 1981, but the majority were initiated after 1989. USAID identified expanding basic education for girls as a special focus and, as a result, has spent $200 million between 1990 and 1996 in this area. A range of strategies and activities were used in the 17 countries and a recent review of the decade's experience indicated that 'the supply of schools—the quantity, their quality, their suitability for girls, and their costs', was the most common obstacle to girls' education. The elements identified as necessary for successful education for girls included making the promotion of girls' education a social norm, political will to make and sustain investments, and broad engagement by community, NGOs, government, business and international donors.

The World Bank has identified girls education as an institutional priority and has a target of lending $900 million each year for programmes to increase girls' access and achievement. While this target has never been met, the Bank has been attempting to work with client countries to help them identify barriers to girls schooling and develop appropriate policies.

Focusing on 31 countries, the World Bank tries to promote a multipronged response including advocacy, reducing the costs of girls' schooling, school and classroom construction, teacher training, quality enhancement and greater involvement of women in school management and administration. Through partnerships, the World Bank has also worked to identify effective interventions, build capacity in effective resource utilization for EFA, try out innovations, and ensure a means of more effective implementation of girls' education programmes in developing countries.

Efforts of the past decade have taught the world community a significant amount about how - and how not - to expand and improve education for girls. For example, funding expensive pilot projects that a country will never be able to afford to take to scale does not work. Many other efforts are successful. Lessons learned since 1990 about educating girls are here grouped into six areas: political will, leadership, supportive fora, new partnerships, using a systemic approach, and conducting careful research and collecting reliable data to support action.

Girls' education is more than an educational issue; it is deeply influenced by poverty, tradition, habit, legal systems, and discrimination, among other things. Political will is required, not just to educate girls, but also to eliminate these non-education obstacles. The lessons that the past decade has taught about policies, programmes and planning will be crucial to providing equitable education for all in the decade ahead. Gender-specific policies that target girls are necessary. Coherent policies (such as raising the legal marriage age) and programmes are required, but it is not enough to assume that girls' education improves as other aspects of primary education improve. A general expansion of primary schools will initially attract both girls and boys, but a certain proportion of girls will remain out of school unless specific barriers are overcome. Simply expanding primary education without specific regard to the factors affecting girls is insufficient to increase girls' enrolment.

Policies and programmes that national and community leaders develop to achieve education goals for girls contribute to the crucial process of building consensus around the importance of girls' education at all levels of society. Political commitment at senior levels from those who make policies and decisions is necessary to move girls' education forward. Policy development and reform need to take place at a central and senior level. It is vital that any policy changes be made within the context of planning and development of the educational system as a whole.

Girls' education policies cannot be excluded from the Ministry of Education or left to a newly formed and disconnected unit or project implementation unit. The education of girls needs to be an integral part of the management of the national educational system. Examples of this include the Ugandan government's National Strategy and Plan of Action for Girls' Education in 1998, and Burkina Faso's National Plan for Girls' Education. This plan aims to ensure access to schooling for all children, improve educational quality, increase community participation in education, and improve capacity building at the national level.

Active, pragmatic leaders who are able and willing to negotiate and compromise in the best interests of girls' education both facilitate and lead the way to improvements in girls' education. Women's strong leadership is particularly important. Leadership takes many forms; some leaders are strong advocates, other quiet reformers. But these differences notwithstanding, the examples of leaders in government, religion, civil society, NGOs, education, and the law, for example, provide extraordinary legitimacy for girls' education. The Forum for African Women Educationalists (FAWE) is one example of an organizational network that captures the synergy of ideas, the influence, and the power of women leaders working to promote the best interests of girls' education. Five African women Ministers of Education founded the Federation of African Women Educationalists (FAWE) in 1992.

The organization now has thirty full members (Ministers or Vice Chancellors), thirty associate members (former Ministers or Vice Chancellors) and twenty-eight male associate members (Ministers of Education). To facilitate national and grass-roots work, national chapters, at various stages of development, are present in more than thirty countries. FAWE has pressed forward on an agenda of policy change and advocacy; it also has a programme that gives awards for innovation. In addition to leadership at international, national and district levels, the leadership of pupils, parents, teachers, community members, school management and administration is also essential to the improvement of girls' education.

Since girls' education is closely related to established patterns of discrimination against women and girls, leaders at all levels need to work to mobilize the entire range of stakeholders around the key educational issues for girls. These stakeholders will together help form a new set of standards and values affirming that girls' have the right to basic education, and that the community has an obligation to provide it in a supportive and enabling environment. Utilizing stakeholders, especially the community, to analyse the situation and intervene in girls' education, has proved very fruitful in expanding educational opportunities for girls over and over again.

Ongoing awareness-raising about girls' education is central to sustaining its impact. Gender sensitization cannot be viewed as a one-time workshop event. Deepening individual, collective, and institutional awareness of girls' issues requires long-term, thoughtful analysis and reflection. Policies and programmes need to emphasize continuing awareness education about educating girls at all levels.

This is especially important for key actors in gender and education issues to ensure that they understand and can communicate the rationale of girls' education. Programme activities need to ensure a gender perspective that points out the need to integrate gender analysis into the beginning stages of programme development. This will help to increase knowledge and to change attitudes, practices, and behaviour towards girls' education at all levels.

The only way to properly combine all five of these key areas (political will, leadership, supportive fora, systemic approach, research and reliable data), in a way that facilitates the kinds of change necessary to give all girls a basic education of good quality, has been through extended and expanded partnerships. New and creative partnerships have brought the necessary dynamism into education systems, defined broadly, and enabled them to expand and reach out to include girls. In the 1990s partnerships developed between unlikely entities: corporations, non-governmental organizations, communities, teacher organizations, governments, students, and international organizations. Partners have sometimes had to adapt to new modes of functioning together, but this has stimulated innovation.

Developing partnerships across sectors is helping to remove obstacles to girls' education. Water, hygiene and sanitation; income-generating activities; health and nutrition services; integrating life-skills education into school curricula (including HIV/AIDS prevention education)—these are some of the areas being linked to girls' education programmes.

The African Girls' Education Initiative (AGEI) is an innovative partnership between UNICEF and the

Norwegian Ministry of Foreign Affairs with CIDA that evolved during the last half of the decade. A comprehensive, integrated structure that links national, regional, and global systems supports the AGEI. Programme implementation combines seven strategies, which operate concurrently at the various levels: ongoing support for country programmes of co-operation; advocacy; partnership; communication; knowledge building; support to NGOs; and resource mobilization. The multi-country programme was designed to implement distinct and coherent vision for achieving change in girls' education in over twenty African countries. Partners associated with national institutions, ministries, NGOs, communities, and individuals formulate and implement the activities that reflect contextual needs and interests. The programme has enabled 6,300 girls in Chad to enrol in school for the first time, increasing the enrolment rate from 65 per cent in 1997 to 70 per cent in 1998 in the sous-prefectures involved. In Swaziland, teachers have been trained in continuous assessment to improve the quality of education programmes. At regional levels, an especially successful dimension of the work has been the development of regional technical assessment teams that build regional and national capacity in monitoring and evaluation (M&E). And, at the global level, UNICEF's Education Section plays a key role in developing programme policy and co-ordinating programme advocacy, communication strategies, and other areas.

A long-term, coherent approach, incorporating all aspects of the education system as well as what will come in the years after, is the best option for making a difference. It is clear that to address issues of quality, equivalence, and demand in ways that can be sustained, it is essential to take a systemic approach to reforms so that girls are no longer excluded. Guinea, collaborating with donor partners, took this approach to education reform in the 1990s. Overall, it is clear that to overcome gender bias and discrimination it is essential to change education systems rather than to work on the margins. This has been an extremely positive lesson learned in girls' education, and has shown that quality and access are inextricably linked. Thus, many actions in support of girls' education have addressed quality, resulting in demonstrable improvements for boys as well as for girls. It is paradoxical that, in some cases, quality improvements for girls' education have actually increased the gender gap.

Staffing schools with female teachers also addresses safety issues and can provide girls with role models of a career they can pursue through their own education. This often means staffing a school with at least one female teacher. Marshalling the political will at all levels to leverage resources that will support these strategies will move the agenda of girls' education forward dramatically.

Increasing the proportion of female teachers in primary schools has a positive impact on female enrolments, as Bangladesh, Nepal, Pakistan, and other countries have seen. In order to augment their numbers, however, recruitment policies for teachers may need to be revised. Some options include reserving a proportion of places in teacher-training colleges for girls, decentralizing recruitment of local females, and revising administrative policies that affect female teachers.

Systematic assessment of the impact of these policies would be useful information for designing future initiatives. In countries like Afghanistan, where extreme fundamentalist religious policies have pushed girls out of school, creative alternatives are needed. In Afghanistan, UNICEF informally supports unemployed female teachers who have set up schools in their homes and where up to 60 per cent of the students are female. While the teaching force in some countries— especially in Southern Asia and sub-Saharan Africa—are dominated by male teachers, countries in Central Europe, Latin America, and other areas report a predominantly female teaching force.

The latter case may represent inequity and lower pay for women teachers, especially at the primary level, and must be addressed. In either scenario the concern is expressed that children should see and have teachers of their same sex as role models. However, to date there is no evidence of parents forbidding sons to enrol in co-educational schools with all women teachers, whereas parents do keep their daughters out of school if no female teachers are present. Perceptions and reassurances of safety are critical for girls, and the presence of women teachers in a male-dominated teaching force—women teachers who value girls and boys equally—must become a high priority.

Enforcing girl-friendly regulations ensures that schools are safe, respectful places for girls. Policies made at the national level, regulations for an entire school, and teacher-made rules for a classroom can all contribute to a school that is friendly to girls. Regulations might include returning girls to their rightful place in school following a pregnancy, constructing adequate latrine facilities for males and females, appointing girls to school leadership positions, or dismissing male teachers or students who sexually harass female students. These regulations and their enforcement are necessary to make a difference in the lives and academic experiences of girls. The safety and security of girls was a major theme in the African Conference on the Empowerment of Women through Functional Literacy and Education, and needs to continue as a major theme in education plans for the next decade.

Community and family empowerment and participation in school management and other activities are key to ensuring that girls enrol in, attend, and stay in school. Family and community participation contribute to the processes of decentralization and the institutionalization of community involvement in education. This, in turn, increases programme quality and sustainability. For example, in the family, a mother's support of her daughter's education is a key factor in girls' attending and staying in school. In disadvantaged communities, members have contributed significantly to girls' education by providing school funds, management, and the land, time and labour necessary for constructing schools and classrooms. Community ownership of schools, (management, control, financing and organization) is an important building block in promoting the educational participation of girls, particularly among populations that have traditionally had low female participation rates. Raising community awareness and responsibility for addressing some of the barriers to education has had impressive results in places like Bangladesh, Pakistan and Mali. Discussions of community involvement is not a panacea, however; communities must be empowered in deed. Adequate human, financial and administrative resources are needed to enable communities to fulfil their roles, as is a clear division of responsibility between communities and local and central governments.

Once communities are empowered to create and manage schools near their homes, with teachers they can trust and a curriculum they believe in, resistance to sending girls to school and keeping them there past puberty appears to melt away. Malawi had historically experienced a persistent gender gap to the advantage of boys. The year the waivers were introduced, girls were a majority in Standard 1 (51 percent) and girls' net enrolment in primary was 60 per cent compared to boys at 57 percent. Two years later, the government introduced free primary education for all and abolished the requirement that school children wear uniforms. The response from boys restored the gender gap, but levels of enrolment for both genders has risen tremendously and Malawi is now close to universal primary enrolment.

Benin introduced a bill that exempted girls in rural areas from paying school fees in 1993. While this is reported to have improved girls' enrolment rates in rural areas, there was also some negative impact since no revenue was available from other sources to replace the lost funds. An unequivocal benefit of any cost reduction initiative, however, is that lowered schooling costs can eliminate the necessity of parents having to choose which child, if any, will go to school.

The quality of education can be improved for all children and sustained over time through the creation of a child-friendly learning environment for girls and boys. This includes using participatory teaching and learning strategies and making use of locally available resources/ materials. Programmes in Southern Asia are placing priority on the quality of education with programmes implementing concepts such as multiple ways of teaching learning (MWTL), joyful learning, and child-friendly schools. Over 16,000 schools in Bangladesh are implementing the Bangladeshi Directorate of Primary Education's Intensive District Approach to Education for All (IDEAL). In 1999 IDEAL worked to build local level management and planning, launch a communication campaign, monitor school quality, conduct studies and adjust the curriculum to be gender sensitive. The formative evaluation has revealed that local level planning has mobilized local funds to provide an average of US $500 per school. In addition, teachers trained in MWTL have shown that using a number of teaching methods (group work, roleplaying, singing) is positive and effective.

Once in school, girls and boys need to learn something meaningful. Issues of learning and achievement are complex, but they need to be addressed. They include curriculum content and the capacity of the school system to implement it; the teaching processes and methods used to convey content; strategies for assessing learning gains and achievement, whether through continuous assessment or final examinations; and concomitant implications for training and recruitment into the teaching service. These issues are being addressed within a wider socio-political context that often contributes to the emergence of workable solutions. With a global push towards democracy and the encouragement towards greater decentralization of political power with the implicit emergence of greater local autonomy and accountability, getting more girls into school no longer seems an intractable problem. As the officers at the community level with the greatest knowledge of the barriers are now increasingly being granted the authority to address them, remarkable innovative solutions evolve almost routinely. In sub-

Saharan Africa, a number of government-sponsored alternative education programmes (COPE in Uganda, PAGE in Zambia and Dina schools in Madagascar) are providing basic education outside the formal system in a manner that recognizes and accommodates local realities. The Bangladesh Rural Action Committee (BRAC) remains one of the most remarkable efforts in successfully providing schooling opportunities for girls outside the formal school system. Good information can support action in a number of ways.

— it can help planners and programme designers develop effective programmes and target those populations that need help.

— public information considerably advances advocacy and promotes community ownership. Third, it can help monitor and assess progress.

Information needs to be collected carefully and recorded accurately and consistently, using sound instruments that allow data to be disaggregated by gender. The data must be analysed systematically and interpreted appropriately. Consumers of the data then must be taught how to use the information prudently. As school systems reach gender parity in access and other measures of girls' participation in school, attention will shift to the qualitative aspects of their participation. It is relatively easy to measure how many girls are in school, and how many are passing examinations. Measuring other aspects of schooling, however, such as the ways in which (and the degree to which) teachers' attitudes, images in textbooks, or interactions with other pupils affirm or erode girls' self esteem and educational aspirations, has been very difficult up to now. Qualitative measurement requires a different kind of process of data gathering and analysis that may not be familiar to those accustomed to dealing with quantitative data and indicators.

CHALLENGES FOR THE FUTURE

Certainly the focus on girls' education from a gender perspective has raised many important issues about boys' education, and it is fully recognized that a gender-sensitive education is one of the things that will make the vision of Education for All a reality. Similarly, the evolution over the decade in girls' education and, in particular, attempts to better understand the gender gap, have resulted in a much better understanding of exclusion—from school, but also in the classroom, even for many who are already in school but who are excluded from effective learning. This work, often pioneered by a focus on girls, can make it possible to adapt what is known to include other excluded and marginalized groups—one of which consists of adolescents, and there are others.

The HIV/AIDS pandemic is presenting unexpected challenges of enormous proportions. Girls are disproportionately negatively affected, whether they are infected or not. Immediate and concerted effort is essential, or more than 10 years' of hard-won gains in girls' education will be eliminated in just a few years. It is very apparent from the work in girls' education that the access to and quality of education are inextricably linked—it would be easier if this were not the case. This relates very closely to two other critical aspects of girls' (and boys') education: the need to understand both supply and demand and how these play out, one against the other. Everybody agrees that quality is important, but the experience of and challenge arising from girls' education is that the very notion of quality must change in some very fundamental ways.

A quality education includes learning the basics and learning how to learn in a safe, secure, gender-sensitive, healthy, and protective learning environment. This finding is an enormous challenge for those educational systems in which it is difficult to offer basic education that meets a conventional definition of quality. New research is revealing that the processes that accompany globalization are capable of increasing disparity and on a tremendous scale. This is particularly alarming, because women already compose the majority of the poor, and globalization could exacerbate this situation. In the face of this challenge and to break the cycle of women's poverty, girls' education has to be given new priority.

On the other hand, the promise of the potential inherent in the new information and communication technologies could make an enormous difference in alleviating unfair disparities. A paradoxical challenge for girls' education is deeply embedded in this possibility, however. There is growing evidence that girls and women are less likely to benefit from these new technologies than boys and men. A challenge not frequently discussed but which is becoming more obvious is a worldwide movement in support of religious fundamentalism, frequently with a concomitant decrease in the rights and empowerment of girls and women. The links of fundamentalism to patriarchy and their implications for educational change deserve more attention if girls' education is to move ahead at an accelerated pace.

To fully grasp these challenges and monitor how they are going to affect girls' education will require more robust data that extend beyond the conventional education statistics. Disaggregated data will also be necessary, so that the nature of challenges can be properly understood.

It is not possible to address every issue simultaneously. Priorities have to be set: some can be established globally, but good analysis at local and national levels will be essential in determining how best to overcome the barriers to girls' education in a particular context, and in what order. Simple access to any kind of basic education remains a major issue for millions of children, the majority of them girls.

Careful and strategic application of the lessons learned to close the gender gap and address educational quality are essential if all are to receive a quality basic education. There is no single intervention that will work everywhere—each context is different, and efforts must be made to adapt what is known to the particular and nuanced circumstances working against girls' education. Moreover, efforts in support of girls' education must now move from what have been limited efforts to efforts on a massive scale. This presents enormous challenges worldwide, but without such an acceleration, the majority of excluded girls will remain excluded from education—and from much more for the foreseeable future.

To make this extra effort, to accelerate progress, will require ingenuity, persistence, ongoing fostering of new partnerships, and significant resource mobilization and utilization. There are probably fewer 'lessons learned' in girls' education with regard to resource mobilization than in any of the other areas selected for discussion. Yet, this topic may present one of the greatest remaining challenges.

It is hard to reach the girls who must be included (poor, with disabilities, affected by conflict or HIV/AIDS, engaged in child labour, for example), and it is likely to take more resources per child to reach them than it took to reach those who were already in school. To reach the goal of Education for All, girls must be included—without this the world will have failed to deliver on the promise of a basic education for all. Girls can be included. It is possible. We can, we must, achieve this goal.

Disseminating the knowledge of (a) what the range of possible strategies to be used with respect to improving girls' education are; (b) what local conditions and opportunities call for; and what the optimal mix of strategies can be, is a continuing challenge. Further, expanding the educational opportunities for girls and women tends to lead to the emergence of issues about the availability of career opportunities. If girls are gaining as much education as boys, then the rationale for excluding them from certain careers becomes less and less justifiable. An underlying challenge in this area is to understand what the key elements of a successful strategy are and which aspects are context-specific.

The increased enrolments that often result when parents are encouraged to send their daughters to school almost always bring into sharp focus a debate on quality. The sudden increase in enrolments can cause acute shortages of classrooms, textbooks, teachers and pedagogical materials. There can be a deterioration of quality on a number of dimensions: performance, repetition and dropout rates, teacher morale and turnover, and parental satisfaction. The challenge then becomes the task of identifying the critical indicator or set of indicators for measuring shifts in quality and assessing which of the many input variables contributes most to maintaining quality. Once this has been established, a national consensus needs to be developed and shared so that limited resources will be effectively spent. This question requires a close collaboration between technical experts, who can assess the impact of different sets of quality indicators, and community and government interests who can use that information to come to political and economic decisions about the organization of schools.

The effective implementation of any new initiative requires close monitoring and processes for continuous review, assessment, evaluation and re-formulation. When carried out in an environment in which stakeholders are empowered to share their views, these processes will lead to a more effective implementation, in which bottlenecks and unexpected consequences are dealt with more quickly and lessons are shared more systematically.

The rapid change in technology, particularly information technology, and the forces of globalization have made the issue of exclusion from basic education even more urgent. Countries without significant numbers of computer-literate men and women are in danger of finding themselves permanently thrust into the periphery. Females are particularly vulnerable because all the available evidence suggests that women, even in the West, are only a small minority of Internet users, computer programmers, web designers, etc. As the gender gap closes, it is becoming obvious that marginal girls need to be reached. This girl is likely to be poor, to live in remote areas—either geographical or culturally—to be of a different religion or ethnicity. Providing an education of sufficient quality and relevance will be more and more challenging and expensive. However, should be encouraged by the success that has already been experienced in educating populations hitherto considered unreachable. We need to be particularly vigilant about viewing 'the girl child' as a unitary concept. As has been noted before, while gender is a very important human parameter, it is not the only one.

The relative disadvantage of each individual girl is mediated by her family's income, her ethnicity, religion and nationality, to name but a few factors. Are the new programmes and policies being utilized by those who need them, or are they simply magnifying the advantage of those who already enjoy high status? In particular, what does it mean when female enrolment increases more sharply at the secondary and tertiary levels than it does at primary, even in countries with relatively low enrolment levels? As we work towards attaining universal primary education, it will be important that each region and country develop reasonable targets and benchmarks for girls' education.

It would be a mistake to ignore the changes that have taken place in the global environment when we discuss the achievement of universal access to schooling. It is patently clear that notion of basic education will need to encompass levels of technical competence that were undreamed of in 1990. In a modern economy, more and more of even the most basic jobs (factories, supermarkets, etc.) require a familiarity with computers.

2

Girls Participation in Primary Educaiton

Where norms of participation are established, girls are likely to be enrolled automatically, while in the absence of strong norms they may stay honk without much parental forethought. When Egyptians were asked to explain the reasons children stayed home or dropped out, many answered vaguely "parental neglect" or "ignorance" to explain what they viewed as a general lack of motivation and interest in education. Contrary to what one might think from reading the literature, it is unlikely that parents spend much time consciously weighing the relative costs and benefits of schooling, even though these factors that ultimately affect their decisions about schooling.

Expressed attitudes are also highly unstable and often unreliable. As example, Egyptian parents who claimed strong resistance to girls' education changed their minds almost overnight when schools were conveniently constructed nearby. Later they blamed school factors while school staff blamed home factors as the major reason for some of the children dropping out. Parents also commonly report "politically, correct" answers to interviewers who come knocking at their door.

In Egypt most parents know from media sources that children should go to school. There are three major conditions should exist to increase the likelihood of girls' enrolling and staying in school:

— schooling opportunities exist and are accessible;

— parents have a positive attitude toward girls' education and are willing to sustain the costs; and

— girls themselves want to complete primary school and are capable of doing so.

Though separated analytically all three categories are interrelated and all affect whether and how long girls participate in schooling. Accessibility of opportunities, for example, both influences and is influenced by parents' and children's attitudes about schooling. The advantage of this framework in a specific context is that once a major condition is satisfied, it may be eliminated-along with its many subfactors-as issues requiring attention.

Following are the factors that encourage girls' participation in some countries:

— Safe schools situated nearby within the community

— Low or no-cost schooling

— Female or trusted male teachers

— Single-sex schooling after grade 3

— Convenient scheduling

— Primary and secondary schools in the same community

— Middle to higher socioeconomic level, urban residence

— Encouraging gender role definitions, late marriage, female role models

— Gender-sensitive instruction and school settings

In developing countries with the lowest educational participation and the largest gender gaps, the problem of non-participation is frequently accompanied by inadequate educational opportur.ities. Studies in Pakistan, for example, showed that what was thought to be a lack of' parental interest in education for girls in conservative Balochistan aid Northwest Frontier Province (NWFP) was rather a lack of accessible opportunities.

In other countries, such as Mali, few schooling opportunities have existed in rural areas until quite recently, making the reason for non-participation all too apparent. Because it is such a critical prerequisite, the accessibility of opportunities needs to be eliminated first as a constraint before addressing other problems of girls' participation. Whether schooling is accessible depends on more than just whether buildings exist nearby.

Parents filter their views of accessibility through a complicated set of perceptions and circumstances. These include at least three considerations: whether opportunities are seen as physically accessible, whether parents are comfortable having their children access them, and whether "institutional" barriers exist that prevent children from accessing them.

Even when circumstances appear the same to an outsider, the outcomes in terms of participation may be quite different because of the differing perceptions of those concerned. There is no guarantee that a supply of nearby schools will inevitably lead to universal education, although it most certainly will lead to higher enrolment rates.

The expectation of educators has been that a nearby school will increase enrolment, especially of girls. However studies suggest a more complex reality. Filmer finds that indeed in six African countries out of the Demographic and Health Surveys (DHS) data he analyses, the presence of a primary school does have a significant effect on the enrolment of 6- to 14year-old children and may even have a larger effect than the relative economic levels of the children's families.

In most countries where there is an effect, however, there is no difference for girls or boys. Deolalikar found that an increase in facilities positively affected the enrolment of the poor but had no effect on the wealthy, possibly because the poor are more likely to live in areas where fewer schooling opportunities are available. A related finding in his study was that a decrease in pupil-teacher ratios had a positive effect on the wealthy and a negative effect on the poor, possibly because increasing teacher costs meant fewer resources available to provide places or incentives for schooling.

Parents find it difficult to send small children to a distant school. What may be accessible to older children may not be so for younger children who cannot walk as far, be counted on to stay out of danger, or find their own way. For example, the Egypt study found that girls' enrolment in primary school dropped off rapidly when the school was more than 1.5 km away. If children were already attending a distant school, and a new school was constructed nearby, parents tended to keep boys in the distant school and bring girls back to the closer school.

In other words, parents stressed what they saw as "program quality" for boys and "protection" for girls. In Mali, 5 km appears to be the outside limit for daily commuting, after which parents who can afford to do so board children near the school. In Malawi, children in one sample walked an average of 2.5 km to school and in some cases even 9 or 10 kin. In Pakistan, enrolment dropped off for girls who lived more than 1 km from Mosque Schools.

The variation probably signals important cultural norms about "safety" and "protection" for children. Streams, highways, railways, and other obstacles make otherwise nearby schools difficult for some children to get to. Even if children enrol initially, difficult access may affect attendance, dropout, and completion. Few public school systems in the developing world have their own transportation systems and public transport is usually not a convenient or affordable option on a regular basis.

Some of these distance and danger concerns are revisited when a child is ready for a higher stage of education located in a building that is separate or at a distance from the earlier stage. Lavy shows that the presence of a nearby secondary school can have a positive effect on primary school enrolment. The proximity of the two schools in an area may also signal long, well-established schooling or possibly urbanized environments. Filmer found that having a primary and secondary school in the same community affected enrolment in only four of 38 countries in his sample, Benin, Burkina Faso, India, and Zimbabwe.

Although girls at this age may be able to walk farther, they have reached puberty when parents view them as sexually, vulnerable. Parents may perceive physical and moral dangers in schooling children, They may believe the road to school is fraught with potential dangers if children must move through isolated or overgrown areas or enter into the territory of rivals. In Upper Egypt and in Yemen, children remain at home when their families engage in revenge feuds with other families.

In Pakistan, children sometimes do not enrol in nearby village schools located in the territory of another family, even when relations with that family are cordial. Parents may require greater protection for daughters by insisting they be accompanied by friends or male members of the household. If appropriate protection is unavailable, they may refuse to send them, abruptly stop sending them, or delay enrolment until they are capable of walking longer distances or protecting themselves better. In all of these cases, the result is fewer years of schooling.

Parents may not allow girls to attend schools where the teachers are male, non-local, or unrelated, or when the teachers are female if they are seen as negative role models because of their dress or behaviour. Although many parents feel more comfortable sending girls to school if there are female teachers, at present only 33 percent of teachers at the primary level are women in developing countries.

These ratios are significantly lower in some parts of Africa, Nepal, and Pakistan, and the gaps are usually more critical in rural areas where the positive effects of female teachers would be felt more strongly. The low percentage of female teachers is related to the low enrolment of girls and the subsequent lack of qualified female teaching candidates in areas where they arc most needed. Several studies have shown that the standards of school buildings and equipment have little effect on girls' enrolment. The poorer facilities in the mosque schools, for example, did not have a differential effect on girls' and boys' participation even when a better government school was nearby.

Even when schools are located nearby, they may not be able to accommodate all children who want to enrol. Departments of education limit enrolment by several means:

— defining minimum and maximum ages for entry into each stage of education
— requiring birth certificates as proof of age
— limiting the number of shifts that can be held in a school building
— scheduling classes at a time of day when some children cannot attend
— setting strict class sizes or fixed student/teacher ratios
— setting promotional quotas for who can move on to the next level of schooling.

Alternatively, they can insist that all children be accommodated in whatever way is necessary, through larger classes, more shifts, or by using temporary class spaces, e.g., on outside verandas or under trees. Local school authorities who feel they are not given sufficient resources, space, or teachers, may also set their own informal limits. They may require unofficial fees (for extra activities, repairs, supplies, school events and hospitality, scouts, special tutoring, etc.) that are enough to prevent poorer children from attending or force parents to choose which of their children to educate. Fees may be graduated so that they, become less affordable as grade level increases. They may set entry criteria such as skill capability, limit the number of students in a given year who enrol, and discourage those who must wait another year or two as they and their parents become accustomed to other uses for their time.

Teachers may discourage students who have disciplinary or academic problems from continuing. Community members may react to scarcity by deciding informally to allocate places to certain groups of children and refrain from enrolling others. When permitted to build additional classrooms, parents who contribute funds determine who will attend. In circumstances like these, where limited resources and places make choices necessary, it is girls more often than boys, and the powerless more often than the powerful, who are denied the opportunity to learn.

Parental attitudes about girls' schooling and their willingness to sustain the costs While parents are the usual arbiters of whether children go to or stay, in school, especially in the earliest grades, they can also be strongly, influenced by what their children want. Thus, one should be cautious about attributing too much foresight or planning to parental decisions about schooling. For example, one Egyptian study showed that a significant number of rural parents simply did not care whether their children enrolled, especially when they were girls.

Most who sent their children-according to teachers-also did not know what was required to do well in school, such as maintaining regular attendance and having quiet time to complete homework. Consequently, many of the early generations of rural children failed, repeated, and eventually dropped out of school. Factors affecting parental attitudes about girls' schooling fall under three main headings: parents' background characteristics, the costs and benefits they see in education, and the general norms and practices of the community that affect parents' attitudes about schooling.

Parents' attitudes are, of course, also affected strongly by the convenience and accessibility of schooling opportunities. Certain background characteristics of parents have been shown in a number of studies to be correlated with educational participation.

The three most important are:

— economic level,

— parental education, and

— residence in an urban or rural location.

Economic level

One of the most important predictors of education participation-both enrolment and completion-is the relative economic level of the households from which children come. Filmer demonstrates that while generalized female disadvantage is confined to certain regions of the world, wealth gaps are large in almost all countries where DHS data have been collected. Sometimes in countries where gender gaps are small there are still significant wealth inequities in education.

Filmer consequently stresses the importance of looking at both gender and wealth simultaneously when addressing inequities of education. Some examples of attainment show this wealth phenomenon. In Mali, for example, only 12 percent of the poor complete grade I , while 60 percent of the wealthy do so. The gap in median grade completed between wealthy and poor is four grades in Mali, three grades in Egypt, and 10 grades in India. Almost all children from wealthy households in Pakistan complete grade 1 and most complete the primary stage, while much lower levels among poorer families do so.

In countries such as Nigeria, Egypt, Morocco,' India, and Pakistan with already large gender gaps in enrolment, wealth deepens the female disadvantage. In India 81 percent of males aged 15-19 and about half of females complete grade 1, and the gap is still significant at grade 5, with 73 percent of males compared to 51 percent of females completing. When wealthy males and poor females are compared, the gap widens to 96 percent for the wealthy males and 29 percent for poor females completing the primary level.

These examples suggest that in some countries, girls' low completion rates might be most productively addressed by narrowing the focus to girls or rural girls from poorer families. In one group of countries, the wealth gap in enrolment is larger between wealthy and poor females than it is between wealthy and poor males. In Pakistan for example the gap is 35 percentage points between the two groups of males and 64 between the two groups of females.

In Egypt, the gap is 17 for males and 39 for females, and in India 34 and 55. Fihner notes that even while wealth gaps in general are much larger than gender gaps, investment in girls' education is still important because of the greater private and social returns that accrue to that investment. As he notes, it is the level of girls' education and not the gap that is important. However, he adds that wealth is also an inequality that needs to be addressed when the objective is universal education.

A few small subnational studies suggest that other factors may at times counteract the wealth effect on education. Anderson and Chaudhry found that poverty did not differentially affect the participation of girls and boys in mosque schools in Pakistan, presumably because such factors as proximity, security, and low cost encouraged most nearby children to attend.

In Egypt, poor urban boys drop out at or before the end of primary to earn income or learn skilled trades, while girls remain in school in hopes of qualifying for "respectable" civil service jobs.' In Botswana a similar female advantage appears at junior high and high school, probably because boys "incur higher opportunity costs by attending the lower quality schools in view of the income producing alternatives available to them in mining and agriculture".

PARENTS' EDUCATION

Another important characteristic of parental background is educational status. Most studies dealing with this factor report that it is the education of the mother that is an important predictor of whether a girl goes to or stays in school, but fathers may also have some effect. Miske and Prouty report that daughters of educated women are as much as 40 percent more likely to enrol in school.

In Egypt, Fergany finds that a better educated (more than minimum literacy) mother improves the chances for children's initial entry and attainment of higher cognitive achievement levels but not necessarily of primary completion. In Kenya, mother's education has a greater effect on the enrolment of children from poor as opposed to wealthy households, suggesting that positive effects on children's enrollments might be obtained by promoting literary classes for females from poor families.

The marginal effect of increasing the average years of schooling of female adults in the household by one year, for example, increased the chances of children's enrolment between one and six percentage points. Overall the effect of adult females' education was significantly greater than males' education on children's schooling in 11 countries. USAID's Girls' and Women's Education (GWE) activity is investigating these relationships in Bolivia, Nepal, and Honduras.

This was not true in countries where either adults' or girls' attainment was consistently low or high without much variation. In nine other countries, the education of adult females had a significantly greater effect on boys than girls, which is partly explained by the overall low level of adult female education in these countries.

URBAN-RURAL RESIDENCE

Where information is available, all measures of participation and attainment show consistently more positive outcomes in urban areas—these indicators include enrolment, dropout, completion, and often even achievement. Even though the differences between urban and rural outcomes are well known and accepted as fact, it is difficult to estimate them accurately because of the way "urban" and "rural" data are reported.

Pakistan demonstrates how schooling outcomes differ in urban and rural settings. At the start of the Pakistan

Primary Education Development (PED) Program in 1989, estimates showed that primary participation rates varied from highs in urban areas to lows in rural areas. Primary dropout rates similarly showed male dropout highest (77 percent) in rural Sind and female dropout highest (93 percent) in rural Balochistan compared to lows for males (12 percent) and females (24 percent) in urban Punjab. A study by the National Education Assessment Program (NEAT') showed that achievement scores also vary by urban-rural location, albeit with small differences and overall low scores. In grade 5 Urdu, for example, urban girls had a mean of 27 percent and urban boys 25 percent against comparable scores of 26 percent and 23 percent in rural areas.

Urban parents are more likely to feel the importance of schooling for both boys and girls. For them the benefits of education are obvious and the constraints fewer: schools are nearby, the household workload is less, community norms favour education, and employment opportunities are more widespread and visible. In Lahore, Pakistan, for example, education is considered so important to urban parents that they make significant sacrifices to ensure their children receive the best quality education possible.

Over 90 percent of Lahore's children go to school including 75 percent of the poorest children. And most go to private schools despite the higher cost and the fact that government schools exist near by. The favourable conditions found in urban areas may be absent in rural environments. In rural areas, child labour is more essential, primary and higher level schooling opportunities may not be accessible or safe, academic programs may be weaker; promotional exams may loom larger, and fewer parents are capable of providing the help with schoolwork that some systems require.

In Bangladesh, for example, BRAC found most rural parents were unable to help their children with homework and so reduced the amount of homework required of students. IMPACT in the Philippines found it difficult to rely on parents who were illiterate or too tired by the end of the day to help their children with homework, and sought out high school students to give remedial help to primary students.

In brief, location of residence and wealth are the strongest predictors of education outcome, with gender often aggravating both of these conditions. Although neither is within the capacity of educators to affect directly, it is possible to create conditions and incentives where disadvantaged children will be more likely to avail themselves of educational opportunities.

BENEFITS OF EDUCATION

Even though parents' decisions about schooling may be largely based on an unconscious sifting of options, it is nonetheless important to review the various costs and benefits as parents may perceive them. Those coming from a cultural perspective that stresses the rights and potentials of individuals sometimes find it difficult to understand that many parents in developing countries base their assessments of costs and benefits on what is good for families as a whole, and only secondarily on what is good for individual children. The focus on family interests may explain why studies in Africa have shown that what was assumed to be community financing of schools turns out in reality to be household financing of education. Parents, not a generalized "community" group, are expected to bear the burden of their children's education.

This is important when it comes to expectations about community support, since involving communities in many cases simply intensifies the burden on parents whose capacity to pay may already be strained. The reasons parents give for their children's non-participation have changed over time and have tended also to differ for girls and boys. A study of rural families in Egypt found that an important current reason for non-participation was "poverty" and that this reason was more important for girls than for boys. "Tradition" was not a prominent reason.

In previous generations poverty was considered more important for males than for females who were constrained by the equal factor of tradition. At least two intervening events may account for this change. First, parents expressing their opinions in the mid 1990s after years of government pressure to educate children, no longer felt it acceptable to excuse a lack of participation with the answer "tradition." Second, the associated costs of education have become so high that many poor families consider seriously whether and how many of their children to educate.

Consequently, poverty had become a justifiable reason for non-participation. When respondents reflect back on the past, tradition seems an acceptable reason for women not to have participated earlier but men need the more compelling reason-poverty-for their lack of participation. In families of actual dropouts, parents said the main reason was an inability to pay fees, while additional reasons included lack of motivation for boys, and early marriage for girls. A similar difference of opinion occurred in Egypt when parents and teachers were asked why specific children dropped out of school. Parents blamed the school while teachers blamed the parents.

THE COSTS OF SCHOOLING

"Costs of schooling" almost always appear prominently in lists of reasons for non-enrolment or limited participation. The costs that might deter poorer children from attending school are well known, and include such expenses as school fees, clothing, supplies, textbooks, snack foods, transportation, and in some cases after-school tutoring.

A study in Egypt found the cost to parents of schooling a child averaged about LE 250 ($75) per child per year. Multiplied by several children in a family and considered in the light of an annual per capita income of $1,200, the difficulty is obvious. In addition, some of these expenses increase with grade level, causing families with lower incomes to consider seriously whether they can afford to continue sending their children to school, especially if they are not doing well academically or if girls "do not especially need or want education."

Though some costs may seem normal, such as clothing and shoes, they are not always so. A school child may be expected to wear a dress or uniform that exceeds the cost of normal dress in poor families and may have to wear shoes when they might otherwise go barefoot. Parents may give children pocket money or buy them special kinds of food to take to school.

Although not always absolutely necessary, these costs may be considered part of the expense of schooling, in order that children "will not be shamed in front of others." Girls' expenses often exceed those of boys if uniforms are required. In Guinea the cost is $2 more for a girl out of a total average of $18. In some countries like Mali, distance to existing schools may be so great that children must be boarded in the vicinity, or daily transport must be arranged at considerable expense to parents.

The costs of village schools in that country are expected to be almost entirely covered by parents as donors reduce their share of the costs in the future. When primary and secondary enrollments declined in Tanzania in the 1990s and educators discovered children starting school on average much later, a study was conducted to investigate the effect of costs on school-going.

Parents also saw dramatic differences between the still-affordable cost of primary and the no-longer-affordable cost of secondary for poor families. The authors concluded that even if more places were provided, without subsidization, the costs of secondary school were high enough to discourage enrolment at both levels, since the returns of primary schooling were not enough without secondary schooling. The late start in the Tanzanian primary school was attributed to opportunity costs which were a more significant problem for girls.

The opportunity costs to the family of doing without the child's household labour or outside earnings has been identified as a significant factor affecting girls' participation. A study in Egypt show girls doing 85 percent of the household work assigned to children in rural areas. In Guinea, 95 percent of girls claim they help in household tasks, 55 percent say they do so on a daily basis, and 50 percent say they come to school late because of these chores.

In cultures with strong segregation of sex roles, the work tasks of girls and boys are not usually interchangeable, although if crossover is required, it is more likely that girls will do boys' tasks. If one parent dies or is ill, the child of the same sex must leave school and take over the parent's work. Since girls are charged most often with caring for siblings, they may have to leave school when a new child is born or when the work of many young children becomes too burdensome for their mothers.

Eldest girls sometimes are withheld or withdrawn from school for these purposes even while their younger sisters go to school. Birth order therefore can be a critical factor when parents only send some of their children to school (although the pattern is not always consistent) (author's experience). Another long-term cost parents must consider is that educated children often refuse manual or agricultural jobs when they become adults.

Overall, parents must come to believe that the benefits of education including the quality of the education their children receive outweigh the costs of schooling. To the question what are the benefits of educating your children, the standard answer of rural Egyptian parents is that boys can obtain jobs and avoid a fixture in farming, and for girls that education "expands their vision" and teaches them "to organize their homes and family life better," and on a personal level that it makes them "cleaner and neater."

Parents also believe educated girls make better wives and mothers. In both Egypt and Pakistan, parents report that educated people in general are more polite, responsible, and rational in their thinking; consequently, school staff see it as a significant part of their mandate to emphasize proper behaviour. The opposite is true in Mali, where parents believe schooling makes children less willing to adhere to the respect behaviours expected in villages.

A factor that in some areas draws educational, economic, and social benefits together is the fact that education is a major marker of class status. In Egypt and India, for example, the easiest way for motivated individuals of the lower classes to make the transition upward is to acquire degrees that lead to higher class occupations. Once they achieve higher status, their children must attain similar educational levels to maintain the family's standing.

This is one of the most important operative conditions in countries undergoing rapid expansion of the middle classes and bureaucratic occupations. Noting this phenomenon, education officials and developers once believed it would only require educating one generation of children to solve the problem of participation. Now, however, other factors-the cost of education, inflation and subsequent lowering of the social value of degrees, the poor quality of education programmes, a labour market that no longer rewards education, etc.-have undermined that expectation.

Among some lower-middle-class urban families in Egypt, for example, where a decade ago parents would have sacrificed much to educate their children, the rates of participation are declining because of the high costs and limited personal returns associated with education. The length of children's schooling is related to parents' expectation, about the benefits of each stage.

Most parents recognize two qualitatively different levels of effort and benefit in formal education. The first-primary or basic education-confers basic literacy and numeracy skills. The second requires longer immersion with concomitantly greater expenditure of resources and effort. The benelll of completing this second level is that an individual qualif:es for professional occupations with their accompanying stable incomes and preferred status-possibly a job in the government bureaucracy.

While most parents may be willing to send children to school long enough to obtain functional literacy, they may hesitate to support the second level of effort, which requires that a child succeed at intermediate, secondary, and even possibly higher education levels before obtaining significant additional benefits. A parent may withdraw a child from primary school when functional skills seem well-enough developed if there is little expectation that the child will continue to higher stages.

Encouraging a child to complete primary school may indicate commitment to completing higher levels of education and the added efforts and expense (tutoring, fees, etc.) of passing national promotional exams. A parent may also withdraw a child before the end of the primary level because "education didn't take"-that is, no apparent learning went on-either because the program was poor or the child lacked the capability to succeed in the system.

There are few private advantages in completing any of the intermediate stages after primary unless children expect to continue to the final level that ensures a job. In the first years of schooling, parents may sanguinely report that they want their children to continue to the highest level possible, but by the final years of primary they often have more realistic expectations. "High repetition rates in major exam years are usually a result of children who continue to hope they can make it to the next level."

Parents are susceptible to the norms and expectations of their communities. Families in several villages in Egypt were asked to recall the educational experiences of members as far back as they could remember. When plotted on a timeline, their answers showed that first, a small group of boys enrolled and persisted, urged on by interested parents and community leaders, and by example became role models for other village boys. This was followed by a second period when a larger group of boys enrolled but many dropped out, and finally a period when a large group of boys enrolled and persisted as education became a village norm.

The periods were similar for girls, but with a time lag until a critical mass of boys was enrolled. The enrolment and persistence stages for both boys and girls could be extended or compressed depending upon such local factors as a newly accessible school in the village, the encouragement of a village leader, or the advent of a popular teacher. However, in these villages other variables such as location near major urban settlements or industrial sites, farsighted community leaders, and the early establishment of schools also played a role in shortening the time lag for girls.

Community leaders played an important role in children's participation in the Egypt study. Wherever a greater than usual enrolment existed in the early 1980s, leaders could usually be found who had supported education by soliciting resources from the official establishment and encouraging parents to send their children to school.

When community members become involved in the establishment of local schools, they usually shape conditions in ways that overcome parental resistance, such as ensuring flexible schedules, overcoming financial hurdles and monitoring the presence of needed materials and staff. A study of community participation shows that indeed involving communities in education delivery tends to have a greater effect on educational participation than any of the other anticipated community participation outcomes of lowered costs, achievement, quality, etc.

Interestingly, decreases in participation also occurred for both males and females at times of major national crises, even when the crises did not especially affect conditions in the communities concerned. The NGO fieldworkers implementing the Community Support Project (CSP) in Balochistan, Pakistan, had to overcome strong parental distrust of government before they were able to win their cooperation. Community leaders, depending on their attitudes, can become effective catalysts or major obstacles to educational participation.

The record of religious leaders-national and local-has been mixed with regard to promoting modern primary, education. The example of Egypt is again instructive. Meanwhile an entire religious school system has been established in Egypt from first grade through university in competition with the "modern" school system. In the last few decades, it has been the fastest growing school system in Egypt, although it only enrolls about 8 percent of those in the public system.

Other religious personnel in Egyptian villages also do not normally become involved in issues of public education, and if called upon to do so, cannot be relied upon to promote girls' participation. Many have themselves been educated in the religious system and consequently may not be positively inclined toward "secular" education. Involving them in campaigns to enroll or keep children in the public system may unnecessarily complicate the issue of participation in some countries, and give them an importance in the matter they would not otherwise possess.

In Pakistan, a study of mosque schools (where a regular teacher is attached) found that 18 percent of imams were against girls' education, 13 percent favoured their education up to age 8 or grade 5, and 60 percent unconditionally supported girls' attendance in mosque schools. Islam as a source of values about educational participation. There are, however, no direct strictures in the Koran or Sunna opposing education. The reverse in fact is true-there is clear encouragement to educate both boys acid girls.

Individuals and special groups, however, often use religion to reinforce their personal views and practices, knowing they will not be criticized if invoking religious rationales. The Koranic injunction for women to be modest, for example, could be interpreted by a person opposing girls' education to mean she should not go out in public and therefore should not go to school. On the other hand, those who support girls' education can cite other Koranic verses saying that both girls and boys should be educated, "even if they must go to China", to do so.

Evidence that Islam itself is not necessarily an obstacle to girls' education can be found in the enrolment figures of culturally conservative countries of the Arabian Peninsula. These countries have a large reverse gap favouring girls over boys in higher education, and little if any gender gap at the primary and secondary levels. Also a number of "fundamentalist" groups in Egypt have demonstrated their support for education by opening tutoring centres to help children of both sexes with exams and homework and by providing financial help for poor children who cannot afford school fees.

Christianity as source of values on education. Christians in Middle Eastern countries have generally been early adopters of education. In Lebanon where overall there now is a reverse gender gap, Christians have had the longest involvement with education. Egyptian Christians were also early adopters of education and before independence constituted a disproportionate ratio of the educated middle and upper classes.

The states in India with the highest female literacy rates (such as Kerala) of these successes to early missionary schools, that even today provide a better quality academic program than most schools in the public system. A widespread belief in traditional societies that educated people should be accorded special respect does much to encourage children and their parents to make the supreme effort to become educated. Teachers are revered in many parts of the developing world, serving; as role models for rural children.

In some countries they wear special clothing in order to be recognized and treated with special deference. In Egypt, a change in dress style automatically accompanies the transition from lower class to middle class to indicate that a person is educated. A well-dressed, respectable-looking woman walking; alone will be called "doctor" to give her the presumption of responsible behaviour that comes with education.

In Nepal, participants in literacy classes begin to see themselves as "educated" and begin to adopt more responsible health and other behaviours. When women who may previously have been denied membership on community councils become educated, they are suddenly given places on the councils and their advice is sought, e.g., India. All these behaviours create a set of assumptions in communities about the respectability and desirability of education for women. They may be sufficient to counteract the negative constraints of poverty and tradition for girls.

"Gender" is not a well-understood concept in many countries. The idea that sex roles are socially defined-not predestined-and vary from place to place may be quite alien. As with any cultural belief, beliefs about social roles are assimilated from childhood, and it is very difficult to redefine gender roles in such contexts.

Since gender roles often make functional sense in the way family life is organized, it is also not enough to say they should change without understanding the part they play in social life. Community resistance can sometimes be overcome by casting the benefits of education in terms of education's contributions to the well-being of all family members rather than only to the well-being of the girls. One of the significant constraints recognized in the literature has been the lower private returns on investment in girls' education.

Girls and their parents in many cases do not see their opportunities measurably expanded by education. Arguments citing the important social returns to the country in improved development indicators are not convincing to family members who may care more about immediate as opposed to hypothetical future benefits.

Parents are especially affected by local views of how education affects the marriage chances of girls.

In many countries men are expected to be more educated than their wives, which causes some women to perceive each level of educational attainment as narrowing the pool of men they might marry. At some level of education, they know they have essentially given up the chance to marry. On the other hand, educated men in some conservative Arab societies have gone from wanting "more malleable" uneducated wives to insisting upon "more companionable" educated wives. The rush to educate girls in these countries and the consequent female advantage in higher education is threatening to make prolonged education there "a woman's activity."

In India an educated women capable of working may receive marriage proposals without bringing the dowry that usually accompanies the woman in marriage. '4 In Guinea the main reason for dropout is marriage, and the second most common reason is household responsibilities. People in that country are reported to have seen more instances of girls who have been "corrupted" by schooling than who have improved their chances for a career.

Schooling, consequently, is seen as giving girls a freedom that makes them less desirable marriage choices. In any case, parents will be affected by prevailing community views of marriage when considering the length of their daughters' education. The strong association between education and employment has made it difficult for rural parents to see why girls would benefit from schooling beyond the primary level.

Increasingly, however, many governments have expanded services in rural areas and have employed educated women. Seeing this, parents begin to view education as a way of ensuring that their daughters will be able to support themselves if necessary as adults." Among the urban poor in Egypt, as noted, prolonged education has come to be seen as a way for women to gain access to respectable jobs. Although women in the Middle East, North Africa, and Pakistan are not expected to provide the main support for families, increasingly urban and even rural men want to marry, educated working women who can contribute at least to a portion of family income.

The community's views on whether women should be employed are a major factor in girls' long term educational participation. Another is the realities of the labour market and the extent to which girls can translate their credentials into opportunities for work. An effective encouragement for educational participation has been the example of community members who acquire higher degrees and demonstrate personally the advantages of acquiring stable, "professional" jobs.

In agricultural communities, "desk" jobs are coveted because employees do not have to dirty their hands or depend upon the vagaries of weather and price controls for their income. In the Egypt study, the local role models admired most by the community were rural residents in such "modern" jobs as agricultural extension workers, irrigation engineers, teachers, social welfare personnel, and other government bureaucrats. Without compelling reasons, community norms prove highly resistant to change, especially if modifying them has a direct effect on family life, as changes in gender roles are apt to do.

One sociologist was surprised to find how resistant Asian family values had proven in the face of the homogenizing effects of globalization. He found that while family values resisted new kinds of development at first, once they had started and their advantages were apparent, the same family values were extremely helpful in spreading new practices rapidly. When rural Malian parents claimed their children needed more relevant education, their first priority was income-earning skills--carpentry, welding, machine work, etc. for boys, and sewing and craftwork for girls-additions to the program that were too difficult and costly for this resource-poor nation to provide.

In all these examples employment occupies a central place in parents' minds when considering the benefits of education. In many contexts that means that boys are automatically considered to need the skills of education more than girls do. A very recent study of adolescents in Egypt reported the main reason for dropout for both sexes in all the regions studied regardless of social-economic level was poor scholastic performance. The reasons girls may feel they want to continue or drop out of school fall into three categories: the schooling environment, the academic program and their performance, and their own personal problems with schooling.

There are a number of physical and psychological elements in the schooling environment that discourage the participation of children. In certain seasons, the schoolyard may become a sea of mud or snow. Children may have difficulty leaving the classroom to go to, the bathroom or, if they go, may find unsanitary conditions with little or no waters' and a lack of privacy. Schools in rural areas of Northwest Frontier Province (NWFP) in Pakistan demonstrate extreme examples of all these conditions, exacerbated in many cases by teachers who have ceased to assume and but a caretaker role. Students are led in memorized texts for a large part of the day by other students beating a recitation rhythm with large sticks.

In the stressful, overcrowded classrooms, teachers spend a great deal of time disciplining students for infractions of behaviour, incorrect answers, inattention, lateness, and a host of other misdemeanours they feel threaten order. The discipline is often harsh and physical, but it may also consist of holding the child up as an example of ridicule or commenting negatively on some aspect of his or her ability. An important determinant of children's willingness to stay in school is their enjoyment of and sense of success in the academic program. When programs are poorly presented and boring, when little real learning goes on and when exams are ordeals, children quickly becoming discouraged with schooling. This is especially true for children who have difficulty adjusting to rigid rote learning formats inherent in many school systems.

Some of the academic problems include the emphasis on rote memorization, poorly prepared teachers, inadequate instructional materials and aids, inability to effectively assess the learning results of the system, poor support for teachers do must cope with large numbers of students of differing ages any liabilities, and high teacher and student absenteeism.

Beginning primary classes have as many as 100 children crowded into small rooms. Classes may have so many children that it is impossible for teachers to provide individual attention. In multigrade classes children may be left for long periods waiting until the teacher is ready to work with their group again. A

Pakistani study found that the time spent engaged in learning in multi-grade classes was only about 60 percent of that found in single-grade classes. Children become bored and listless waiting for their turn while trying not to engage in activities that might attract the discipline of a teacher.

Tests are developed and administered by classroom teachers until the end of the primary level when for the first time a national test makes it possible to see how individual schools and children fare. Pass rates are set at about 30 percent, because few children are expected to do any better. Studies conducted in Pakistan in the late 1980s attempted to link educational inputs in schools with student achievement. Few inputs proved statistically significant. However, one that proved to have positive effect was the length of the teachers' academic training.

Rural female teachers produced students with the lowest achievement levels, probably because on average they had fewer years of schooling. Students of male and female urban teachers with about the same years of schooling scored roughly the same. In Pakistan, Afghanistan, and elsewhere instructional materials compound the already serious difficulties of teachers and children.

Indeed because of system-wide expectations for progress, teachers dog not have the time to compensate for the textbooks' deficiencies. Overall, the books have no systematic link to learning objectives or skill-building, contain few practice exercises, arc teacher dependent, and have no way to adequately assess what children have learned. When it comes time for promotional exams, memory and "trick" rather than competency-based test items make exams an ordeal for children.

For the Pakistani children who enter the system, survival requires fortitude to surmount all these hurdles. For girls who have "no real need for education" even greater stamina is required. Unfortunately these symptoms of a poor learning environment and subsequent poor skill development are seen in a wide spectrum of countries. In Egypt, the adolescent study found that although 61 percent of the children had never failed an exam in any subject, one quarter had to retake exams, and 15 percent had to repeat a year.

An aspect of schooling that has become well recognized in recent years is the differential treatment of boys and girls in schools and classrooms. Besides affecting their learning outcomes, these biases affect girls' feelings about school and their desire to continue. There are a number of ways that gender bias makes the academic environment less attractive for girls than for boys. Biases are found in how the curriculum is presented; how teachers interact with students; how school opportunities, places, activities, timings and the distribution of resources are organized; staff expectations about the needs and capabilities of girls and boys; and how schools are decorated, staffed, and administered.

In addition to these in-school experiences, girls may come to school having less practice than boys in the languages of instruction or of speaking in front of an audience of peers. Society may have encouraged shyness and accommodation in girls while rewarding aggressiveness in boys. Girls, as already noted, may be given less time during the day to devote to learning outside of school because of their household chores, and in school because they are asked to do more of the school's housekeeping chores.

They encounter problems with sexuality more often than boys do, including sexual harassment by male teachers in some countries. Girls who become pregnant are far more likely to bear the consequences than the males who impregnate them.

Teachers also tend to reinforce gender stereotypes in their interactions with students. In school they may segregate girls and boys in different rooms or areas of classrooms, where they receive different kinds of education, disproportionately less of the teacher's attention and reinforcement, or disproportionately more negative reinforcement.

Insidious and often ingrained in the unconscious of adults, these different treatments arc often difficult to identify and even more difficult to remedy, and they inevitably lead to an attitude that closely replicates the views of the prevailing society. Girls, as a consequence, experience schooling vary differently from boys, and school rather than having a liberalizing; effect on societal views, continues to confirm them. Community values, as one would expect, affect girls' treatment in school.

Overall teachers provide less support for and have fewer positive expectations for girl students. A study in Nigeria showed that although the positive interaction, between teachers and boys and girls in the early years were about equal, by the sixth grade they were significantly more positive toward boys than girls. Other differences included boys taking more of the teachers' time, teachers viewing boys as more scholarly and competent than girls, and girls remaining more passive and doing less hands-on activity and consequently being judged as less competent.

Personal factors affect children's desire to remain in school. A child, for example, may have chronic health problems. A study of adolescent children in Egypt found that 46 percent were infected with parasites and the incidence was higher among rural as compared with urban children. Children may have handicaps, or even single bouts of illness that stare a cycle of absenteeism, failure, repetition, and dropout.

In NWFP, a major health problem affecting large numbers of children is iodine deficiency, which leaves children lethargic and with IQ levels reported to be reduced on average by as many as 15 points. Overall, girls in developing countries are known to be at greater risk for malnutrition, and they tend also to receive less medical care than boys. In African countries, HIV/AIDS has decimated large numbers of the adult population-out of 2.6 million who died worldwide in 1999, 85 percent were in Africa. In Africa, 10.4 million children under age 15 have lost either their mothers or both parents. Many of these children are left to scavenge for food on their own with no time left or supervision to encourage their attendance in school.

Women in Africa are infected with HIV at higher rates than men, and adolescent girls are five to six times more likely to be infected than boys because they are preyed upon by older infected men. Girls tend to bear more of the burden of this epidemic than boys by being asked to assume a larger share of the household responsibilities of missing adults.

Individual children may also have difficulties attending school from the fatigue of walking long distances or because they fear real or imagined dangers along the way. They may face teasing by fellow school mates or feel threatened by those they believe will harm them. They may have household duties that make it difficult to arrive on time with completed homework, and they may fear the punishments this and other infractions elicit from their teachers.

A child may speak a language different from the language of instruction, or from other classmates, or from the teacher. This is particularly true in African countries with a multiplicity of tribal languages and a lingua franca that is unknown to many rural children. With their greater range of mobility, boys may have more opportunities to pick up these languages than girls who are usually confined to areas closer to home. As noted already, school systems and staff also tend to be less welcoming and encouraging of girls. Girls may leave school early to marry in some countries, although in Egypt where early marriage used to be common, adolescent girls. Children are only dropping out when a unique set of circumstance forces them to do so.

INITIATIVES OF GIRLS' PARTICIPATION

Most initiatives aimed at increasing girls' primary participation fall into four categories, those that expand the supply of schooling opportunities, mobilize support and/or provide incentives for girls' education, improve the quality of schooling programs, and increase the resources available for girls' education. Initiatives that expand the supply of schooling opportunities. Schooling can be organized almost anywhere-in buildings meant for other purposes, temporary facilities, people's homes, and under trees.

Many ministries of education, however, insist upon fully constructed, government-dedicated buildings before committing the other resources needed for formal schooling. Consequently, the high cost and time required for construction denies education to millions of children who become "too old" while waiting for schooling opportunities to materialize. In addition, capital development budgets consume a large share of education budgets that might otherwise be available for program improvements or the search for more cost-effective delivery methods.

Kane and Yoder in a literature review, noted that of 78 interventions implemented to improve access, 23 did not report results, 4 failed to produce results, 1 had mixed results, and 50 reported they increased access. The interventions consisted mainly of provision of schools (buildings and programs) and community involvement. Other interventions included recruitment and training of local female teachers, bilingual education, curriculum revision and provision of textbooks. They also reported 70 interventions aimed at girls' persistence.

Of these, 17 provided no information on results, 7 had mixed outcomes, and 4 did not produce results. Forty-two interventions in 11 projects reported actual increases in persistence. The persistence initiatives focused more on teachers and less on schools. Community initiatives were the most common effective interventions, including economic incentives, sensitization campaigns and community. In the 1960s, most of the World Bank investments were in civil works construction.

By the 1970s and 1980s investments turned more to textbooks, teacher training and supervision and community support. Now the demand is for better organization of the inputs, for decentralized decision-making, for better teaching techniques, and assessment of outcomes management of education combined with other interventions. Also effective were alternative education programs and scheduling flexibility.

Initiatives to expand the supply of schooling opportunities are by far the most common means by which educators and developers attempt to increase girls' participation. A well-constructed school houses children for years and consequently its impact extends almost indefinitely.

The two largest donor-supported school construction projects were mounted in Egypt and Pakistan in the 1980s and 1990s with support from USAID. During the 1960s and 1970s, the Government of Egypt constructed very few schools soy it was not until USAID supported the cost of constructing almost two thousand schools that capacity was measurably increased. An assessment of the Basic Education project estimated that girls' enrollments increased in rural primary schools from 35 percent (897 thousand) in 1981/82 to 42 percent (1.4 million) of total enrollments in 1990/91, or by an increase of 60 percent.

In the same period, urban female enrollments grew by 26 percent while urban and rural boys' rates grew by 19 percent.' In 1996 Save the Children/US (SC) took over the management of Afghan Refugee Village (RV) schools as an implementing partner with UN High Commissioner for Refugees (UNHCR) in Pakistan. After an assessment of the status of the existing formal schools, SC embarked on an initiative to increase access, promote gender equity and improve program quality in the schools. As one of the first steps in this effort it built upon an already established program of nonformal education to open Home-Based Girls' Schools (HBGS) in Balochistan in 1997.

The present 52 one-classroom schools spread over five of six refugee settlements (one still resists the schools) accommodate roughly 1,037 girls in grades one through four. The aim of the initiative was to provide primary education opportunities for girls in conservative Afghan refugee communities who for reasons of distance and/or the presence of boys and men in RV schools were unable to access formal schooling. HBGS classes take place in the homes of literate women who are given student textbooks, teachers' guides, blackboard, chalk and writing supplies, and from grade 3 a tin trunk library of books. The children sit on the ground on a tarpaulin.

Children and teachers receive edible oil as an early incentive to encourage participation but this incentive will phase out soon with little anticipated effect on enrolment levels. Teachers receive small stipends to teach classes that meet three hours a day, five days a week, 11 months of the year at a time of day convenient to the teacher and the girls.

Conditions in the Afghan refugee communities of Balochistan are similar to those found in other developing countries where education services are difficult to deliver:

— Girls require special circumstances if they are to enrol at all, and especially if they are to continue beyond grade 3.

— Resources are scarce both for the implementing agency and in the communities served by the initiative.

— Distance to and between communities makes schools difficult for supervisors to monitor and support.

— Qualified female teachers are hard to find and those candidates who exist may have serious gaps in their education.

— Most parents are illiterate and therefore cannot help their children with schoolwork.

Between 1990 and 1994 the USAID-supported Pakistan Education Development Program (PEDP) had as one of its aims to increase primary school enrollments, especially of girls and rural children. It expected to do this through school construction in two low-literacy provinces. The schools were to be constructed in rural communities where schools had not existed before but where there were sufficient children to support a school. Previously the small number of primary schools had been mostly dedicated to boys, although a significant number of girls attended the boys' schools.

Officials believed two schools would need to be constructed in each village to deal with what they believed were parents' desires for single-sex schools for girls. To assess this view, PEDP was preceded by a Human Resource Survey (HRS) of all villages in both provinces to determine where schools were needed, where potential staff were available, and whether parents would agree to educating girls in the more cost-effective alternatives of coed schools taught by male teachers.

Negotiations to develop a contracting process delayed school construction in NWFP, but the results of HRS convinced educators to change their policy and open boys' schools to girls, an act that effectively opened opportunities for them in a number of villages. An assessment, however, found that by the time USAID withdrew, the inherent biases toward boys continued in the distribution of opportunities in Balochistan and NWFP.

In both Egypt and Pakistan, there were two subsidiary benefits to the construction effort. Preceding the construction, formal mapping surveys were undertaken for the first time to determine where schools existed and where they were needed relative to areas of unserved population. In some cases these assessments provided a defence against political efforts to site schools where they already existed and to ignore areas of need where residents were less influential.

In both countries, also, construction was preceded by the development of a more transparent contracting, implementation, and supervising process to cut down on graft and substandard construction. Despite these efforts, informed observers believed that construction contained 5-25 percent of "unseen" costs. To these costs have to be added the expense of overbuilding in anticipation of poor construction and private supervision services whose aim was to catch the more egregious problems of poor building practices.

In the end, schools cost significantly more than their actual cost. An additional difficulty arose in Egypt when the government reneged on its agreement to maintain the buildings and they began to deteriorate. In Oman, political will and increased resource allocations made it possible to increase schooling participation very quickly. In 1970 when the national education program started, there were three boys' schools with 909 students. By 1988/89, there were 703 primary and secondary schools with 294,934 students.

The gross enrollment rate for females at the primary level by 1988/89 had reached 95 percent, and girls comprised 46 percent of primary and 51 percent of secondary enrollments. Oman is not a wealthy country, and therefore the allocation of funds to provide schooling places meant sacrifices in other sectors. In Kenya, rural communities attempted to duplicate the high quality facilities and opportunities of urban, government schools.

The harambee (self-help) movement started as a result of the rural population's frustration at being left out of the country's modernization schemes. Communities in Kenya' gathered funds and constructed their own secondary schools, the expectation being that they would then receive resources from the government for the academic program. However, as harambee schools increased in number, fewer government resources were available and communities found it difficult to sustain the expensive schools. Roughly half failed before they were completed. There was no doubt that the harainbee schools increased the participation of rural children significantly.

However, most harambee schools could not afford the quality inputs such as good teachers and special facilities like science labs that allowed students to compete successfully for places at higher education levels. Significantly, when the government decided to support the schools with inputs such as teacher salaries, the results were only marginally improved, and at the same time the government was left with fewer resources to spend on equalizing opportunities for poorer communities who could not afford their own schools.

In the long run, the community initiatives helped some children while deepening the differences based on gender, region, and wealth without significantly opening up the opportunities villagers sought. The harambee initiative demonstrates very vividly how mortars and brick do not guarantee educational access or quality. Despite these difficulties, school construction is still a significant intervention in the future plans of some countries.

The Government of Morocco, with help from the World Bank, for example, plans to raise girls' enrollment by almost 20 percent between 1996 and 2001 by constructing schools and increasing access to clean drinking water and sewage. The intent is to increase girls' enrolments in rural areas from 34 percent in 1996 to 55 percent in 2000, through building schools closer to girls' homes and improving; access to clean drinking water and improved sanitation facilities.

To encourage girls' participation in particular, some communities are also building boundary walls, latrine, wells, and canteens. Similarly in Egypt, after a hiatus on major construction, USAID will support the construction of roughly 800 new classrooms in a new community schools project.

A number of initiatives have aimed at reducing school construction costs. Many countries now find it impossible to afford standard schools for all children. Donors and lenders have made up some of the shortfall in the past, but it is unlikely they will be willing or able to continue doing so. Perhaps this is why they have been at the forefront of effort to find less costly alternatives and to model their advantages to local governments.

COST-SHARING INITIATIVES

Cost-sharing initiatives tend to be of several kinds, with benefits accruing; to different groups. The costs .of some may be ,roughly equivalent to those incurred in constructing normal government schools, but cost sharing arrangements lower the cost to governments. Or they may use less costly materials to the benefit of everyone. Or rarely, the government may take on more of the costs to the benefit of parents. The prevailing trend is to assign more of the burden to parents, often accompanied by use of less costly construction materials. One study has warned against the approach of expecting parents in African countries to assume more of the burden of education costs. What has been thought of as community financing of education, it reports, turns out to be household financing, i.e., parents pay the bulk of community contributions.

In Mali, the cost-sharing burden falls more heavily on parents, yet with some cost effciencies in school components. There are four ongoing community school models in Mali, three in the south and one in the north. One major cost saving derives from community-constructed schools. In three initiatives, rural parents contribute their labour and local materials while the donor pays for corrugated roofs and wooden window and door frames. The final initiative in the desert regions of northern Mali is supported through loans and facilitation by CARE. Local communities purchase tents to use as schools.

There are similar initiatives to reduce costs through community support in Ghana, Guinea and Malawi. USAID supports these projects as a way of demonstrating to local governments that there are ways to expand places, improve learning, and at the same time reduce the costs to governments. One of the common methods governments use to reduce the costs of establishing rural schools is to require communities to donate a plot of land for the school. Critics of this approach say that urban communities are not required to make land available and it is therefore unfair to ask poor rural communities to do so.

In Mali, educators answered these complaints by proposing fees for urban students equal to the amounts contributed by rural students. Proponents say that land is much more costly and difficult to find in urban areas, and therefore the community could not afford the cost. Without rural land donations, they say, schools would be significantly more expensive, and there would be far fewer of them.

Another approach to cost-sharing is to ask villagers to provide an- interim or temporary school facility. The Community Support Project in Balochistan required communities to show their seriousness in educating girls by providing such a facility for several years before the government constructed a standard school.

Since a number of girls' schools had previously been opened and then closed for lack of teachers or students, this interim school ensured not only that costly schools would ultimately be used, but also that education could be delivered to girls expeditiously without waiting for schools to be built. Egypt's community school project also required communities to build or donate a facility, in this case for as long as the school was needed.

One of the most cost-effective approaches to the problem of schooling venue is that used by BRACE in

Bangladesh. For a three-year cycle of roughly 30 students taught by one teacher, BRAC rents a low-cost room that has been renovated by parents. At the end of the cycle the room reverts to its owner if there are not enough children ill form a new cycle.

The Government of Pakistan opened mosque schools in 1978 to provide schooling access at low cost to village children. The schools:

— were staffed with regular primary teachers;

— taught normal curriculum with free materials;

— paid the imam a stipend to teach religious subjects;

— were supervised by the District Education Office; were held for four hours a day so as not to interfere with prayers; and

— had a three-year course from which qualified students could enter formal schooling.

Girls' participation increased when no school had been available before, when the schools were located nearby, and when imams encouraged their participation.

Pakistan similarly rents a number of primary schools, especially in urban areas, classifying them by the misleading name of "shelter-less schools." However education officials disapprove of these schools and try to replace them as soon as possible with new construction or by purchasing; existing buildings.

In Punjab a project to use prefabricated materials in school construction is failed when it met resistance from local government officials, and ill Egypt efforts to encourage community-supported school construction also met with the resistance of the Ministry of Education, which favoured standard school designs. In Kenya, temporary classrooms were said to be far less sanitary than standard classrooms. It seems premature, however, to condemn "temporary" buildings for human problems that are not a consequence of a particular building type.

Critics argue that interim schools are usually not built to withstand the wear and tear of many children, that they require more maintenance and are less comfortable in extreme weather than standard schools. Some very creative minds, however, including the famous Egyptian architect Hassan Fathy, have developed school plans are more functional, comfortable, inexpensive, and aesthetically pleasing than standard schools, and yet these too have failed to gain acceptance.

Much of the resistance, to the so-called substandard schools comes from government bureaucrats who believe that educational quality is linked to presentable schools. The problem may also be related to the inability of many ministries education to prepare the cost-comparisons necessary to make informed judgments about different options. A rented school appears as a permanent drain on education budgets, whereas the costs of a built school disappear after it is completed.

Many schools in Pakistan hold classes on school verandas or under makeshift rush shelters outdoors. Younger children occupy these makeshift arrangements while the few children persisting to the upper grades and seriously engaged in preparing for promotional exams occupy large classrooms furnished with desks and chairs. IMPACT encouraged parents to build study shelters to accommodate larger numbers of children and make it possible to implement a new kind of teaching-learning methodology.

One of the most common and practical ways to solve the problem of inadequate space is double-shifting. Egypt, with its high population growth rates, has resorted to two, three, and sometimes even more shifts. In Egypt double-shifting involves two separate "schools" using a single facility, one in the morning and one in the afternoon. Most recent five-year plans have called for eliminating multiple shifts in Egyptian schools, believing it produces an inferior academic program.

Studies have shown, however, that double-shifting can be organized so as not to negatively affect learning as long as different sets of staff are used in the two shifts and care is taken to allot the same amount of time to instruction as in a single-shift school. Girls, however, have tended to suffer more from "shift" solutions than boys, because they may have incompatible household work schedules or, if assigned to the later shift, may be tired from their chores.

Nevertheless, shifting is a practical solution to the high cost of construction, especially where governments have not yet been able to extend schooling to all children of a community. Other unique approaches Egypt has adopted two other approaches in trying to solve its space problems. The most unusual one used by some schools is the so-called "flying classroom," where one class moves from room to room occupying the places of students who are taking physical education.

In 1987, Egypt decided to drop the sixth grade from primary schooling, hoping thereby to expand places at the primary level. The experience was not successful: first, the Ministry of Education found that the transition to fewer grades left gaps in the learning of some children who suddenly skipped to higher grades; second, it produced an enormously difficult to accommodate "double-cohort" moving through the system up to and including university; and finally, overall learning deteriorated as a result of fewer years of primary education.

In the near future Egypt plans to revert to a six-year primary system. Some circumstance make it difficult to provide schooling because settlements are scattered, remote, nomadic, transient, or in other ways difficult to reach. There may be problems finding qualified teachers or the supply of teachers may be limited and girls in some conservative societies may have difficulty appearing in public after a certain age.

Some governments have solved these problems through flexible delivery systems that focus more on the needs of the populations being served and less on rigid expectations for formats of schooling. India has experimented with a number of ways to approach difficulty-reach communities, using "barefoot" teachers to accompany nomadic groups, extracting indigenous children from their communities, training them in boarding schools and sending them back to teach, and assigning teachers to travel with brick-making construction workers to the next job.

India has thousands of NGOs and other voluntary groups dedicated to teaching children in communities where it is difficult for them to obtain an education or to persist for long in the system. Most school construction programs have criteria (whether strictly observed or not) for locating schools, usually conforming with parents' feelings about proximity and the safety of children.

Where it is practical, some education districts separate lower and upper primary sections into small feeder lower schools near the child's home and consolidated upper primary schools further away but accessible to children coming from the feeder schools (Pakistan). As far as we know there is no research to indicate whether this separation of stages leads to higher dropout as children make the transition from one to the other.

BRAC schools serve as de facto neighbourhood feeders for the fourth grade of the formal system, as do Community Schools in Egypt into formal intermediate schools. Increases in primary enrollments also put pressure on the next higher stages of education. Governments (e.g., Pakistan and Egypt) are beginning to look for ways to construct facilities for these higher stages nearer primary schools to encourage graduates to continue.

In Pakistan there is higher likelihood that children will continue their education after the primary level if they study in a grades 1-12 school than if they have to move to a separate location.

Mali's community school models compare favourably for cost effectiveness with current government primary schools (and they cost much less for the government). Altogether 1,500 three-year community schools are supported by USAID in the south of the country through Save the Children (STC), World Education (WE), and Africare. The variations in the three models create an interesting basis for comparison. The WE model is essentially the same as the government schools except for the help provided by WE in establishing the schools. STC schools have enhancements to the basic model in the form of specially prepared materials and beginning classes conducted in the local language.

Africare schools have just started, and their model is not yet well defined, but it includes a comprehensive service approach that includes not only education but visits by health specialists. These "low-cost" models cost $36 per child in the WE model and $54 per child in the STC compared with $42 per child in the government schools. Although the community models have several cost-saving elements (community-assisted construction and furnishings, and lower teacher salaries) these are offset by the increased costs of training and teacher support, and in the case of STC students, the specially prepared materials they receive.

To make this a cost-effective input would require that children show a 30 percent higher achievement than in WE schools. Parents now pay a large share of the costs and in the future will be asked to pay even more, raising equity concerns about the costs to poor parents. The WE model could eventually make it possible to educate twice as many children at the same cost to the government that it now pays.

In Afghanistan, conditions are unique both because the government has banned girls and female teachers from public schools, and because the government provides practically no support for a public system of education. In response to this situation, Afghan educators, with the support of the international assistance community, are developing a quality "package" of tested materials, teacher instructions, and assessment items that with minimum orientation for the teacher can be used to provide primary schooling for Afghan children in almost any setting within or outside of Afghanistan.

This package reduces primary education to its essential elements and makes it "transportable" so that children under difficult conditions will be able to pursue the equivalent of a formal education under the supervision of a minimally prepared adult. Programmed materials may be the next step for older children.

INTERACTIVE RADIO INSTRUCTION (IRI)

Interactive Radio Instruction (IRI) in recent years has focused more attention on gender issues and programs for women. IRI has been used in more than 20 countries since 1974 including early childhood programs and primary level courses in math (Thailand, African countries, Haiti, Nicaragua, Honduras, Bolivia), science (Papua New Guinea), language arts (Haiti), foreign languages (Kenya, South Africa, Dominican Republic, Costa Rica, Pakistan, and Bangladesh), health (Bolivia), civics (Haiti), environmental education (Costa Rica), and critical thinking skills (Ecuador).

IRI has also been used for teacher training (Indonesia) and adult education (Honduras). The transportability of the programs either through broadcasting services or audiotapes means children can obtain quality instruction even when fully qualified teachers are not available or the small numbers of students or their remoteness make it difficult to afford a normal program.

The advantages of IRI are its cost effectiveness, its demonstrated academic results that are usually equal to or higher than comparable formal programs, and its potential teaching-learning benefits. For example, it can compensate for poor teacher preparedness and a lack of specific skills (such as foreign languages). It can model new and perhaps more effective teaching methods, and provide a more uniform teaching standard across regions so that a poor rural child theoretically can receive the same quality of lesson as a well-to-do urban child.

Critics have pointed out the weaknesses of IRI: the time that may be wasted in waiting for the broadcast; the fact that some children may not respond well to IRI's participatory methods, and the fact that some skills such as reading and writing cannot be taught by radio. Thus, IRI, cannot substitute for good materials and teachers. Another downside of IRI is that officials of some countries have difficulty accepting the idea that radio technology can be effective when it differs so radically from traditional delivery. They may also resist the high costs of program development.

Nonetheless, under certain conditions IRI can be a potent instructional tool. IRI's potential has not been fully tapped. It might also help girls continue their education in environments like Afghanistan where schooling may be interrupted before the end of primary not only because of conservative attitudes but also because teachers cannot cope with the more difficult subject matters in the upper primary grades. By the third grade many Afghan girls may be secluded at home.

Donors are often urged to improve physical facilities in the belief that better infrastructure attracts more girls and improves program quality. However there is little evidence that structures alone increase girls' enrollment or improve program quality. Anderson and Chaudhry, for example, found that the standards of equipment and buildings in mosque schools did not have a differential effect on girls' and boys' participation.

Girls' enrollment appeared to depend less on the quality of the facilities than on the fact that they existed and were nearby. The Asian Development Bank's girls' schools in Pakistan were not any better attended than others, even though they were built on the premise that large, well-endowed schools would be more attractive to girls. Similarly Warwick and Reimers found no evidence that a school's facilities related in any way to student achievement.

Rugh, however, found that the physical appearance of a school influenced supervisors' impressions about the quality of the academic program in them and that there was some relationship between their perceptions and actual student achievement. One explanation for this effect may have been that supervisors preferred large, well-staffed schools, characteristics that Warwick and Reimers also found related to higher achievement.

Overall however it is unlikely that construction in and of itself is responsible for good student learning. A number of non-construction physical inputs have been provided to schools in an effort to make learning more attractive and to encourage more enrollments. Textbooks are perhaps the most important input. It is not uncommon in rural areas to find several children sharing textbooks, to find books missing altogether or arriving several months after school has started.

The Government of Balochistan provides textbooks to rural children to encourage their enrollment but, compared with NWFP where parents buy books from private dealers, Balochistan has more difficulty getting the books to schools on time or in sufficient numbers. Because the books are made of poor quality materials, they often do not last the year, nor can they be reused. Nevertheless, they provide an important incentive for many children. Their cost, however, is becoming prohibitive for the government, and the need to keep production costs low has affected their quality in the past schools, which ultimately overburdened existing NGO capacity to follow-up and monitor the paraprofessional teachers.

BRAC has also implemented a successful program of upgrading under-qualified, usually female, teacher candidates from villages where BRAC schools are established. BRAC pays its teachers considerably less because they lack full qualifications. A problem with these teachers in any system is that they often do not have the academic skills to teach above the early grades of primary where more complicated coursework and the addition of foreign languages requires a more sophisticated knowledge.

Social scientists have been interested for a long time in how social norms change and whether governments can do anything to change people's values. A new field called behavioural economics suggests that people tend to imitate other people's behaviours and that they "often act more like sheep than like rational individuals." With elaborate computer models, one scientist is trying to understand what happens when "norm cascades" occur-when communities shift rapidly from one norm to another.

Malawi's GABLE project is the best-known effort to mobilize communities in support of girls' education. Through local rallies, radio broadcasts, and a theatre-for-development group, it brings messages supporting girls' education to individual communities. The theatre group lives for several days in a village, taking part in daily activities and learning about education issues and barriers to girls' education. At the end of this time they play out these issues in skits, and convey messages about girls' education using adapted local songs and dances. Communities develop action plans and community development officers follow up and support their implementation.

During the time this program was first being implemented the government announced fee waivers for the primary level, which led to large increases in enrollments for boys and girls. GABLE specifically addresses "completion" issues by working with initiation counsellors and parents to show the benefits of girls completing their education. Some of these counsellors have become effective advocates for girls' education. A significant amount of the NWFP budget was allocated to school furnishings in new schools. Blackboards and teachers' desks and chairs were useful and generally appreciated items.

However, many of the children's desks and benches were piled in corners because they took up too much space and couldn't accommodate the numbers of children in the lower classes. They thus occupied classroom space and the attentions of supervisors who had to inventory them every year. Since most rural children sit on the floor at home and are not accustomed to benches and desks, this was a needless expense. Another largely unused input was kits with instructional aids a teacher might use to demonstrate subject-matter concepts.

Teachers were often untrained in the use of these materials, were not accustomed to using these items in teaching, and were afraid they might have to pay for any damage that occurred to the items during class. Libraries of selected books met the same fate, many remaining unused and locked up in head teachers' offices.

In parts of Afghanistan UNICEF provides writing supplies to children, and while these are undoubtedly useful, the example of next-door Pakistan shows that renewable materials such as quills, slates, and wooden writing boards may be better and longer-lasting investments.

In general there are limitations to the accomplishments that can be expected from physical inputs alone. Construction can have an impact where schools did not exist before, but it will not in itself improve academic performance, nor is it necessarily the best use of resources. Provision of textbooks can have an effect where few existed before or were too costly for parents. Only some furnishings and supplies-in particular ones related to instruction such as blackboards-are likely to be worth their cost. All diminish as an incentive over time if the costs of sending children to school relative to family income becomes a burden.

Lack of qualified female teachers who are willing to work in rural areas has been a major deterrent to girls' programs. The Directorate of Primary Education in Balochistan, with support from UNICEF, organized a Mobile Teacher Training Program (MTTP) to support minimally educated local women to become primary school teachers in community schools. The program consisted of short intensive workshops, starting with "emergency" support, and over time building the practical as well as theoretical skills of teaching.

Eventually the young women were expected to complete other requirements to gain their credentials, including completing matric diplomas and participating in further teacher training. The government of Balochistan waived its usual requirements for teacher selection in order that these teachers might be paid and begin teaching immediately. This program has had difficulty over the years keeping up with the large expansion in girls'

Communicating messages about the value of girls' education Several countries have used the media-radio and television-to promote messages about education explicitly or indirectly. Egypt has broadcast messages about the importance of education and indirectly as themes in the story lines of popular television series. The "soap opera" series has proved successful in establishing the importance of education for girls.

Pakistan has used billboards to promote education. In both .countries, however, a general distrust of government reduces the impact of direct messages about education. Involving communities in-the establishment of schools As already noted in the costsharing section above, a number of initiatives worldwide have incorporated community involvement as a major component in their design, usually to reduce the costs of education to government but also as a way of mobilizing support for primary education generally, and in most cases especially for girls.

In Egypt, 1992 the Ministry of Education, with support from UNICEF, opened four schools for 121 students. By May, 1995, there were 34 schools with over one thousand students. The initiative, targeting girls in rural communities, aimed to:

— involve communities in the construction and management of schools;

— use NGOs to facilitate the hiring, training, and support of local staff;

— employ a child-centered approach to learning organized around learning centres, self-instructional materials, and regular assessment;

— provide a program equivalent to primary schooling, yet scheduled according to the needs of the community;

— have teacher-facilitators selected by local school committees; and

— develop a model that is easily sustained and replicated.

Community School Projects in Egypt, Mali, Malawi, and Ghana. For the most part communities provide labour and financial resources, select sites, identify students and local teachers, determine school schedules, and provide monitoring and local oversight over the schools. They may also troubleshoot problems and establish a link with education officials. NGOs usually are necessary to facilitate this involvement.

The expectation is that when parents have a stake in creating the conditions for and managing the local school, they will be more likely to enrol all their children, especially girls. Enrollments do appear to have increased in education projects having a community involvement component. The major criticism of these initiatives, especially those supported with outside help, is that they are likely to have sustainability problems when the support is withdrawn. The problem may be due to the lack of attention in project designs to the long-term incentives and structures that need to be in place before support is withdrawn.

Fey Algeria is perhaps unique in its efforts to become involved with the community. To make sure the school is lodged in the local context, staff members live within the community, develop special programs to meet local development needs, and ensure that the school is at the centre of local festivals and celebrations. Parents are actively involved in all its programs and activities. Fey Algeria views its institutional role as primarily supportive and communicative of good ideas that originate in local communities, rather than authoritarian or directive of what should take place.

Another effort in Tanzania encouraged communities to take responsibility for their own schools. A community education fund was established by a donor to provide funds on a matching basis with funds raised by communities. The aim was to encourage community improvements in local schools. Communities were given double the total in fees they collected from students, after they submitted a plan for the use of the money. The results were that parents' contributions increased considerably, acceptable plans were developed, and improvements (usually consisting of construction) were made.

The activity seemed highly motivating to parents. The drawbacks were the costs (to be sustained they would have to be taken over by the government), the potentially less-effective future implementation by non-NGO bureaucrats, the questionable use of funds for building rather than for textbooks, etc. Villagers continued to believe that governments should provide these other inputs, and the fund in the end only supported those activities for which the community was already responsible.

In some countries school may be seen as an alien arm of the government, staffed by outsiders, and teaching content that has little relevance in the lives of local people. Escuela Nueva tries to overcome this feeling by starting the school year with a community meeting where maps are drawn on the school wall depicting the village and every family's home. During the year students interview community members and develop reports on the socioeconomic and cultural aspects of the village.

The NGOs in Balochistan also expended considerable effort in overcoming local suspicions about projects involving the government. They did this by setting up a fully transparent system of selecting a teacher, testing the candidate and publishing the result, and following a step-by-step process providing evidence from every side-government, NGO, and community-that commitments would be kept. The NGO as a trusted local entity was essential in this process of anticipating the reactions and resistance of parents and overcoming them.

Programs for adult female education have been proposed as a way to support girls' education. Parents' educational level has been suggested in a number of studies as promoting enrollment and persistence. Fergany notes that an educated mother in Egypt also exerts a significant impact on cognitive achievement. Deolalikar adds that mothers' education seems to be more important in poor households. In all of these cases education was probably acquired in childhood rather than as an adult. Adult education may not have the same impact on daughters' education.

In Nepal, for example, literacy classes are believed to have increased the schoolgoing behaviour of participants' daughters, and from self-reports of having involved the mothers more in homework and other supportive behaviours. In Bolivia and Honduras, longitudinal studies are now being carried out under USAID's Girls' and Women's Education (GWE) activity to find out the effects of providing literacy courses to adult females.

One would need to look carefully at these initiatives, if they are intended mainly as a way to increase girls' participation, since mothers may enter these programs only after all their children have exceeded school entry-age or dropped out of school. If this were the case, the effect would be negligible. And there may be other factors such as whether women entering these classes are not already more interested in schooling or have not become motivated to take the classes because of their daughters' schooling.

At issue also is what kind of adult education class would be most supportive of education, and whether alternative approaches (for example discussion rather than literacy groups) might not be equally effective in promoting girls' education. Institutional and cost barriers have sometimes served as potently as lack of facilities in preventing children from taking advantage of public schooling. In recent years governments have become aware of these barriers and in some cases have instituted reforms to correct or compensate for them. Initiatives are of two kinds: those that remove barriers discouraging participation, and those offering material incentives for girls to go to and stay in school.

For years Egyptian rural children faced rigidly enforced age requirements related to schooling: a child could not enter first grade before the age of 6 or after the age of 8, and similar restrictions applied to intermediate school. To prove age, children needed a birth certificate which many did not have. Even if they possessed one, the dates were often inaccurate, at the same time. School officials now allow doctors' certificates in lieu of a birth certificate and are more willing to relax age restrictions in special cases.

Girls in Malawi commonly leave school at puberty or even younger to take part in initiation ceremonies into sexual adulthood. GABLE convinced initiation counsellors to delay the ceremonies and to become advocates for girls' staying in school. The National Commission for Women in Malawi was instrumental in convincing the Ministry of Education to change a policy that prevented a girl from continuing in school after it was discovered that she was pregnant, while the male impregnator was not punished. Now both must drop out of school until she has had the baby, and then they both can return to school after arrangements have been made to care for the baby.

A number of initiatives aim to reduce the cost of education to parents. Kenya's program to provide uniforms and books increased enrollment, improved attendance, and significantly reduced dropout rates in experimental schools. The Government of Malawi waived fees for primary education, and made uniforms optional, both of which had been major expenses for rural families. The response overwhelmed the school system, which had neither the space nor teachers to cope with so many children. Malawi's experience shows some of the unintended consequences that may attend abrupt policy changes.

The "free school" policy was understood by parents to be part of Malawi's new democratization, which was interpreted to mean that everything would henceforth be free and that the government was now financially responsible for education, health, and all other services the people needed. Some villagers felt they had also been freed from customary responsibilities related to the school such as financial support for extracurricular activities, ensuring students' regular attendance, and accepting staff discipline of their children. The schools had suddenly become "people's schools."

The implementers of BRAC believe fees are a major reason poor children have not enrolled in the formal system. Its program selects poor children, especially girls (70 percent or more of enrollments), and requires no fees other than the replacement cost of materials that are damaged by children. When graduates want to move into the formal system, BRAC provides scholarships as needed to help with fees.

BRAC derives its support from donors, and to a certain extent from the profits of small industries it owns. The trade-off in providing free schooling for the poorest children is that BRAC lacks long-term funding security. It suffers also from the ambivalent feeling of the education bureaucracy that believes BRAC siphons off international assistance the formal system would otherwise be receiving.

BRAC handles only about 8 percent of primary students in Bangladesh, so it still provides for only a small share of school-age children. The high costs of "special lessons" is a major deterrent for poor children in all areas of Egypt. Male teachers tended to exploit this opportunity more, and women teachers less because they had less time to spend in after-school activities. The government tried to prohibit tutoring with little effect, and then decided to allow schools to organize tutoring in afternoon group classes in school with a set fee. The Ministry of Education claimed group learning would make tutoring more affordable, but was not true for children whose parents have difficulty sustaining any extra expenses. One of the pernicious influences of tutoring is that it creates a disincentive for teachers to teach well during class time.

Some religious groups in Egypt-Islamic and Coptic-compensate by providing help for children with their homework or with money for school expenses. Some countries have laws that set a minimum age and other requirements for work. These are intended to keep children in school and remove them from competing at cheaper rates in the labour market. Egypt, for example, has legislated a minimum age for work and in government-run industries has required basic literacy for employment.

The effect in areas where national industries exist is to keep most children in primary school until the minimum age is reached, and then for boys to drop out and try for places in industry. In poorer neighbourhoods of cities and in rural areas where work in harvesting or workshops is available, the laws are ignored. Not many initiatives specifically address the issue of the lost opportunitycosts of child labour. Some initiatives reduce the amount of time required, to complete the primary level.

India has set up early education classes near or in primary schools, one of the stated goals being that these programs will substitute for the child care that prevents girls from attending school. Usually, however, these centres do not take children before the ages, of 2 or more, by which time the intensive care girls provide for their siblings may be over. Toddlers are often left to roam freely in villages. Probably a more significant consequence of these centres is that targeted poor children from illiterate families are brought into the orbit of the school and tend to enter and continue on into the primary program.

3

Role of Education in Girls Primary Education

A child's right to education is enshrined in a number of declarations and conventions. The Universal Declaration of Human Rights of 1948 outlines the right to free, compulsory elementary education, and states that education should work to strengthen respect for human rights and promote peace. Parents have the right to choose the kind of education provided to their child.

The Fourth Geneva Convention of 1949 states that, in situations of military occupation, the occupying power must facilitate institutions devoted to the care and education of children. The rights of refugee children are protected in the 1951 Convention Relating to the Status of Refugees, which guarantees the right to elementary education, and states that they should be accorded the same opportunities as nationals from the host country. Beyond primary school, refugee children are treated as other aliens, allowing for the recognition of foreign school certificates and the awarding of scholarships.

The Convention on the Rights of the Child of 1989 calls for states to make primary education compulsory and free to all, and to encourage the development of accessible secondary and other forms of education. The Convention mandates an education that builds on a child's potential and supports their cultural identity. The Convention emphasises psychosocial support for conflict-affected children, and outlines the principle of nondiscrimination, including access for the disabled, gender equity and the protection of the linguistic and cultural rights of ethnic minorities. The Convention also protects a child's right to recreation and culture. Finally, the Rome Statute of 1998 outlining the legal jurisdiction of the International Criminal Court (ICC) includes protection for educational institutions under Article 8, which covers war crimes. The ICC protects against 'intentionally driven attacks against buildings dedicated to religion, education, art, science, or charitable purposes'.A number of regional agreements also address issues of education.

Education has also been subject to a series of international conferences and agreements. In 1990, the World Conference on Education for All (EFA) in Jomtien, Thailand, agreed to universalise education and reduce illiteracy. Aggressive targets were set aimed at achieving universal basic education by the end of the decade. The global commitment to basic education was revisited ten years later, at the World Education Forum in Dakar, Senegal. When considering EFA, the Forum's 1,100 participants clearly meant education that went beyond merely formal schooling. Thus, according to the Dakar Framework for Action, delegates committed themselves and their governments to:

— 'expanding and improving comprehensive early childhood care and education, especially for the most vulnerable and disadvantaged children;

— ensuring that by 2015 all children, particularly girls, children in difficult circumstances and those belonging to ethnic minorities, have access to and complete free and compulsory primary education of good quality;

— ensuring that the learning needs of all young people and adults are met through equitable access to appropriate learning and life skills programmes;

— achieving a 50% improvement in levels of adult literacy by 2015, especially for women, and equitable access to basic and continuing education for all adults;

— eliminating gender disparities in primary and secondary education by 2005, and achieving gender equality in education by 2015, with a focus on ensuring girls' full and equal access to and achievement in basic education of good quality; and

— improving all aspects of the quality of education and ensuring excellence of all so that recognised and measurable learning outcomes are achieved by all, especially in literacy, numeracy and essential life skills'.

The goals of universal primary education and gender parity were adopted as Millennium Development Goals by the UN General Assembly on 6 September 2001.

Education in emergencies (often used interchangeably with emergency education) is primarily carried out in situations where children lack access to their national and community education systems due to the occurrence of complex emergencies or natural disasters. Because modern conflicts are chronic and recurring, the sector tends to use the word 'emergency' in its broadest sense, encompassing not only the first days or months after an event, but also the effort to deal with the on-going effects of the crisis, and reconstruction. Within the context of EFA, emergency education does not negate states' responsibility to educate their people; rather, it provides the space for the international community to assist where the government is unable or unwilling to provide education. Attacks on schools are one of the most easily quantifiable ways of gauging the effect of a conflict on education.

During 2001, for instance, Israeli soldiers shot at nearly 100 schools in the Occupied Territories, using rubber bullets, live ammunition and tear gas. Another 71 schools came under attack through tank shelling or rockets fired from helicopters. In East Timor, the violence of September 1999 destroyed between 80% and 90% of school buildings and related infrastructure. The impact of conflict on education may also be felt more indirectly, as part of a wider pattern of disruption and dislocation and the effects of state collapse. Some argues that formal education is at risk during war 'because it relies on consistent funding and administrative support that is difficult to sustain during political turmoil. During the fighting in Somalia and under the Khmer Rouge regime in Cambodia, public expenditure on education was reduced to nearly nothing'. In Mozambique, wartime damage to schools left two-thirds of the country's two million primary-school children with no access to education.

Children's reduced enrolment and attendance at schools is another potential measure of conflict's impact on education. Emily Vargas-Baron of the RISE Institute claims that, of the approximately 115m children worldwide who are out of school, a large majority are living in nations affected by complex crises. The Oxfam Education Report states that two-thirds of countries in Africa that are experiencing or recovering from conflict have enrolment rates of less than 50%. Just 3% of refugee adolescents -some 50,000 children—attend anything beyond primary school. For internally-displaced children, the prospects can often be worse; access to education in parts of Angola, the Democratic Republic of Congo, Somalia and southern Sudan are minimal. In Somalia, it is estimated that only 9% of school-age children (and only 6% of school-age girls) are attending school.

Enrolment ratios are based on comparisons of registered children against often inaccurate figures of the numbers eligible for schooling. Moreover, they give a poor reflection of actual attendance patterns. Existing measures of the impact of conflict on education also say nothing about quality. Where children in areas of conflict are lucky enough to go to school, their learning is often hindered by trauma or hunger, untrained or ill-prepared teachers, or the lack of sufficient learning materials and infrastructure. Even when officially open, schools can be closed down periodically, and days and terms can be shortened. Despite these weaknesses, it is clear that children living in conflict are systematically denied the right to education: as Vargas-Baron puts it, 'in every failed state there is a failed education system'.

RISKS IN EDUCATION

While education is generally considered a force for good, conflict can distort its benefits and introduce additional risks. Schools may not always be safe: for example, Chechen schools have been bombed during class hours because they were deemed to be sheltering military targets, and grenades have been thrown into classrooms. Teachers too may be at risk; in Colombia and Sudan, teachers have been threatened and killed. Education may be connected to recruitment by facilitating access to children; in southern Sudan, for instance, schools have been used as a convenient way of assembling young men for military service. In the Democratic Republic of Congo (DRC), schools have been a common site of child recruitment by Rwandan-backed rebel groups. Propaganda teams from the Liberation Tigers of Tamil Eelam (LTTE) in Sri Lanka have positioned recruitment booths near schools, and used street theatre to induce children into joining the military.

In northern Uganda, fighting forces have kidnapped schoolchildren directly from classrooms. One rebel group in Burundi abducted more than 150 students from two schools in November 2001, setting fire to several classrooms as they did so. The prospect of education may itself serve as a rationale for joining an armed group. In southern Sudan during the 1980s, boys were lured hundreds of kilometres from their homes by promises of education, only to find that the 'schools' promised to them were also military training camps.

The stress that conflict places on communities can make the school environment itself more threatening. Corporal punishment, for instance, seems to become more common in schools during times of conflict. While teachers in many countries may see caning and slapping as an appropriate disciplinary tool, war can exacerbate its use as teachers take out their frustrations and stress on their pupils. In conflict areas of West Timor, Buton and Ambon, teachers' use of physical punishment, ridicule and humiliation to control and discipline children appears to be connected to the stresses they themselves experience.

The risk of violence or abuse in an educational context may be particularly acute for girls; in West African refugee camps, teachers regularly ask female students for sexual favours in exchange for good grades. In Kosovo after 1999, fear of rape or abduction kept many Kosovar minority children, especially girls, away from school.

The broader economic pressures people affected by conflict face may also inhibit schooling. War-affected children from the most economically disadvantaged backgrounds are discouraged from attending school due to the expense. In extreme cases, such as the exploitation found in West Africa, young people may deliberately put themselves at risk, for example through prostitution, to pay school fees. Even when officially 'free', hidden costs remain, such as for uniforms, books and transport.

Survival pressures may cause children to be removed from school and set to productive work; girls may be married off earlier than usual, or parents may be forced to exclude one child from school for the sake of the education of other family members. Bedreldin Shutta of Save the Children recounts one instance in Sri Lanka where a mother reported that she would not hesitate to encourage her elder child to join an armed group if it meant money to pay for the education of her two remaining children.

In societies in conflict, education systems may themselves be politicised. A UNICEF report highlights a variety of ways in which education can be manipulated to the detriment of children:

— the uneven distribution of education as a means of creating or preserving positions of economic, social and political privilege;

— education as a weapon in cultural repression;

— the denial of education as a weapon of war;

— education as a means of manipulating history for political purposes;

— education as a means of diminishing self-worth and encouraging hate;

— segregation in education as a means of ensuring inequality and inferiority; and using textbooks to inhibit children from dealing with conflict constructively.

Thus, during the crisis in Rwanda and Burundi education was used to heighten ethnic tensions between Hutu and Tutsi, conditioning the population to accept ethnic discrimination and propagating a culture of mutual fear and pre-emptive self-defence. In Serbia, the education system was used to subjugate the Kosovar Albanians; in Sri Lanka in the 1970s and 1980s, government textbooks presented Tamils as the historical enemy of the Sinhalese.

Governments may deliberately block access to education for certain groups. In the mid-1990s, for example, the Zairean government sought to prevent Rwandan refugees from having access to schooling. Many young Palestinians in schools in Lebanon have a 'distorted and unclear perception' of their own history because curricula are required to teach from a Lebanese perspective.

The relationship between protection and education in conflict as two-fold, involving both protecting a child's access to education amid conflict and displacement, and using education to protect a child from the risks that such situations present. In recent years, protection has occupied an increasingly important position on the humanitarian agenda, with agencies going 'beyond the conventional view of how people are dying, to embrace ... how people are living'. This humanitarian concern for protection arose out of the horrors of the 1990s: ethnic cleansing in Bosnia, the Rwandan genocide, atrocities in Sierra Leone. Since then, humanitarians have begun to explore what kinds of practical actions can be taken to protect civilians both from physical harm, and from wider violations of their human rights.

PROTECTING CHILDREN

Children constitute a particularly vulnerable group in times of war by virtue of their dependence on adult care. Conflict and displacement can present particular threats, such as separation from family, abduction or recruitment by fighting forces, or exposure to targeted violence or landmines. At the same time, preexisting threats, such as sexual or gender-based violence, labour exploitation or malnutrition and disease, may increase. Efforts to protect children in times of war date back to the early years of the twentieth century; in 1924, for instance, the League of Nations adopted the Geneva Declaration on the Rights of the Child.

Declaration of Human Rights and the subsequent International Covenant on Civil and Political Rights and the International Covenant on Economic, Social and Cultural Rights. Regional instruments such as the European Convention on Human Rights also make specific reference to children. Following Machel's landmark UN study in 1996, a number of key initiatives have been taken. The appointment in 1997 of a Special Representative of the UN Secretary-General for Children and Armed Conflict.

The UN's adoption of the CRC's Optional Protocol prohibiting the participation in hostilities of those below 18 years of age. This was spearheaded by the Coalition to Stop the Use of Child Soldiers, a network of humanitarian agencies. High-level meetings to focus attention on the plight of children in war, such as the Oslo/Hadeland Conference 'Protection of Children and Adolescents in Complex Emergencies' in 1998 and the 'International Conference on War-Affected Children', held in Winnipeg, Canada, in 2000.

Action for the Rights of the Child (ARC), a rights-based training initiative by UNHCR, Save the Children, the UN High Commissioner for Human Rights (OHCHR) and UNICEF, which has developed a series of resource packs on conflict-affected children's rights and needs. The Watchlist on Children and Armed Conflict, an NGO initiative that prepares reports on the situation of children in specific conflicts, and makes recommendations to UN and international actors to improve child protection.

A set of Inter-agency Guiding Principles on Separated Children developed by the Working Group on Separated Children, as a means to strengthen the tracing and reuniting of separated children. The particular needs of children are being incorporated as a cross-cutting sector in current revisions. A number of innovative agency-based initiatives, including the Emergency Stand-by Teams of Save the Children Sweden and Norway, and the Norwegian Refugee Council (NRC); UNICEF's Child Friendly Spaces initiative; and the series of participatory adolescent field studies led by the Women's Commission for Refugee Women and Children.

In practice, children's protection is variously seen as a legal, social and physical concern. Defining its scope beyond the legal framework is, however, difficult. In an external evaluation of UNHCR's efforts to protect refugee children, for instance, there was confusion among staff as to what child protection meant, and what the agency's policy actually entailed. Few written definitions of child protection exist. The Oslo/Hadeland Conference described the international protection of children and adolescents as 'the gamut of activities through which ... rights are secured by the international community'. Save the Children has developed a draft definition of child protection as 'action to prevent or address harm caused to children because their rights to security, survival or development are threatened—directly or indirectly—by the acts of third parties, including armed groups'.

Child protection as a 'continuum'. At one end lie efforts to address violations of a child's rights, such as tracing and reuniting separated children, demobilising child soldiers and ensuring that schools are safe zones for children. Other protection activities focus on securing governmental and community respect for children's rights through training, advocacy and strengthening local mechanisms of enforcement and dissemination. These activities are often combined with the delivery of assistance and services to address gaps in the rights of specific groups, such as girls, minorities and children with disabilities. Protection-related elements are often included in these activities, but not as their primary aim.

EDUCATION IN PROTECTING CHILDREN

Within the international humanitarian community, there are increasing calls for education to play a role in enhancing child protection, both as a service to be supported and delivered, and as an 'enabling right' which assists children in accessing their other rights. The Oslo/Hadeland conference on child protection in November 1998 claimed that 'Experience shows that education has a preventive effect on recruitment, abduction and gender based violence, and thereby serves as an important protection tool'. In UNHCR's Global Consultations on International Protection, education is similarly described as 'an important protection tool'. Materials produced by the ARC declare that education has a 'direct protection function in monitoring the development and progress of children'.

Certain aspects of education can inherently protect children: the sense of self-worth that comes from being identified as a student and a learner; the growth and development of social networks; the provision of adult supervision and access to a structured, ordered schedule. Maintaining education and its 'built-in' protective components can thus provide vital continuity and support for children living through crisis. At the same time, education can offer an adaptive response, addressing some of the particular conditions that arise from conflict. Thus, teaching in a conflictaffected environment can pass on potentially lifesaving information, or impart basic skills in literacy and numeracy that may be crucial to a child's survival.

Child-focused humanitarian activity in conflict situations tends to assist a relatively limited number of children most affected by the crisis.Vulnerable groups might include child soldiers, separated children, children living on the streets, the sick or malnourished, those with a disability and child-headed households. The urgency of their predicament, along with their high profile and discrete numbers, makes them an appealing focus. However, efforts that target vulnerable groups without taking into account the needs of their peers tend to create inequity and foster resentment. Jane Lowicki of the Women's Commission for Refugee Women and Children points out, for example, that in Sierra Leone a number of demobilisation projects have provided free education to former child soldiers. Non-combatant young people who are not able to attend school seem to resent this; they see themselves as the real victims and as more deserving.

The international community is increasingly aware that all children living in the midst of war are vulnerable and need protection. Schools and recreational activities can bring some elements of physical protection to the majority of children - providing a safe place to play, offering an alternative to destructive behaviour, giving access to nutritious meals or providing regular adult supervision. For children who have been especially victimised by the conflict, coming together for educational activities may make it easier to identify those needing special help, and programmes can be tailored to their specific needs. Follow-up work to find children who do not attend school will further aid in identifying the at-risk, while education staff from the community can be invaluable in identifying children facing threats due to separation from their families, susceptibility to military recruitment or experience of sexual exploitation. They will also understand the impact of gender, ethnicity or disability on children in their own community.

In terms of a child's psychosocial health, education offers a regular routine, opportunities for self-expression and the chance to engage with peers. The very status of 'student' can be valuable, protecting a child from forced recruitment, or bolstering a sense of identity and inclusion; in Liberia, for instance, former combatants sought to attend school to redefine themselves as something other than soldiers. By gathering children together, education programmes can support socialisation, establish peer networks and encourage children to understand and accept views other than their own. Regular routines enhance children's development and assist in their recovery from conflict. Education activities are important in establishing daily schedules that create a familiar and comfortable rhythm and establish a sense of structure and purpose. For families, schooling provides a schedule for the week, while also marking special times such as weekends, holidays and school breaks.

A child's attendance at school also grants parents the time and space to rebuild their livelihoods, re-establish sources of income, or simply come to terms with their experiences. School attendance also encourages children to regain some hope in the prospect of a better future. Goals such as completing homework, preparing for exams or completing a school certificate, regular assignments and tests and rewards such as gold stars and celebrations at the end of term provide children with achievable short-term and long-term objectives. These can be essential when finding a reason to continue the struggle to live in a conflict-affected society. This sense of hope can extend into a child's relationship to the community.

During conflicts, children lose the sense of what it means to be a good citizen and how to live in a non-confrontational way. In places where war has lasted for years, some children will never have seen how a stable family or community functions. Education can respond to this need through building children's skills in listening, problem-solving and conflict resolution. Instruction also transmits vital basic skills, such as literacy and numeracy and the capacity for critical thinking, as well as imparting important information. In circumstances of crisis, academic learning is not a luxury. Knowing how to read, write and do basic maths is essential for children in protecting themselves. Reading skills enable children to gather information about their environment—whether from signs, newspapers, health brochures or medicine bottles. Writing skills enable children to sign for services and write letters seeking assistance. Children may need basic mathematical skills to manage their household's flow of money.

Every day, children make decisions about what is in their best interests based upon their knowledge and life experience. Deciding to volunteer for the military or to venture into a heavily landmined area may be logical decisions, based on need. Children's responsibilities can also extend to caring for younger siblings, especially when separated from their parents. Providing children with accurate information from sources that they can trust strengthens their ability to cope with conflict at a practical level, to analyse situations and make decisions. In crisis situations, thousands of children fall victim to dangers which simple health and hygiene education could have prevented. In most cases, these children are living in a new environment; they do not know the location of landmines, the importance of immunisation or hygiene or how to minimise the risk of a disease like HIV/AIDS and cholera. They might not understand the consequences of sexual activity or drug use. Education in schools is one of the most practical means of conveying the kind of messages that enable children to make safe decisions.

HUMANITARIAN PROGRAMMING IN EDUCATION

Although education has long been an important component in development work, its appearance on the humanitarian agenda is relatively recent; even a decade ago, few humanitarians considered education within their scope of action. Education had been seen as neither indispensable to human survival nor required for subsistence. In recent years, however, attitudes have started to change and education has begun to emerge as an issue of humanitarian concern. Thus, for educational activity to be established as a priority component of all humanitarian assistance. The absence of education for children dooms them to remain recipients of assistance; the Humanitarian Charter and its call for the right to life with dignity serves to support the inclusion of education in humanitarian response.

Emergency education seeks to give shape and structure to children's lives, preparing them with skills to survive conflict, and promoting justice, stability and respect for human rights. Its aims tend to be threefold: fulfilling a child's right to education in the immediate response phase, mitigating the psychosocial effects of conflict and achieving protection related objectives. An increasing number of assistance agencies have included education as an emergency response. There is, however, no standard definition of 'education in emergencies' at the inter-agency level. Other activities might include recreational and cultural programmes, human rights and peace education, landmine awareness, HIV/AIDS prevention, out-of-school literacy classes and skills training.

Education began to gain recognition in humanitarian terms in the early 1990s, with initiatives such as 'RAPID ED', a working group which hosted a series of meetings on emergency response; the NRC's campaign to include education as the 'fourth pillar' of humanitarian response, in addition to food, shelter and health care; a 'Declaration on Principles of Education in Emergencies and Difficult Circumstances', proposed at the Oslo/Hadeland Conference; and the Global Information Networks in Education (GINIE), which serves as a 'virtual learning community' for education innovation in countries in crisis and transition. Agencies continue to show a strong commitment to working together and developing the emergency education sector. Two more recent initiatives—the Interagency Network on Education in Emergencies (INEE) and the Working Group on Standards for Education in Emergencies—facilitate informationsharing between organisations and the establishment of consensual standards for education response.

The INEE was established at the Interagency Consultation on Education in Situations of Emergency and Crisis, held in Geneva in November 2000. Against the backdrop of the Convention on the Rights of the Child, the EFA Declaration and the Dakar Framework, the INEE aims to 'promote access to and completion of education of high quality for all persons affected by emergencies, crises or chronic instability'. Its objectives are:

— to share knowledge and experience;

— to promote greater donor understanding of education in emergencies;

— to advocate for education to be included in emergency response;

— to make teaching and learning responses available as widely as possible;

— to ensure attention is paid to gender issues in emergency education initiatives;

— to document and disseminate best practices in the field; and

— to move towards consensual guidelines on education in emergencies.

INEE's members include UN organisations, international agencies, national NGOs, research institutes and universities, advocacy organisations, bilateral funding agencies and national governments. It is led by a steering group comprising UNESCO, UNHCR, UNICEF, CARE US, IRC, NRC and the Save the Children Alliance. It operates four task teams covering networking, materials, monitoring and evaluation, and post-primary education. INEE's secretariat is based at UNESCO in Paris. From

2003, the INEE is to host the Working Group on Standards for Education in Emergencies. This group emerged from a meeting in March 2002 organised by key NGOs - CARE, IRC, SC UK, SC US, NRC and Catholic Relief Services (CRS) - and involving a broad range of non-governmental and UN agencies.

The meeting identified a commitment to ensuring a level of quality and accountability among education programmes serving children and adolescents in situations of crisis; and a belief that education in emergencies could not remain outside the mainstream of humanitarian programming, but must be seen as a priority response. Inspired by the Sphere model, the Working Group on Standards followed in January 2003, with representatives from ten NGOs and three UN agencies. Developing standards is expected to take two years.

The main UN agencies involved in education in emergencies are UNICEF, UNHCR and UNESCO (including its institutes). WFP also plays an important role in emergency education through its school feeding programme. UNICEF protects the rights and best interests of children living in poverty in developing countries, including children affected by armed conflict, who are identified as a vulnerable group in need of special protection. According to Pilar Aguilar, head of the organisation's education responses in emergencies, UNICEF is 'moving more towards working intersectorally'; to this end, it has developed an integrated services model in the form of 'child-friendly spaces'. There is also a focus on rapid educational response, as demonstrated by UNICEF's commitment to ship emergency education and recreation kits within 72 hours of an emergency. The 'School-in-a-Box' supplies materials for up to 80 students and a teacher. Contents include pens, pencils, chalkboards, chalk and paints. Using a locally developed teaching guide and curriculum, teachers can establish makeshift classrooms almost anywhere. In 2001, 19,000 kits were delivered to over 30 countries.

UNHCR and UNICEF have a Memorandum of Understanding, which assigns UNICEF the primary role for incountry situations, and UNHCR in refugee situations. This has helped to organise overall response in recent emergencies. UNHCR coordinates international action for the protection of refugees, part of which includes ensuring primary education for all refugee children.

UNHCR's Department for International Protection (DIP) has included education in its recently-adopted Agenda for Protection. UNHCR's education work has included developing curricula initiatives in the areas of education for peace, conflict resolution and human rights, and environmental awareness. However, the review of UNHCR's child-related efforts in 2002, while seeing education as one of the keys to 'operationalising' the protection function, warned that budget reductions threatened this capacity.

UNESCO's emergency education work emphasises the need to extend support beyond the short term. The Programme for Education in Emergencies and Reconstruction, based in Nairobi, has developed a set of mobile teaching learning materials called the Teacher Emergency Package (TEP). In 2002-2003, the UNESCO International Institute for Educational Planning (IIEP) and Section for Support to Countries in Crisis and

Reconstruction are developing a joint programme to 'build governments' capacity to plan and manage education in emergencies'.

Beginning with the documentation of case studies that illustrate different emergency profiles, researchers will review education responses in East Timor, Honduras, Kosovo, Palestine and Rwanda. In addition to drawing out lessons learned and producing a series of policy studies, materials will be developed to conduct training with ministries of education. Concurrently, the UNESCO International Bureau of Education is undertaking a study on curriculum change and social cohesion in conflictaffected societies.

The World Food Programme is the largest organiser of school feeding programmes throughout the developing world. In 2001, 15m children were fed in schools in over 57 countries. WFP provides food for students and teachers, usually in the form of school meals, as part of its emergency response. WFP focuses on increasing girls' enrolment; in Pakistan, for instance, a programme providing edible oil to girls was credited with increasing the school attendance of Afghan refugee girls.

The ICRC's work in education is part of its mandate under the Geneva Conventions. The Exploring Humanitarian Law project designs curriculum materials on international humanitarian law for adolescents. In selected crises, ICRC provides assistance for schools, such as in the Mindanao region of the Philippines, in Chechnya and in Bosnia.

International NGOs working in the emergency education sector include the Academy for Education Development (AED), CARE International, CRS, the Christian Children's Fund (CCF), IRC, NRC and the Save the Children Alliance. A number of regional and local NGOs also play a lead role in implementing education response in their areas of operation. As this group is vast, this section looks at the work of some of the more prominent agencies engaged internationally.

In 1999, the post of education technical advisor was established, and the scope of IRC's work in this area has continued to expand. With a focus on rapid response and displaced populations, IRC operates education projects in nearly 20 countries. In Africa, it has formed a protection consortium, which includes education, along with CCF and Save the Children US. IRC will host the focal point for the Working Group on Standards. The NRC includes education as one of its 'four pillars' of humanitarian response. It operates Norwegian and African Standby Forces, ready for deployment in 72 hours, many of whom are seconded to UN agencies. The NRC is operational in 11 countries around the globe, and has developed Teacher Education Packages and human rights education programmes. NRC has been a major advocate of the sector, and currently chairs the INEE steering group.

In 2001, the International Save the Children Alliance began to work closely together on strengthening their education response. Since then, a joint set of training materials has been prepared, and shared principles for programming developed. Of the national member organisations, Canada, Denmark, Norway, Sweden, the UK and the US actively support education in emergencies. Save the Children Sweden and Norway each maintain an Emergency Stand-by Team that seconds community services officers, who look into education as part of other social service-related needs, to UNHCR for three to six months. Save the Children UK supports education in around 30 countries affected by emergencies, and has produced a guide drawing on its experiences. In 2002, the agency hosted an emergency education officer for the Alliance. Save the Children US implements emergency education in some 24 crisis affected countries. The agency has also produced a field guide on education as part of a series on children in crisis.

Refugees represent a particular area of emergency education programming. Organisations with this focus include the Jesuit Refugee Service (JRS), which works with refugees and displaced people in over 40 countries, with special strength in Africa. In Nairobi, the JRS has what is probably the world's only resource centre for education in emergencies, with material specifically related to populations in crisis. The Refugee Education Trust, established by UNHCR but now operating independently and reexamining its role, was originally conceived as a major refugee education fund, channelling resources to those in the field engaged in secondary and vocational education. Finally, the Women's Commission for Refugee Women and Children advocates for education as essential to the protection of children and adolescents affected by armed conflict. It has conducted participatory field studies among adolescents in Kosovo, Uganda and Sierra Leone. It has also undertaken a global survey on education in emergencies in an effort to build a database detailing the sector's scope of work.

Because education has traditionally been seen as part of development work, not humanitarian relief, humanitarian donors have generally been reluctant to fund emergency education responses. Moreover, few bilateral donors have a policy specifically on education in countries in, or emerging from, conflict. A notable exception is the Swedish agency Sida, which has produced guidelines for humanitarian assistance in the education sector. These list the right to education as the basis of grants, and highlight that protection can serve as a further justification for education programmes in humanitarian situations. Other bilateral agencies have shown interest in the sector, and have funded emergency education projects. The Norwegian aid organisation NORAD, has supported the sector through its partnership with the NRC emergency team. The UK's Department for International Development (DFID) has explored the impact of conflicts on education in a study partly meant to inform internal policies on the subject. The US Agency for International Development (USAID) and the Bureau for Population, Refugees and Migration (BPRM) have both shown signs of interest; they are major funding sources especially for US NGOs, as is the Canadian International Development Agency (CIDA) for Canadian agencies. ECHO has also shown a new openness to including this sector in its work.

As collaborative initiatives between agencies advance, the best practices necessary to provide quality education in times of crisis will become increasingly clear. Even so, the diversity of crisis, agency mandates and funding mean that it will be impossible to put forward a generic approach to education in emergencies. Factors such as the capacity and priorities of the local or host government, the availability of facilities and the presence or otherwise of pre-existing education systems and staff will all influence implementation decisions, as will the level of distress and violence the affected population has experienced. That said, general frameworks have begun to emerge.

The phased approach to education in emergencies seeks to develop programming through the different phases of a crisis. The three-phase model of Rapid Educational Response was first proposed in a joint publication by UNESCO, UNHCR and UNICEF. Suggested for use in the initial months following large-scale displacement, this model proposes that education in emergencies should focus initially on establishing recreational programmes, which then move into non-formal education and eventually the establishment of formal education. This model includes the caveat that phases may be implemented simultaneously, and implies that at some point no educational services exist for refugee and displaced children. The matrix includes the overarching themes of protection and psychosocial support that were not addressed in the earlier model. Additionally, it posits that, within emergency education, there are certain core areas - including academic subjects, life skills and capacity-building - all of which must be included regardless of the context. Implementation follows a general progression, but is not bound to a specific timeframe.

While useful in articulating how education programmes can be rapidly implemented and how they can change over time, the phased models used in isolation focus on the operations of the humanitarian agency, rather than the children and their communities. The 'Circle of Learning', proposed in work for Save the Children, provides an alternative that puts children at the centre of the decisions determining the response.

LINKS BETWEEN EDUCATION AND PROTECTION

Education programmes can protect children, but they can

also put them at risk. Recent humanitarian interventions, in West Africa, Guinea or Sierra Leone, for example, have shown that education activities may subject children to abuse, or make them more vulnerable to military recruitment. These risks deserve serious attention, but they should not cause education to be discounted as a tool of protection. Programmes should be designed to enhance education's inherent protective aspects, while frankly and simultaneously addressing the potential risks.

Protection is a developing field, and humanitarian agencies have few frameworks to guide them in integrating protection into their activities. The recent IASC publication Growing the Sheltering Tree: Protecting Rights through Humanitarian Action provides a possible framework through a series of practical field-based examples. In encouraging an integrated approach. The four areas identified as central to putting protection into practice are: leadership and collaborative work in protection; negotiating access to people under threat and ensuring the right to humanitarian assistance; 'conscious' presence (the strategic implementation of programmes to promote protection and prevent violations); and programme process (assessment, planning and evaluation).

Applying these areas specifically to education in emergencies and its potential to enhance child protection, considers:

— the leadership potential within the education structures of conflict-affected communities;

— education's role in enhancing access for vulnerable children;

— the importance of visible presence as a deterrent to violence against children; and

— the role of teachers and schools in implementing education efforts and gathering and giving out protection-related information.

A community's concern for its children can be one of the best protection resources, and can be reached through schools. Education committees would make ideal allies in such a protection role; indeed, they may themselves become an important psychosocial tool. In some situations, such as the Community Education Committees in the Belet Wayne district of Somalia, committees have received psychosocial training to enable them to enhance their parenting skills to deal with traumatised children within their community. Education committees are likely to comprise community leaders with an interest in child protection, as these are the same issues that affect their own children. The first role of the group should be to encourage children to attend school, and parents to participate in education activities. While they may not initially be familiar with the idea of protection, individuals from the committee could be trained, in turn training others, on children's rights, local laws or the identification of vulnerable children.

Education committees can potentially play a larger role in protection. As an example, humanitarian organisations typically include child rights in their training of education committees; what is lacking, however, is follow-up to make protection manifest. This lack of follow-up can make school education committees believe that their purpose is to mobilise resources to build the school or raise money, rather than taking a more comprehensive view of providing for the welfare of their children. In Liberia, IRCtrained Parent Teacher Associations (PTAs) identified students not attending school, and teachers followed up with the individual families. For girls, this was commonly due to pregnancy; in some instances, PTAs were instrumental in young mothers returning to school.

By their nature, education committees are wellplaced to identify allies and extend local networks concerned with protection. In Kosovo, where PTAs were poorly developed, the IRC supported local women's groups to conduct house-by-house surveys of the educational needs of all the girls and women in their villages. This identified girls who had never gone to school, as well as those being prevented from attending. In both instances, the women's groups worked with local schools to develop appropriate programmes and advocacy. In Rwanda, UNICEF developed partnerships with education committees to identify at-risk children, as well as potential interventions. The Committees then developed projects which linked education and protection. Examples include support for the education of orphans, domestic workers and child-headed households, and accelerated learning for children who had dropped out of school or who had missed their first chance of enrolment (Baldah, personal communication).

Children can also take the lead in their own protection, and often address a wide range of education focused goals through their activities. At an Afghan refugee camp in Bajaur Agency, Pakistan, for example, Save the Children supports groups of children to participate in 'reflect-action' circles to identify their protection concerns. Important issues typically span a range of topics, from latrines to early marriages, but many centre around schooling. Thus, the group brought its concerns about teaching aids being resold by school staff in the market to the attention of community leaders, who have since taken action. In Liberia, Don Bosco facilitated the formation of a child protection network through elections of school representatives, called junior counsellors.

When providing protection, access to vulnerable children is vital. This is usually thought of in terms of humanitarian space: the use of aid to reach vulnerable people and so increase a sphere of influence. UNICEF, has promoted the concept of children as 'zones of peace' and facilitated ceasefires or 'days of tranquillity' that enable the provision of services to children. In the DRC, initiatives such as these have enabled students in rebel-held areas to sit for state exams. In education, access also means such issues as school enrolment and attendance. In conflict areas, this may be acutely difficult as 'many children who should be in school are hard to find, hard to get into school, and it is hard to make sure they remain there until completing, at the very least, their primary education'. Whatever their source, barriers to children attending school are indicative of larger protection issues—discrimination, security, poverty or geographic isolation.

Education programmes need to be aware of obstacles to access, and incorporate strategies to overcome them. Thus, emergency support may seek to eliminate barriers such as school fees or difficulties around nonpayment of teachers or lack of equipment, for example, thus facilitating access for children who might not otherwise be able to fully participate. The concentration of people within refugee camps may offer an opportunity to expand educational access to children who previously did not have it due to poverty or a lack of schools in their areas. Sometimes, the challenge can be as basic as a failure to recognise a school as a school. In Tanzania, for instance, it took two years for the government to permit refugees from Burundi to receive 'formal' primary education. Previously, schools in the refugee camps had been referred to as Child Activity Centres, which were not able to provide children with the same certification as formal schooling. The government still does not allow refugee children to receive formal secondary education.

Presence, most commonly understood as the presence of outside observers, can offer a sort of 'protecting witness' for civilian populations. In the protection lexicon, this means that international witnesses are on the scene. Thus, visible support of schools and safe areas places the participating children under the protective umbrella of the supporting organisations.

This presence, shown through agency stickers and flags and by monitoring in marked humanitarian vehicles, may be a deterrent for individuals or parties wanting to harm children. Local groups or communities may play this role themselves. In Sri Lanka, for example, the LTTE was less likely to conscript children from areas where international organisations were involved with local partners.

Although international actors were not physically present at all times, it was clear that local groups were in easy contact with them. Similarly, in Kosovo IRC and CCF sought to generate community support for the education of Roma children. This took many forms: in some communities, Roma children were escorted to school by other children; in more hostile areas they were escorted by parents. Both organisations also sought to include the Roma in wider community activities, such as sport or cultural activities like dance.

Assessment, dissemination, reporting and monitoring Multi-sectoral assessment should include an effort to understand the capacities of existing community services, such as schools. This helps to identify where the international community is not needed, and areas where support can be offered for a limited period of time. As a means of identifying potential violations and threats, OHCHR's training manual on human rights monitoring states that the assessment of children's rights should include reference to the role of 'structures', including 'access to schools and health care; the strength of immediate and extended family structures; and the effectiveness of government ministries with responsibility for issues affecting children. Analyses should be aware of both modern and traditional structures'. Humanitarian actors should also survey beneficiary communities to determine protection concerns.

Educational activities can ensure daily attention is paid to children. In this respect, education differs from health programmes that monitor only the sick, and from food-distribution programmes with their periodic character. Teachers at schools are aware of children's needs and can facilitate screening for children who require special assistance. If children do not come to school, teachers should be asking where they are - and following up. Teachers can also provide information about:

— where families can be registered, or where a child tracing form can be submitted;

— how to obtain medical and social services, and information on food distributions;

— where tq report crimes, including general security information;

— news from home, such as the current status of peace negotiations;

— announcements from community groups, such as women's group meetings; and

— human rights education, on such instruments as the Convention on the Rights of the Child or the Refugee Convention, translated and explained.

If the proper mechanisms exist, teachers and students can report abuses, rights violations or general concerns. Essential to any such process is trust, confidentiality and follow through on the part of the agency. Because this could potentially become too political or unsafe, proper oversight is important. In Pakistan, IRC's protection unit learned of domestic violence from the agency's extensive teacher network. Teachers knew that the abuse was happening, but did not know where to go or what to do with the information. Women's centres were eventually created to help deal with this issue. In early 2003, the IRC piloted a protection reporting form for teachers.

Monitoring educational activities can provide a barometer of children's protection needs in the larger community. For example, marked drops in the attendance of girls could be an indicator of stress, if scarce financial resources lead families to invest in boys over girls. In some countries, UNICEF maintains databases of children enrolled in school to provide information to monitor and prevent recruitment. This kind of monitoring needs to happen at the local level; collecting national or regional statistics has limited direct effect on child protection. The value of monitoring lies in empowering local communities to identify issues and the means to address them. If the government or an NGO monitors school attendance, the information and its interpretation are theirs and the community tends to expect them to take action. If a community collects the information and interprets the results, the community itself is in a position to react, with outside organisations in a supportive role.

By their very nature, educational activities in conflict-affected societies can place children at increased risk. Schools may be a target of attack, while gathering school-age children together to teach them may offer easier opportunities for military recruitment than are present when children are dispersed. The importance of education to conflict-affected communities may be such that the prospect of schooling splits up families that might otherwise stay intact, or the education expenses may leave children with little alternative but to put themselves at risk, through prostitution for example. Depending on the circumstances in which they are developed, emergency education programmes need a realistic appreciation of these potential risks, and need to take precautions to minimise them. Whether in a family, a school, a church or a mosque, individuals with access to children can help, or they can hurt. The more that protection is considered as a crucial element of education, the more likely it is that schools will be safe places.

Attacking a school not only endangers students, but also creates fear within the community at large. Ultimately, the security of schooling depends on the larger security environment, which is a question of politics and the mechanisms of reconciliation, disarmament and demobilisation. But on a local level, opportunities may be available to improve the security of emergency education programmes. Thus, advocacy may encourage belligerents to accept education as an illegitimate target, for instance emphasising that attacks on schools are considered a war crime. Lessons may be moved to a safer place, such as a local home. Communities can be encouraged to take steps to ensure the safety of their children on the way to and from a school, perhaps by escorting them.

Education may facilitate recruitment, but it may also be an important mechanism of prevention. As with attacks on schools, it is unlikely that the presence of an emergency education programme will prevent a determined effort to recruit children, though agencies may help reduce the risk by, for example, making sure that lessons are not conducted in isolated areas, or on the edge of a community, and that steps are taken to ensure the safety of children travelling to and from school. Monitoring school attendance may indicate when children have been abducted, and this information may be important in negotiations for the return of abductees.

Education may be more important in the case of voluntary recruitment, and when efforts are being made to discourage former child soldiers from reenlisting. Thus, the some argues that 'education, vocational opportunities for former child combatants and the economic security of their families' are the 'determinants' of successful social reintegration and the prevention of re-recruitment. The UNHCR has recommended that efforts to prevent recruitment should include 'educational, vocational ... and recreational activities', particularly for adolescents.

In crisis situations, communities commonly perceive education as their only tangible hope for a better future. In its pursuit, children can be separated from their families, potentially exposing them to greater risk than had the family stayed together. In south Sudan, an extensive survey of 1,000 'Lost Boys' by Save the Children identified education as their 'first priority in life, even more than a chance for family reunification'. In many cases, these boys, now men, have never regained contact with their families, though they have retained the desire for education. To minimise the risk of separation, emergency education programmes should as far as possible be planned so as to keep families together. In Chechnya, the significance of family was emphasised, with children identifying a close, caring and respectful relationship within the family as the most significant factor in their well-being. To minimise separation, special arrangements may be needed for students in their last years to help them complete their courses. In refugee or IDP areas, repatriation should be coordinated with the end of the school year so that children can complete the term and remain with their families. Boarding schools should be discouraged.

In areas of conflict or crisis, children and their families may compromise or endanger themselves to pay for school fees, uniforms, materials or books. Teachers may be implicated in this; in West Africa, for example, teachers have been found to abuse their pupils. In response. female teachers assistants may be placed in the classroom, as has happened in refugee camps in Guinea. In this way, opportunities for sexual exploitation are curbed, the teaching pressure is decreased and children receive more individual attention. A code of conduct for humanitarian personnel has been developed by the IASC

Task Force on Protection from Sexual Exploitation and Abuse, and its applicability to teachers and other education professionals involved in humanitarian programmes could be explored so that harassment is clearly defined and punishments for transgression laid out. Workshops on children's rights, as well as on more practical subjects such as classroom management techniques and supportive learning, may be helpful in addressing issues around the increased use of corporal punishment in emergency settings.

Education can play an important role in enhancing the protection of conflict-affected children. In many conflict situations where state systems have collapsed or are inaccessible, communities themselves organise simple schools and educational activities for their children. It is the responsibility of humanitarian organisations to build on these efforts - not only so children can learn, but also to strengthen the protection which communities, families and children themselves can provide. A right in and of itself, education can also be a valuable means of realising children's other rights.

Through schooling, children can learn about the human rights to which they are entitled and the obligations which these entail. Education helps to develop children's ability to express themselves, contribute to their culture, and care for their health. For older children, education can help in the transition to adulthood by providing leadership, reproductive-health training and job skills. Education also plays a role beyond just preparing children to attain their own rights—it offers a structure that can potentially guard against abuse, neglect and exploitation on into adulthood.

ROLE OF WORLD BANK

Education is at the heart of the World Bank's mission to reduce global poverty. It is central to helping countries invest in growth and invest in people. The World Bank is the largest single external financer of education. Since its education funding first began in 1963, it has provided over $30 billion in loans and credits.

The World Bank portfolio constitutes nearly $10 billion in commitments under implementation in 79 countries; the World Bank makes more than $1 billion in new commitments each year. The Bank is committed to helping countries accelerate progress in educational attainment. For the poorer countries, a high priority is to help-together with other external partners-achieve universal primary completion by 2015, with a strong focus on closing the gender gap. In mutually reinforcing ways, the Bank helps countries:

— design and implement sound policies and needed reforms

— build capacity within countries and strengthen institutions

— knowledge generation and dissemination including lessons in worldwide experience in development

— mobilize financial resources, both through its own lending and its ability to leverage other financing

The Bank's education programs are wide ranging in nature. Examples include support for classroom construction, increasing the supply and distribution of textbooks, support for teacher education, increasing female literacy, building the knowledge-based economy through investments in higher education reform programs, transform education systems through investments in modern technologies, and expansion of access in rural areas, emphasizing girls in particular.

Investment in education benefits the individual, society, and the world as a whole. Broadbased education of good quality is among the most powerful instruments known to reduce poverty and inequality. With proven benefits for personal health, it also strengthens nations' economic health, by laying the foundation for sustained economic growth. For individuals and nations, it is key to creating, applying, and spreading knowledge-and thus to the development of dynamic, globally competitive economies. And it is fundamental for the construction of democratic societies.

Education greatly benefits personal health. Particularly powerful for girls, it profoundly affects reproductive health, and also improves child mortality and welfare through better nutrition and higher immunization rates. Education may be the single most effective preventive weapon against HIV/AIDS.

Increases productivity and earnings: Research has established that every year of schooling increases individual wages for both men and women by a worldwide average of about 10 percent. In poor countries, the gains are even greater.

Reduces inequality: Education is a great "leveler", illiteracy being one of the strongest predictors of poverty. Primary education plays a catalytic role for those most likely to be poor, including girls, ethnic minorities, orphans, disabled people, and rural families. By enabling larger numbers to share in the growth process, education can be the powerful tide that lifts all boats.

An educated and skilled workforce is one of the pillars of the knowledge-based economy. Increasingly, comparative advantages among nations come less from natural resources or cheap labour and more from technical innovations and the competitive use of knowledge. Studies also link education to economic growth: education contributes to improved productivity which in theory should lead to higher income and improved economic performance.

Has synergistic, poverty-reducing effects: Education can vitally contribute to the attainment of the Millennium Development Goals. While two of the goals pertain directly to education, education also helps to reduce poverty, promote gender equality, lower child mortality rates, protect against HIV/AIDS, reduce fertility rates, and enhance environmental awareness.

Contributes to democratization: Countries with higher primary schooling and a smaller gap between rates of boys' and girls' schooling tend to enjoy greater democracy. Democratic political institutions (such as power-sharing and clean elections) are more likely to exist in countries with higher literacy rates and education levels.

Promotes peace and stability: Peace education-spanning issues of human security, equity, justice, and intercultural understanding is of paramount importance. Education also reduces crime: poor school environments lead to deficient academic performance, absenteeism, and drop out-precursors of delinquent and violent behaviour.

Promotes concern for the environment: Education can enhance natural resource management and national capacity for disaster prevention and adoption of new, environmentally friendly technologies.

INVESTMENT IN GIRLS' EDUCATION

Investment in girls' education yields some of the highest returns of all development investments, yielding both private and social benefits that accrue to individuals, families, and society at large:

Reduces women's fertility rates: Women with formal education are much more likely to use reliable family planning methods, delay marriage and childbearing, and have fewer and healthier babies than women with no formal education. It is estimated that one year of female schooling reduces fertility by 10 percent.

The effect is particularly pronounced for secondary schooling.

Lowers infant and child mortality rates: Women with some formal education are more likely to seek medical care, ensure their children are immunized, be better informed about their children's nutritional requirements, and adopt improved sanitation practices. As a result, their infants and children have higher survival rates and tend to be healthier and better nourished.

Lowers maternal mortality rates: Women with formal education tend to have better knowledge about health care practices, are less likely to become pregnant at a very young age, tend to have fewer, better-spaced pregnancies, and seek pre- and post-natal care. It is estimated that an additional year of schooling for 1,000 women helps prevent two maternal deaths.

Protects against HIV/AIDS infection: Girls' education ranks among the most powerful tools for reducing girls' vulnerability. It slows and reduces the spread of HIV/AIDS by contributing to female economic independence, delayed marriage, family planning, and work outside the home as well as greater information about the disease and how to prevent it.

Increases women's labour force participation rates and earnings: Education has been proven to increase income for wage earners and increase productivity for employers, yielding benefits for the community and society.

Creates intergenerational education benefits: Mothers' education is a significant variable affecting children's education attainment and opportunities. A mother with a few years of formal education is considerably more likely to send her children to school. In many countries each additional year of formal education completed by a mother translates into her children remaining in school for an additional one-third

Getting children into school is not sufficient-what matters are learning outcomes, which depend on the quality of education. And education of higher quality-measured by an increase in test scores-fosters economic growth, according to Robert Barro, Professor of Economics at Harvard University.

Notwithstanding considerable progress in primary enrolment and adult literacy, more than 113 million children remain out of school and nearly a billion adults are illiterate. Two-thirds of the out-of-school children are girls-and the majority of them from poor and vulnerable groups. A third of pupils drop out of school before they are functionally literate.

HIV/AIDS, armed conflicts, and a widening knowledge and digital gap are some key challenges increasingly demanding urgent attention.

Basic education is the foundation of a healthy, skilled, and agile labour force; lifelong learning enables countries to continually assess, adapt, and apply new technologies; and tertiary education is central to creation of intellectual capacity, on which knowledge production and utilization depend.

4

Challenges of Primary Education

The elimination of poverty and progress towards sustainable development will only take place with increased and improved levels of education. The commitment of the international community to this end has been reaffirmed on many occasions but for millions of the world's poorest people, Education for All remains an unfulfilled commitment.

The International Development Targets encompass the expansion of educational opportunity for all children. They are:

— Universal Primary Education in all countries by the year 2015

— Progress towards gender equality and the empowerment of women demonstrated by eliminating gender disparity in primary and secondary education by 2005.

One sixth of the world's population is unable to read and write. Over 20% of school age children, two thirds of them girls, do not benefit from primary education-within formal schools or elsewhere. Children who do attend school often fail to achieve literacy, let alone develop broader skills and values. This is a huge impediment to sustainable development and is a denial of fundamental human rights. At the World Education Forum, the international community reaffirmed its collective commitment to the achievement of the international targets.

It elaborated the targets to emphasise the importance of inclusion, equity and quality. Ensuring that by 2015 all children, particularly girls, children in difficult circumstances and those belonging to ethnic minorities, have access to - and complete - free and compulsory primary education of good quality. Eliminating gender disparities in primary and secondary education by 2005, and achieving gender equality in education by 2015, with a focus on ensuring girls' full and equal access to, and achievement in, basic education of good quality.

Improving all aspects of the quality of education and ensuring excellence for all, so that recognised and measurable learning outcomes are achieved, especially in literacy, numeracy and essential life skills. The two international education targets do not represent the totality of individual and national aspirations, needs and goals. Education for All includes adults as well as young people.

Literacy and the acquisition of new skills are important for the elimination of poverty and for enabling poor people to reap the potential benefits of globalisation. Nevertheless, UPE is the first priority for widening the life chances of those who live in poverty, an absolute precondition for sustainable development and, an essential step on the ladder of lifelong learning.

Education is at the heart of development. The countries which have made the greatest progress in reducing poverty in recent decades are those which have combined effective and equitable investment in education with sound economic policies. Education enables people to use and extend their capabilities, develop skills, improve their livelihoods and increase their earning potential.

And it also empowers them to participate in decision-making and in the transformation of their lives and societies. Education is central to the achievement of greater equality in society, including between men and women. Investment in education for girls has been shown consistently to be one of the most important determinants of development, with positive implications for all other measures of progress.

World Bank research has demonstrated that education increases the likelihood of women choosing to have smaller, healthier families and deciding to send their own children to school. Education contributes significantly to the improvement of health by enhancing peoples' capacity to care for their own health and that of their families, and to make more effective use of health services.

Good primary education can help to foster agricultural innovation and improve the capacity of people to make use of their environment in a sustainable way. The processes by which education can effect such changes are complex. It must involve a meaningful learning process which develops not only literacy and numeracy, but also life skills and the capacity to think and to reflect.

Education should encourage initiative, flexibility and adaptability, the personal qualities which are conducive to greater empowerment, behavioural change and access to a wider range of livelihood opportunities. The human costs of failing to enable all people to realise the right to basic education on an equitable basis are incalculable.

All other efforts to improve health and nutrition, address the causes and impact of HIV/AIDS, reduce infant, child and maternal mortality, enhance opportunities for more productive livelihoods and promote a civil society committed to democracy, good government and the achievement of other fundamental rights, are undermined. Inequitable access or discriminatory practice contribute to social polarisation. The importance of education to individual, community and national development is reflected in its recognition as a human right.

The right to a primary education is enshrined in the Universal Declaration of Human Rights (1948:Article 26) which states that at least in the elementary and fundamental stages education should be free. The UN Convention on the Rights of the Child (1989: Article 28) makes it clear that it is national governments or States Parties which are responsible, on the basis of equal opportunity, for making primary education compulsory and free for all.

Universal Primary Education (UPE) contributes to the progressive realisation of other rights while progress towards gender equality in schooling sharpens the wider focus on women's rights as human rights. Declarations on the goal of UPE have been made as long ago as the 1960s, with an initial target date of 1980. A later target of UPE by the year 2000 was set within the World

Declaration on Education for All in Jomtien in 1990.

Globally, 80 million more children were in school at the end of the decade than in 1990, but approximately 113 million children are still denied the opportunity of a primary education. The decline in enrolments in sub-Saharan Africa during the 1980s has been arrested but economic decline, conflicts across the region and the impact of HIV/AIDS on children and education systems are major threats to the achievement of UPE.

There has been some progress towards greater gender equality at school although in sub-Saharan Africa recent evidence suggests that the gender gap has widened slightly since 1990, where household labour, early marriage, unwanted pregnancies and sexually transmitted diseases continue to threaten schooling. Nonetheless, UPE is achievable if the lessons of the past are learned, and provided governments, with civil society and the support of the wider international community, take appropriate and urgent action. A business as usual approach will fail to meet the target.

A more strategic approach is required; one which recognises the centrality of education within wider development policies and gives it strong political backing together with appropriate resource priority. The question of what it would cost to achieve UPE, and whether governments can afford it, is difficult. The United Nations Children's Fund (UNICEF) and some international non-governmental organisations (NGOs) have estimated that to meet the UPE target, national governments and funding agencies need to find an additional US$7-8 billion annually.

This is an approach which assumes that the problem is a lack of resources per se rather than national political commitment. In reality, sustained progress is only possible with strong political commitment at the country level and a clear recognition of the very different costs of providing education in different countries. The important message is that all governments can afford UPE if they choose to give it priority, and if they make effective use of their own resources, and if funding agencies deliver on their commitment, made in Dakar, that no country seriously committed to Education for All will be thwarted for lack of resources.

Progress can be made towards greater gender equality, although achieving the 2005 target will be problematic in many countries. Recent global figures from the World Bank estimate that girls will make up 47% of combined primary and secondary gross enrolment by 2005. This will demonstrate significant progress. Placing a gender target ahead of UPE is strategically advantageous. It focuses attention and effort on tackling gender disparities, the benefits of which will serve to reinforce efforts to achieve UPE.

Monitoring progress is an integral part of achieving the targets. There are three main indicators for UPE and two for gender equality. These have been agreed by the international community as minimum benchmarks for the monitoring of progress at the global level, and, by extension, for assessing the performance of governments and agencies. This has been difficult in the past because of lack of timely, reliable figures.

The development of national and international capacity to collect and analyse data is critical. Each country needs to be able to assess its own progress and identify trends in order to be able to concentrate its efforts on the most effective strategies. Good data is also essential to improve accountability, particularly of governments to their citizens, and of agencies to the taxpayers who fund them. The international indicators need to be supplemented at the level of country planning, particularly to inform judgements on quality and participation.

Country and context specific indicators and benchmarks are needed, especially in relation to measurable learning outcomes. Indicators of school attendance, retention and attainment are even more difficult to obtain, but it has been estimated that in sub-Saharan Africa, one third of children enrolled in primary school drop out before reaching the fifth grade. Despite the question mark over the validity of the data, it is clear that the magnitude of the challenge of UPE is greatest in sub-Saharan Africa, where net enrolment rates are lowest and 42 million of the 113 million out-of-school children live, and in South and West Asia with 47 million.

Africa also faces a large projected increase in primary school age population between 1998 and 2015, while a stable demand for education is expected in Asia. In both regions, there is a strong correlation between low enrolment and the incidence of poverty. In sub-Saharan Africa, population growth and an increase in the proportion of the population which is very young and economically dependent, set a daunting demographic challenge.

Governments are faced with the problem of educating an ever-growing school population within tightly constrained budgets. To achieve UPE will require major and sustained increases in enrolment, year on year, akin in some countries to the rapid expansion that took place in the post-independence years of the 1960s. Maintaining progress will be a major task, unless fertility rates, in part a consequence of a failure to retain girls in school, fall substantially in the early years of the new millennium.

In South and West Asia, while there are still nearly 50 million children out of school, primary enrolment is approaching 75%, and the demographic picture is less daunting. In India, for example, the school age population is projected to remain at about the current level, but the proportion of the population which is economically active will increase, thus reducing the dependency ratio, and potentially making more resources available for education. In the Arab States and North Africa the annual average demographic growth rate is 2.5% per annum.

To attain an 80% enrolment rate by 2010 will require that primary education opportunities be made available for an additional 29 million students; this in the context of many countries being afflicted by conflict. In South East and East Asia, declining fertility rates in China should result in a major decline in the school age population by 2015, from 220 million to an estimated 183 million, although this projection may underplay the circumstances of minority groups.

In Latin America and the Caribbean, it is the slow expansion of secondary education that represents a significant brake on the pace of development. In the island states of the Pacific primary enrolment is high, and the main issues are quality, equity and the expansion of secondary and higher education. Assessment of the effectiveness of primary education and the quality of learning outcomes is difficult, although rates of dropout from school, the proportion of pupils who have to repeat years, rates of primary completion and transition to secondary education, are useful proxy measures.

The gender gap is most pronounced in sub-Saharan Africa and South and West Asia. Of the 25 countries worldwide with the poorest girl: boy ratios in primary and secondary education, are in sub-Saharan Africa. In 1998, 54% of school age girls in sub-Saharan Africa were enrolled in primary school, compared with 66% of boys. In most high-income countries and Eastern Europe there is near parity of enrolment, and a relatively small difference in Latin America and the Caribbean.

According to figures from the United Nations Educational, Scientific and Cultural Organisation (UNESCO), the total number of adult illiterates fell from an estimated 962 million in 1990 to 887 million a decade later. Despite this, over one in five adults is illiterate in the year 2000 and the majority of these are women. Regionally, Eastern and Southern Asia combined have an estimated 71% of the world's illiterates. This literacy gap is an enormous barrier to sustainable development and is compounded by the very substantial gender gap in adult literacy. And illiteracy in rural areas is more than twice as high as urban areas.

In the countries with the worst education indicators, most children from the poorest households have no primary education. Households with limited education are more likely to be poor. The gaps between the attainment of rich and poor children can be enormous. In India, for example, 15 to 19 year olds from the richest 20% complete on average 10 school grades more than the equivalent cohort amongst the poorest 40% of students.

In Senegal, the enrolment of 6 to 14 year-olds from the poorest households is half that of children from the richest households. Of the children who do enrol, it is the poor who overwhelmingly drop out of school. For the poorest households, education may be a lesser day-to-day priority than basic survival. In cases of extreme poverty, children may contribute up to 40% of family income.

Girls in particular contribute unpaid labour, mainly in domestic and agricultural activities. Thus direct and indirect costs can make education prohibitively expensive, while lack of access to a school or the poor quality of education on offer may discourage those parents who might have been willing to bear these costs. Where poor children do manage to enrol in school, poor nutrition and health can hinder their full participation and learning. Formal education systems are often inefficient in recognising and addressing the special circumstances of working children. The International Labour Organisation (ILO) estimates that there are up to 250 million children working full or part-time in the developing world.

UNICEF estimates that 140 million of these are between the age of 6 and 11. Around 23% of these children enrol at school but 77% of those subsequently drop out. In most societies, men and women differ in the activities they undertake, their access to, and control of, resources, and in participation in decision-making. The position of women is often characterised by unequal power relations, limited mobility, restricted access to political power, confinement to domestic and subsistence spheres and inequality before the law. Girls contend with a complex mix of barriers to their right to education.

Patriarchal systems of social organisation, a high value on women's reproductive role linked to customary early marriage (and pregnancy), and relatively low regard for the value of female life in some societies, are all formidable obstacles. Poor parents may not be willing to incur the direct and opportunity costs of educating their children, particularly girls. Where decisions to send children to school are weighed against labour contributions, girls are often the last to be sent to school and the first to be withdrawn.

Parents sometimes anticipate that their investment in a daughter's education will be lost when she marries into another family. Girls who do go to school are more likely to be withdrawn for seasonal labour. Legal inequalities, the lack of female role models and limited job opportunities for women, allied to the lack of policies to eliminate gender discrimination within schools and more widely, compound the range of challenges confronting girls.

Of the 880 million illiterate adults, some 600 million are women. This is a direct consequence of their not having been able to benefit from a primary education. The prevalence of female illiteracy is a good guide to gender inequality at school level and the disadvantage of girls. Thus, home background has a strong influence on opportunity at school. Illiterate parents are severely disadvantaged in assisting their children in developing literacy and numeracy skills. Those who have been excluded from educational opportunities themselves may have had less opportunity to assess its potential for their children.

Some study indicate that women participating in adult literacy programmes are more likely to send their children to school and keep them there, than illiterate mothers. They are also more likely to encourage their children to read and study at home. Children may be disadvantaged due to their class or caste, or because they belong to an ethnic, linguistic, cultural or religious minority. Migrant families and nomadic communities face specific difficulties.

In multi-language societies, the choice of language for initial instruction may privilege majority groups, either more numerous or more powerful, and disempower minorities. Children with disabilities have the same right to education as other children, and these are enshrined in the Convention on the Rights of the Child. While education data on children with physical or learning disabilities are poor, it is clear that very few, perhaps less than 2% globally, are in school.

HIV/AIDS is having a devastating impact on poor people. In sub-Saharan Africa, the UN has declared that it "is a problem that dwarfs all other problems in the region". The prolonged sickness, and death, of those infected, in addition to the human tragedy, exacerbates and deepens existing poverty, through the direct costs of illness and the loss of labour. The effect on young adults of child-bearing age has increased the dependency ratios in poor communities and left many children orphaned. At least 95% of AIDS orphans live in Africa.

In Zambia, for example, 30% of children are likely to lose at least one parent by 2010. In many countries infection rates continue to increase, and even where these are beginning to be checked the impact will continue to be severe. HIV/AIDS is a very significant challenge to achieving UPE, especially in sub-Saharan Africa. Where traditional community safety nets are disrupted, children may become heads of household, be cared for by relatives or neighbours or be kept at home to care for sick family members.

Increasing numbers of children are taking to the streets. Where attendance at school is possible, it is likely to be disrupted, and there is clear evidence of declining attendance rates of girls in particular. These direct impacts, the more pervasive deepening of poverty and the increased sense of irrelevance of much traditional formal schooling in the context of HIV/AIDS, combine to work against progress in education.

The impact of HIV/AIDS on performance of education systems is dramatic. High sickness and attrition levels among the teaching force threaten to undermine efforts to improve the quality of schooling.

THREATENS FOR EDUCATIONAL DEVELOPMENT

Conflict has severely disrupted education, particularly in sub-Saharan Africa, but also in Afghanistan, Colombia, the former Yugoslavia and parts of the former Soviet Union. Schools are often targeted and teachers put at risk in conflict situations. The supply of educational materials may be affected along with the disruption of education management, and the school environment may become unconducive to learning.

Widespread and severe conflict may result in the collapse of formal education systems; where conflict is confined to a specific part of a country, it will likely result in increased inequity in national development. Education may actually contribute to conflict through language policies which discriminate against minorities or through a curriculum which prejudices their standing in society.

Unequal national development, including education provision, may also exacerbate conflict in less well served districts. The effects of war on children, including massive violations of their rights, are well documented. Children are vulnerable to death, rape, mutilation, unlawful recruitment, displacement and separation from family, disabling injury and malnutrition.

Adolescents are at extreme risk; girls are especially vulnerable, as are children with learning disabilities. They may be put at risk of HIV infection. The impacts of conflict can be long lasting and need to be addressed as part of any education programme with war-affected children. Globally the number of children who are displaced is around 30 million.

In Africa alone, there are over 23 million refugees, returnees and displaced persons. Effective responses which include education require accurate and timely information on war-affected children which is disaggregated by sex and age. There is a lack of a systemic approach to data collection which affects subsequent resource planning and mobilisation. The magnitude of the challenges set out here underlines the importance of learning from the experience of governments and funding agencies; both what has worked, and what has not.

There is no escaping the fact that the achievement of UPE and gender equality, and indeed poverty reduction more broadly, depends in large measure on the will and commitment of a country's political leadership. Strong and consistent commitment, manifested in a willingness to allocate sufficient resources to education, and to use these resources effectively and efficiently, has been evident in all of the countries which have achieved and sustained UPE. There are a number of key issues here.

First, the nature of primary education, with the high potential returns to society, argues for a central role for government. This does not mean that the private sector and civil society have no part to play, but experience shows that only government can ensure universal, equitable and sustainable provision.

Second, primary education must as far as possible be free. Experience from those countries, including Malawi and Uganda, which have moved to abolish direct charging, is that user fees had been a serious deterrent to participation. Moreover, analysis of budgetary allocations in many countries shows that fees at the basic level have been frequently imposed as an alternative to tackling the skewed distribution of public funding within the education sector, which too often favours better-off, but politically vocal, groups.

Third, UPE is not just about numbers. Simply providing a bad quality education to more children risks wasting scarce resources. Unless governments are committed to improving quality, education outcomes will not be delivered, and the broader developmental impacts in terms of growth, better health and so on, will be jeopardised.

MAINSTREAMING GENDER EQUALITY IN PRIMARY EDUCATION

Achieving gender equality in school and society more broadly involves more than adding gender components to funding agency programmes, launching special initiatives, or establishing gender units in government ministries. It requires no less than a fundamental change in mindset in government, and throughout society.

Real progress can only be made by mainstreaming gender through the development of all policies, strategies and institutional practices to ensure that boys and girls are accorded equal opportunity. Guinea managed to double the percentage of girls enrolled in school over the period 1991-98. It did so by taking action to redress discrimination, and to cater for the particular needs of girls; for example, by providing separate latrines.

Even governments committed to UPE may miss out a lot of children if they focus exclusively on rolling out the existing formal system. Including all children requires a flexibility of response which recognises the diverse circumstances in which children live. It is also clear that the cost of reaching marginalised children is higher than the average, and resource-constrained governments may need to look at cost-effective and imaginative alternatives to the formal system.

The use of low cost suitcase radios in Northern Uganda offers one model. There is much to learn about inclusion from experience in India with non-formal programmes, which are condensed, but use curricula and materials similar to those in the formal system. Lessons are delivered through part-time teaching, including by volunteers, at a time and place convenient to learners, using village and local community facilities.

A range of experimental approaches is being piloted in other countries, but flexibility and variety in design and delivery are the key common characteristics. Governments and funding agencies have often tended to think of primary education largely as a service which is supplied. Poor households face significant opportunity costs if they decide to send their children to school rather than retain their labour in the home or send them to work elsewhere.

For this reason, the perception of both parents and children of the quality of education on offer is crucial. Their views on what constitutes quality may often be at variance with those of government officials or funding agencies. Recent consultations undertaken in Uganda and India both showed that parents place a higher premium than expected on adequate, waterproof school buildings. Parents are also concerned about the availability of opportunities to progress on merit to secondary education or vocational training.

Economic incentives are very important for poor households, and demand is very much influenced by the likelihood that children will be able to acquire marketable skills. It has also been recognised increasingly that greater participation of parents and communities in the education of their children plays a central role in stimulating demand at a local level, in building pressure for improved quality, and in developing accountability.

There is evidence that this is so even where parents are illiterate, but it is clear that literate parents are more likely to recognise the benefits of education and to demand their right to be consulted, and to hold teachers and officials accountable. Heavily centralised approaches to education planning and management are often ineffective. A more promising approach, which some governments are now adopting, involves central agreement on core objectives, priorities and budget levels, but with decentralisation of responsibility for the management of schools, and for the spending of at least some resources, to the local level, including by school managers.

Again, a sector strategy is likely to be effective where there is strong community and parental involvement in schools and in local decision-making. Experience with the application of new technologies to education over the past decade has been limited and difficult to evaluate. The evidence is that computers in schools appear to be most effective at the higher levels of the system. Where there has been dramatic improvement, it has been with established technologies, including radio.

One key issue is that new information technologies can involve significantly higher recurrent costs, which has clear implications for affordability. The greatest potential for harnessing new technologies to improve quality at the basic level exists where there is a substantial multiplier effect. There is a growing body of evidence that locally managed and maintained technologies, such as radio and electronic networking of teacher and community resource centres, can facilitate and sustain distance learning and reduce or contain the costs of teacher education.

HIV/AIDS has the proven potential to undermine all efforts to achieve UPE through reducing the demand for, and the supply of, education. Education, however, can play a key role in preventing the spread of HIV/AIDS and coping with its effects. It can promote behaviour that will reduce the risk of infection, strengthen people's ability to cope with personal or family infection, and help to deal with grief and loss. Importantly, it can generate hope.

World Education Forum judged that international assistance for education since 1990 has been limited in its impact. It has been co-ordinated poorly and has failed to give priority to initiatives that benefit the poor - either directly or indirectly. Many interventions were developed in isolation without consideration of the education sector as a whole or of wider poverty frameworks. There were numerous projects which could not be sustained, and which burdened governments with disparate demands and reporting requirements.

Most funding agencies would accept this criticism, and many have already begun to move towards more coherent, government-led sector-wide approaches in education, involving more flexible funding, and greater harmonisation of financial procedures and reporting. Although this is a recent phenomenon, many important lessons have already been learned at the country level. It is essential that funding agencies do not treat the sector as a giant project, but are prepared to engage in a long-term process of government-led change.

A sector-wide approach is not about developing a rigid blueprint for the sector, but rather is an ongoing process of putting in place frameworks and mechanisms which will help to make a difference at the point of educational impact. Ensuring that there is sufficient consultation, participation and ownership at decentralised levels, and by civil society, is proving crucial.

Primary education as a foundation for development carries greater weight internationally than it did ten years ago. The World Declaration on Education for All and the UN Convention on the Rights of the Child are significant reference points and provide a basis for performance assessment and accountability. International awareness campaigns have sustained and heightened understanding of the linkages between education, human rights and development. Setting national and international targets has influenced the thinking and the actions of agencies and governments.

Moreover, the connections between education and health, sustainable livelihoods, gender equity, security and democracy have been recognised in the major development fora of the 1990s. NGO campaigns have helped to popularise these values and have gained public support for investment in UPE. Achieving the education targets will require governments to place basic education at the heart of their development policies.

The international community will also need to give priority to UPE in their support for national poverty reduction plans and programmes. There is no single short-term solution, no one strategy that ensures success. A combination of measures is required, backed by a collective commitment to sustain support for Education for All.

There is a growing body of knowledge on the importance of primary education and gender equality for poverty reduction. Strong international commitments have been given to the achievement of UPE. The practical experience of countries that have given weight to UPE in their development policies and resource allocations offers valuable comparative data. Together, knowledge, commitment and know how point to ten key priorities, addressed primarily but not exclusively to governments.

The governments of developing countries have prime responsibility for formulating and implementing strategies for UPE and gender equality. Much depends on the political will to make the hard choices necessitated by resource constraints, manifested in a broad-based policy response to poverty which accords appropriate priority to education, and to basic education in particular.

Sustained government commitment to Education for All is more likely to come about if there is a strong voice for UPE from its citizens. Governments and representatives of civil society have the responsibility to enable all citizens to have an effective voice in the development of policies and strategies that will ultimately lead to sustainable UPE. One clear demonstration of a government's political commitment to education is the willingness to reallocate resources, both to education and within the education sector itself.

To make faster progress towards UPE and other Education for All goals, many countries will need to increase substantially the resources that they commit to basic education, to enable all children to gain access to a quality education. A number of governments could achieve this through the re-orientation of funds away from less productive expenditures, e.g. military spending. But there is also considerable reallocation that can be achieved within the education sector.

Too often, the needs of primary education are not met because higher education has more vocal and politically influential constituents. The willingness of governments to take hard policy decisions, such as reforming the financing of higher education, is a clear signal of a determination to establish sustainable systems of primary education. In all cases, improved efficiency in the use of resources is critical.

Mechanisms for targeting of resources to specific regions and disadvantaged groups, to offset educational disadvantage, will be an important indication of commitment to education. In countries committed to poverty reduction where, even with increased efficiency and effectiveness, financing from domestic sources is simply inadequate, resources from international funding agencies will be required.

FREE PRIMARY EDUCATION

Inclusive education strategies must take into consideration the interrelated dimensions of cost and access. No child should be denied access to a basic education because she or he, their parents or guardians cannot pay for it. Even where education is nominally free, however, some direct costs are often passed on in the form of charges for books, uniforms, exams and transport. These direct costs can reach up to 20% of a family's income, making education unaffordable to many.

The International Forum on Consensus on Principles of Cost-Sharing in Education and Health in Africa asserts that general taxation and other forms of government revenue are more effective, efficient and equitable ways of raising revenue for basic social services than cost-sharing. The allocation of scarce financial resources should be targeted at primary and other components of basic education. Cost recovery should be promoted at higher levels in the education system.

Free education implies not only that states have a policy of provision for per capita expenses, but that measures are taken to ensure this is not undermined by schools raising compulsory levies from poor parents. While the aim is free primary education, the instant introduction of fee abolition may not be the most appropriate in every context.

During a planned transition to free education, targeted incentives and exemptions can lessen the burden on poor people. This is particularly important for retaining girls in school, through scholarships, provision of free textbooks and removing the requirement for uniforms. It can also be effective to focus on merit-based secondary scholarships for poor girls as an incentive for primary enrolment and to help to reduce the gap at the post-primary levels.

Achievement of UPE requires unwavering commitment to gender equality. It needs a consciousness throughout the education system that changes of attitude and practice are necessary. Sector strategies should be underpinned by comprehensive gender analysis. Raising awareness and commitment to support gender equality at all levels of the education system needs to be integrated into such startegies.

Gender analysis may lead to the conclusion that specific interventions are needed, such as gender awareness training for teachers and school management committees or the development of gender-sensitive learning materials and pedagogy. Interventions that focus specifically on rectifying the disadvantages faced by girls and women are likely to include: programmes to research and raise demand for, and acceptance of, girls' education; support for women's literacy and empowerment; programmes to raise girls' self esteem and life skills; increasing opportunities for women teachers and head teachers; and better protection of girls from sexual harassment by teachers and fellow pupils.

Increasingly, the need to develop methodologies for addressing boys' and men's attitudes to girls is being recognised as a vital strategy. To improve access will involve tackling a range of issues, including addressing the shortfall of schools or classrooms, and poor maintenance of physical infrastructure. Schools need to be located near where children live.

Long distances between home and the nearest school often deter children, and girls in particular, from attending school, or dissuade their families from encouraging their education, for fear of mishap, violence or abuse. School facilities must take account of the special needs of girls, since they are more likely than boys not to attend school or drop out altogether at puberty, if, for example, separate latrines and clean water are not available.

Education should be 'inclusive', responding flexibly to the needs and circumstances of all excluded children. Complementary or non-formal primary or pre-primary education programmes acting as alternative delivery structures or bridges into school provide important routes into education and valuable lessons for the formal system. Schools and other educational programmes may need, for example, to adopt flexible calendars and time-tabling, support pre-school education, initiate awareness-raising activities to change attitudes to disability or to minority groups, or develop ways to include a number of languages in the classroom.

For schools to be able to respond flexibly to the needs of the excluded implies a degree of decentralisation of management and decision-making to schools. Guidelines for accountability are needed which give incentives for schools to be equitable and inclusive. The needs of working children have to be addressed. Approaches to child labour which involve applying sanctions or throwing children out of work with no other means of support are likely to be counterproductive.

The UN Convention on the Rights of the Child and Convention 182 of the ILO, on the Elimination of the Worst Forms of Child Labour, require governments to eliminate the worst forms of child labour, meet the basic health and education needs of working children, ensure their protection and enable them to participate in decisions which affect their lives. Governments should place greater emphasis on understanding the different priority which poor people may accord to education, and on stimulating demand through community involvement and genuine ownership of education.

National participatory poverty assessments yield valuable information on the perspectives of the poor and include views on the quality of schooling. They can lead to strategies to ensure that parents understand stated entitlements to education and are in a position to be able to challenge schools that turn away children or demand illegal fees. The interfaces between primary and secondary education, and primary education and employment, need to be the subject of wider national research to inform policy.

Both have implications for the type and quality of primary education provided, especially for those children for whom primary schooling is the limit of their formal schooling. The demand for primary education is reflected in children's enrolment and retention rates at school. There are many complementary activities which encourage parents to send their children to school, and to keep them there. These include: early childhood care and development programmes; activities which highlight the value of girls' education; the availability of local and accessible secondary education; adult literacy programmes; community-level interventions to promote health and reduce the workload of women and girls; and strong school-community partnerships with the representative involvement of parents, particularly mothers.

Civil society should be encouraged to develop its key role in supporting these strategies at local levels. The quality of education offered to children is another major determinant of demand. Many children, particularly those from the poorest households, drop out of school or fail to enrol as a direct result of poor quality schooling. Parents will be unwilling to invest in their children's education unless they are convinced of its quality and value.

Investing in improving the quality of schooling makes good economic sense if it promotes greater efficiency and affordability by reducing repetition. In Bangladesh, a World Bank study found that four out of five children who had completed five years of primary education failed to attain a minimum learning level. In sub-Saharan Africa, it is estimated that up to 60% of children leave primary school functionally illiterate. This is a waste of human potential, and also a waste of scarce resources.

The actual learning experience of each child is at the heart of education. Quality implies developing an ethos and learning practices which will be acceptable and understandable to communities, take account of language and culture, and ensure an environment where all children feel safe, valued and hence able to learn. This includes actively promoting equality, respect for fundamental rights and the all-round development of children.

Promoting community participation in education is an essential part of this. Community participation in school governance can be an important catalyst for their involvement in local decision-making. Poorly trained, or demotivated, teachers reduce learning opportunities. Improving the quality of teaching and learning means putting teachers at the heart of the learning process. Teachers need to be able to teach effectively, using appropriate methods to help children achieve measurable learning outcomes, particularly in literacy and numeracy.

However, they also need to be able to develop good relationships with pupils and the wider community, with an understanding of the disadvantage that accompanies poverty, to promote gender equality, respect diversity and support community development. This requires effective teacher training. Teachers need support close to their schools and ongoing professional development opportunities.

Training teachers within their schools as part of a wider process of school development is likely to be particularly appropriate. The design of teacher development programmes should recognise broader issues affecting teacher motivation especially where pay levels are tightly controlled. For teachers to be effective, the curriculum should be manageable, and adaptable to changing local and national contexts.

It should provide real learning outcomes, based on adequate teaching and learning time. Improving and sustaining quality requires capacity to assess learning outcomes, and to use assessment to enhance teaching, not just for selection and promotion purposes. It also means making sure that children have access to appropriate and stimulating textbooks, which has been shown to have a significant effect on outcomes.

Access to other basic learning resources such as readers, exercise books, pencils and pens will reinforce this positive effect. A child's mother tongue, or widely understood local language, should be used for effective early learning and the acquisition of literacy. Poor learning environments are the norm throughout much of sub-Saharan Africa and South Asia. The active management of the broader physical assets and environment of the school is important. Appropriate low-maintenance buildings, classroom furniture and the provision of clean water and adequate separate-sex latrines are vital, and are often perceived by parents, children and teachers as a significant component of the quality of the service on offer.

The development and maintenance of physical learning infrastructures benefits from strong partnerships between communities and those - usually, but not always, governments - who provide the bulk of the resources for school development. The location and the long-term sustainability of new schools benefit from community involvement in resource mapping and the choice of effective construction systems. A more systematic approach to the planning and maintenance of physical assets is needed.

Enhancing quality at the school level and practising whole school development are dependent upon sufficient decentralisation of responsibility and resources to local and school levels. Support for headteachers is important. There is strong evidence that they are one of the key determinants of school effectiveness, but few have the resources, the training or the delegated authority to manage their schools well. It is important that decisions on school management are taken in response to local needs and priorities, and to facilitate co-ordination with other sectors at the local level.

Education policies and strategies are often set after limited consultation with poor people, and fail to incorporate a sound social analysis that identifies those who are marginalised and excluded. The capacity of governments to listen and learn is not always well developed, and the representative bodies of civil society face the challenge of developing a strong in-country voice in support of UPE and gender equality in education.

Adult illiteracy constrains poor people from having this voice, with women being particularly disadvantaged. A weak civil society cannot challenge corruption and inequitable allocations of resources. Consultation with civil society, including children and their parents, so as to ensure participation in policy-making and in the monitoring of delivery on government promises for education, is a key starting point for developing a sector-wide policy and strategy for change. The way in which this is best carried out varies according to context.

Sometimes using education personnel at decentralised levels may be effective. In other instances, a national process of poverty assessment incorporating educational issues, and feeding these back into policy-making at national as well as sector level, may be appropriate. Civil society bodies will have an important, proactive role to play in this process. However, consultation should not be considered a one-off event.

Mechanisms are needed for ongoing processes of dialogue on policy. This is as important at school level as at national level, and may imply a focus on developing literacy and the ability of poor people, particularly women, to participate in school and local governance. Developing stronger legal frameworks for UPE can be effective for ensuring that people can access their entitlements and hold their governments to account.

Education is an integrated sector: appropriate early childhood education can help to develop children's capacity for cognitive learning and promote positive attitudes to school; opportunities to continue to secondary education, or into vocational training, motivate students to complete the primary phase; improved adult literacy encourages parents to send their children to school. This means that UPE cannot be achieved and sustained in isolation.

Unfortunately, many primary education development strategies and programmes designed to enhance equitable access and quality remain isolated from each other and from the rest of the education system, sometimes with disconnected or contradictory objectives.

Very few countries have mainstreamed gender analysis within their education policies, strategies and sector management processes. A strong commitment to attitudinal change, and to the development of educational institutions that mainstream strategies for attaining gender equality in schooling, is still relatively rare.

While there are often international lessons to be learned, sector policy and strategy needs to be based on very specific sets of country circumstances. Nevertheless, key features of a successful strategy are likely to reflect fully the priorities of poor people, encompass sufficient gender and social analysis, articulate linkages across the sector and, within a framework of common objectives, provide the flexibility that allows for a diversity of responses at decentralised and school levels.

FINANCE FOR PRIMARY EDUCATION

Constraints on public resources have limited the ability of many countries to address the challenges of UPE. This particularly applies to sub-Saharan Africa. Since the mid-eighties, public expenditure on education as a proportion of GDP in Africa has decreased in 15 countries, and is now less than 3% in 12, some of which have low levels of primary education provision. But the challenge is not just about how much funding is allocated to education, but how efficiently and effectively these resources are used.

In many of the countries with the worst education indicators, education expenditure is skewed towards the upper levels, where participation is low and dominated by high-income groups. This is often the result of a lack of political commitment to tackle vested interests, exacerbated by insufficient capacity within governments to develop and implement pro-poor education strategies. Within the education sector itself, hard choices will have to be made.

In many countries, teachers' salaries consume the vast majority of the primary education budget, leaving few resources available for learning materials. Difficult trade-offs need to be made in such cases between, for example, class size and non-salary expenditure. There are choices to be made also about the pace of school construction and between technologies. More broadly, governments need to make decisions about the allocation of budgetary resources between the different levels of education. Willingness to address these complex and difficult issues is itself a strong indication of commitment.

The potential role of the non-state sector as a provider of services, or as a source of finance, is neglected in many national policy frameworks. The extent of involvement of the private sector (including non-governmental organisations and religious institutions) is often seen as an indicator of poor provision, access and quality in the state sector. But the private sector's role need not be restricted to 'mopping up' those failed by government schools. It can be a vibrant addition to the education sector, including as a source of replicable innovation.

The resources needed for education cannot be treated in isolation. Governments face a range of legitimate competing claims on their limited budgets. They have to make decisions about what allocations to key sectors they can afford and sustain. The evidence from local analysis of the effects of different policy decisions on poor people is vital, as is the use of international evidence on the use of 'gender budgeting', social analysis and the relative effectiveness of different strategies in different contexts.

A further challenge for governments is to make allocations between regions on the basis of need, to offset disadvantage. A simplistic focus on allocation by sector without examining allocations within sectors, or on specific targets for allocation of aid and the proceeds of debt relief, can undermine governments' capacity to manage their own development and lead to short-term expansion which cannot be sustained.

Furthermore, differing cost structures and different levels of institutional capacity may mean that roughly similar levels of educational expenditure in a group of countries will not necessarily result in similar outcomes. Governments need also to begin to evaluate their expenditure against educational outcomes and accept accountability for their actions.

The Education for All Assessment 2000 has held governments up to scrutiny for their performance towards achieving UPE, and governments have reaffirmed their commitments. The UN Convention on the Rights of the Child presents another means of holding governments to account through its reporting arrangements.

Strengthening the capacity of institutions for planning, management, monitoring and accountability. Capacity-building and the strengthening of education institutions at all levels needs to be an integral part of effective educational reform. Key areas include sector policy analysis, managing processes of change, and effective monitoring within systems which are becoming increasingly decentralised.

Capacity to plan, manage and report on expenditure is critical not only to the achievement of greater effectiveness, but also to improved transparency and accountability. Real ownership by governments requires capacity to lead effective partnerships with funding agencies, NGOs and the private sector, and to manage the recruitment and deployment of technical assistance. Capacity-building efforts will be most effective within a broader context of public service reform which includes training, staff development and appropriate incentives for performance, at all levels in the system.

Developing effective public-private partnerships will often be an important concern. In some countries private and religious foundation schools sustain education, and many have, for example, helped communities to apply for government-aided status. The private sector may be able to relieve pressure on government by developing sustainable private education options, offering choice, specialism and the sharing of facilities and expertise. However, private schools can also attract the best teachers from the public sector and draw influential community members away from support for state schools.

Certain NGOs may be able to support governments in meeting the needs of some of the most difficult to reach children, piloting approaches that can be scaled up and sustained. More broadly, the education sector is increasingly served by private consultants, textbook publishers, Information and Communication Technology (ICT) providers and construction firms. These may offer positive implications for efficiency and quality, and a clearer focus of governments on their core tasks of policy setting and monitoring.

But, there will need to be strong leadership from governments in the development of such partnerships to ensure that the goals of achieving equitable access and quality in education remain paramount. Development in the education sector cannot be viewed in isolation. It has to be connected with poverty reduction and development initiatives in other sectors. Good economic policies conducive to private investment, to growth, to innovation and to job creation, are of paramount importance.

There is clear evidence that in deciding whether to send their children to school, which, even if nominally free can still carry significant opportunity costs, parents take into account the differences in wage and job prospects between educated and uneducated workers. Good policies, including openness to trade and ideas, coupled with effective investment in education, can create a virtuous circle: higher growth potential raises the perceived rate of return from education, which increases demand and the willingness to pay both via taxes and private contributions, which permits higher investment.

Health and nutrition policies have an important influence on education. Early childhood nutrition and basic care impact strongly on children's learning capacity.

Strategies to give access to reproductive health care tend to stabilise population growth, which has positive implications for sustaining education, and for individual families' ability to feed and educate their children.

Policies on agriculture, the environment and rural livelihoods can reduce the workload of the poor, particularly that of women and girls. This in turn can improve their access to, and retention in, schools. Policies on infrastructure will be important where this affects asset planning and management, school design and construction and the availability of water, sanitation and latrines. The Habitat Agenda for Sustainable Human Settlements (UN 1996) offers important reference points for linking community well-being with education. The availability of clean water and sanitation in homes and schools greatly affects child health and performance in school.

Unhealthy children cannot learn and the reduction of waterborne diseases will have a positive impact on learning opportunities. The impact is particularly important for girls who also bear the burden of having to collect the water. National gender policies and strong equal opportunities legislation which inform and emphasise the value of increased gender equity for individuals and society have the potential to impact on attitudes to, and practice of, girls' education.

Studies indicate that the benefits of educating girls accrue from generation to generation. Gender aware policies and strategies can increase opportunities for women teachers and managers and give access to literacy for adult women, allowing them to play a stronger role in their children's education. They can also catalyse childcare initiatives, freeing girls to attend school and encouraging better preparedness of young children to enter school.

Cross-sectoral programmes are needed to help to meet children's physical, emotional and educational needs whilst facilitating their transfer into schooling or into employment as young adults.

COMPULSORY EDUCATION

The twenty-first century began against the failure to translate promise into performance, to secure at least primary education free of charge for all children. Promises generated by world conferences are seldom translated into performance by governments acting collectively. Individual governments also tend to forget promises made in their electoral platforms once they are elected. Promises then fall into oblivion, highlighting the importance of human rights law which defines individual rights and the corresponding governmental obligations.

Human rights law requires rights to be precisely defined so that they can be effectively claimed, their violations exposed, remedied, and prevented, so that people would have effective means for holding their governments accountable. Human rights law defines rights as claims addressed to governments; these specify what governments should and should not be doing. Law is symmetrical and rights cannot exist without corresponding governmental obligations. Inattention to the right to education of children who have no access to any schooling is therefore addressed in this publication. It aims to elucidate the necessity of merging normative and empirical worlds.

All children should-'but do not have'-the right to education. The principal method of human rights work has always been exposing the abyss between normative and empirical worlds. In attention to the right to education is evident form the absence of worldwide overviews showing the scope and depth of this abyss. Economic and social rights necessitate addressing governmental human rights obligations on two levels -on the domestic level, as is customary in human rights work, and also on the global level because decisions on development finance or debt relief considerably affect the leeway of individual governments to comply with their human rights obligations.

Moreover, universality of human rights requires universality of human rights obligations, thus encompassing governments acting collectively, as donors or creditors. Problems in guaranteeing free and compulsory education to all children revolve around funding. The worlds of human rights and fiscal allocations are separated by an abyss at the global or domestic level. Funding for education tends to be treated as discretionary, contrary to what international human rights law demands.

Few countries in the world have effective constitutional guarantees which oblige the government to allocate to education a determined proportion of its budget. A rare example is the 1947 Constitution of Taiwan which has specified: Expenditures of educational programmes shall not be in respect of the central government, less than fifteen percent of the total national budget, in respect of each province no less than twenty-five percent of the total provincial budget, and in respect of each municipality, no less than thirty-five percent of the total municipal budget. The purpose of human rights law is to transform allocations for education from discretionary into obligatory.

This process entails acceptance of human rights correctives in decision-making, which is a political process at all levels, from local to global. Securing a match between governmental human rights obligation in education and fiscal allocations requires another step-according priority to primary education. The objective of international human rights law is to alter political choices by bestowing legal rights upon those actors who have the least access to decision-making, such as children.

Primary-school aged children who should be 'but are not' in school are easily marginalised hence their legal claim upon governments. This claim is detailed in a number of international and domestic legal instruments. These are, as the term 'instrument' indicates, tools whose value increases with their utilization. The inverse is also true, such tools have no value unless they are known and used. Promoting human rights requires knowledge about the existing international obligations of states and this knowledge can be imparted through a summarized overview of key international treaties, accompanied by country-specific tables.

The 1962 UNESCO Convention against Discrimination in Education is the oldest global treaty guaranteeing free and compulsory education. It was followed by the International Covenant on Economic, Social and Cultural Rights, adopted in 1966 and abbreviated as ICESCR. Within the Organization of American States (OAS), similarly to the Council of Europe, the American Convention on Human Rights had included only civil and political rights to be in 1988 supplemented by the Protocol of San Salvador on economic, social and cultural rights.

The Organization of African Unity created its own human rights treaties and organs, starting in 1981 with the African Charter on Human and Peoples, Rights, which merged collective and individual as well as civil/political and economic/social/cultural rights. The Charter on the Rights and Welfare of the African Child was adopted in 1990 to come into force ten years later, with the committee that should be established on the basis of this Charter expected in the year 2001.

The Convention on the Rights of the Child (CRC) was ten years old in 1999 and has thus far been ratified by the largest number of states (191). These treaties map out the international legal framework of the fundamental requirement of right to education, to secure free and compulsory education for all children. From the Universal Declaration of Human Rights in 1948 to the European Social Charter of 1966, the requirement for education to be free and compulsory never wavered. However, changes have been in the specific designations of various stages of education.

The Universal Declaration has used the term 'elementary' which later became 'primary' and in the African Charter 'basic.' Although the wording of international treaties demands only primary education to be free, compulsory education has been prolonged in practice, thus lengthening free-of-charge education. Because law is symmetrical, the right to education entails corresponding obligations. Making education compulsory requires parents and governments to perform their obligations towards children.

Making education compulsory was thus contingent on making it free. In the drafting of the foundation for all human rights treaties, the Universal Declaration of

Human Rights, there was never a question about education being made compulsory without being free. The International Covenant on Economic, Social and Cultural Rights has prompted more than a dozen states parties to submit reservations to its provision on the right to education. These range from acknowledgments that financial constraints to access to primary education were beyond the capacity of the state, to assertions that education should be treated as the monopoly of the state, or that parents should be allowed to educate their children themselves, in their own home.

The Convention on the Rights of the Child lays down the full scope of the right to education. The principle of nondiscrimination is followed by general provisions on the access to education, its purposes and objectives, which is accompanied by specific requirements upon education to protect children from abuse and neglect or illicit use of narcotic drugs, and followed by safeguards against work that interferes with children's primary education.

An illustration of the demanding nature and scope of states' obligations concerning education is the number and variety of reservations. The consequence of the number and variety of reservations is that a mere ratification of a treaty does not mean that it is binding in its entirety for a particular country. Information on ratifications then has to be supplemented with indications of their limited scope through reservations. Moreover, some reservations, especially those relating to the human rights of children and women, are so wide-reaching that their compatibility with the spirit and wording of the treaties has frequently been challenged and their withdrawal urged.

Many belong to the poorest and/or most heavily indebted countries, with school-aged children constituting a large proportion of the population and too little public funding available for their schooling. A mere ratification of a human rights treaty may be of little value to the domestic population because the rights guaranteed therein cannot be accessed and enjoyed. The remark 'UN Special Rapporteur' in the right-hand column denotes countries for which the United Nations Commission on Human Rights has established a country-specific mechanism, which reflects the Commission's concern about the overall human rights situation in that country.

Within the United Nations, there are two treaty-based procedures: the Human Rights Committee (HRC) deals with communications related to the International Covenant on Civil and Political Rights, while the Committee for the Elimination of Racial Discrimination examines communications alleging breach of the Convention on the Elimination of All Forms of Racial Discrimination (CERD). The third one is starting under the Convention on the Elimination of All Forms of Discrimination against Women (CEDAW), whose Protocol establishing such a procedure has recently come into force for the first dozen states parties.

Within regional organizations, two distinct procedures exist within the Inter-American human rights system, one before the Commission and another before the Court. The Council of Europe has recently altered this pattern and there is only the European Court of Human Rights for violations of civil and political rights guaranteed by the European Convention. The European Committee of Social Rights has recently started processing collective complaints of violations of social rights.

For African countries, access to the African Commission on Human and Peoples' Rights follows from the ratification of the Charter, which also does not allow reservations; access to international remedies is thereby automatically broadened. The coming into force of the Charter on the Rights and Welfare of the African Child entails setting up a committee which will also receive complaints. Experiences at the regional level, in Europe and the Americas, and more recently in Africa, have undoubtedly contributed to the internationalization of human rights enforcement.

The lack of a regional organization with powers to define and enforce human rights in Asia is reflected in the large number of Asian countries listed in the right-hand column. The interplay between international and domestic human rights guarantees represents a fascinating area for research because assumed correspondence between the two tends to be an exception rather than a rule. It would be easy to assume that human rights safeguards from ratified international treaties are reflected in domestic constitutions but this assumption is belied by facts.

Those states that have ratified all international treaties which guarantee free and compulsory primary education to all children, without any reservations, do not necessarily repeat this commitment in their constitutions. The postulate of the Convention on the Rights of Child whereby all children should have guaranteed access to education regardless of their legal status, or that of their parents, is gradually being translated into the practice of states.

In Africa, children of primary-school age may constitute close to half of the population and the majority is living in rural areas. Making primary schools available to dispersed rural communities, some of whom may be nomadic, illustrates the scope of the challenge. If the intake capacity of primary schools is below the number of primary-school aged children, legal provisions on compulsory education will not be translated into practice and access to education will remain a need or a wish rather than, being a right.

Investment in educational infrastructure requires considerable initial capital but yields benefits after a long time. The recurrent costs and maintenance of schools as well as teachers' salaries add to the cost. The requirement that primary education be free of charge is thus costly. Economists often apply the criterion of affordability to free-of-charge education, and questions have been raised in the past two decades about compatibility between fiscal and educational policy, that is, between fiscal targets defined in terms of reducing public expenditure and funding necessary to ensure universal primary education free of charge for all children. While international law requires primary education to be free of charge, education cannot be free-of-cost in theory or in practice.

For governments, it is one of the major items in their budgets. Parents finance their children's education through general taxation, and routinely pay the cost of books, transportation and school meals, uniforms, pens and pencils, or sports equipment. The requirement upon governments to make primary education free implies that governments should eliminate financial obstacles in order to enable all children 'no matter how poor to complete primary schooling.

A great deal of controversy has been generated regarding the human rights obligation to finance primary education. The requirement that primary schooling be free of financial cost for the child has generated a great deal of consensus, but that it also be free of financial cost for parents triggers dissent. One reason is parental primary responsibility, financial as well as any other, for their children, affirmed in the Convention on the Rights of the Child. Another reason is parental freedom to choose non-state schools for their children, or establish their own or else educate their children at home, routinely at their own expense.

Primary education should be free for children because they cannot possibly pay for themselves. This does not imply that education is free for parents, community, society or the state because schools and teachers' salaries have to be financed. Rather, this means that primary education should be prioritised in resource allocation.

Direct charges in primary education, under whatever name, impose upon parents the obligation to fully finance the education of their children. School fees are named differently, as user charges, registration fees, school maintenance or development levies, but whatever name they bear, their effect is to openly question the explicit requirement of international human rights law that at least primary education be free. The duty to financially contribute to the cost of primary education is spread among the whole population where education is financed by the state out of general taxation, which is the model envisaged in international human rights law. International human rights law assumes that states are both willing and able to generate resources needed for education through general taxation.

There are few which are unable to impose and enforce taxation upon their wealthy population, many more are unwilling to do so. This is precisely why human rights have been defined as governmental obligations. The assertion of the Universal Declaration of Human Rights that all individuals have duties towards their community has, regretfully, fallen into oblivion. And yet, states cannot finance education unless they generate resources, they cannot generate resources unless companies and individuals pay tax.

Today's dominant ideology seeks the withdrawal of the state from generating and allocating resources, thus jeopardizing access to education, particularly in the poorest and youngest countries. The financing of education is in many countries within the remit of local or regional authorities, whose tax base and tax revenue may be profoundly different from those of the central government. Nevertheless, no internationally comparable data have been generated in this area. From the human rights viewpoint, the state is responsible for human rights hence its obligations encompass the whole territory and all the people.

Because local communities may not be able to raise revenue sufficient to guarantee to all children free and compulsory primary education, the state ought to redress their lack of capacity. The same rationale extends to the world at large because human rights are universal. International co-operation has been envisaged as the method for redressing inability of individual states to comply with their human rights obligations.

Distinguishing between inability and unwillingness thus obtains a great deal of importance. Those who do not earn enough to be liable to taxation are not taxed, thus taxation applies the logic of distributive justice. Where fees are charged in primary school, those who are too poor to afford the cost nevertheless have to pay the charges. If they cannot afford them, their children will be penalized by denied access to primary school. Where exemptions are nominally provided, they may be too cumbersome to comply with or too expensive to administer.

The Convention on the Rights of the Child has specified for health that children should not be denied access to health services because of the inability of their parents to pay its cost, and there is no indication that the Convention envisaged a lower standard for primary education, on the contrary. The Committee on the Rights of the Child requires governments to report on 'the measures taken to ensure that children, particularly those belonging to the most disadvantaged groups, are protected against the adverse effects of economic policies, including the reduction of budgetary allocations in the social sector.'

The cost of primary schooling is considerable. Mark Bray has estimated that at least 20% and often as much as 90% of the financial cost of primary education is borne by the parents and/or families. Parental financial contributions towards primary education of their children depend on their ability to contribute, not only their willingness to do so. Their inability to afford sending their children to school deprives their children of access to primary education and highlights the essence of governmental human rights obligation to be the provider of last resort.

Parental choice may be exercised to the detriment of girls and requires governments to act so as to alter parental choices. Efforts to increase primary school enrolment for girls have included subsidizing direct, indirect, and opportunity costs (namely, the loss of the value of the girls' work) for their parents and/or families. The distribution of the cost of primary education between the government and parents depends on budgetary allocations. The budget exemplified the translation of political choices into financial commitments.

Education is often the single largest item in governments budgets although in heavily indebted countries it tends to be dwarfed by debt repayments. A group of senators in the Philippines challenged in 1991 the constitutionality of the budgetary allocation of P86 billion for debt servicing, while P27 billion was allocated for education.

The inevitable consequence of insufficient public funding for primary education is slanting financial obligation to bear the cost of schooling towards parents and families. There are, of course, exceptions, such as United Arab Emirates with a low allocation out of a sizeable budget, while Lesotho has a proportionally large allocation and yet primary education is not free of charge. Piecing together the mosaic needed to portray the full panorama of free primary education in today's world demands a great deal of painstaking search for important questions and answers. Regretfully, this has not yet been done despite the crucial importance of securing free education for all primary-school children. As far as possible, the documentation generated by the reporting procedures under human rights treaties or reports by ministries of education have been used so as to keep the sources authoritative.

The documentation of the World Bank and other international agencies has been used where no governmental reports have been found. For countries, such as Angola, where no recent information is available, reports by journalists have been the only available source. Education should be compulsory until children reach the minimum age for employment Similarly to the requirement that primary education be free of charge, information about the requirement that education be compulsory is routinely confined to international treaties and domestic laws while there is no review of the gap between normative and empirical worlds.

Compulsory education has much longer tradition than the right to education. This was reflected in the 1959 Declaration of the Rights of the Child, which laid down the entitlement of the child to receive education, articulating the vision of the child of the time as a passive recipient of education. The changed vision of the child as a subject of rights, embodied in the Convention on the Rights of the Child, is slowly being translated into domestic laws and policies. As noted at the beginning of this publication, the requirement that primary education be compulsory forms part of international human rights treaties and this is reflected in domestic laws of a vast majority of countries in the world. The capacity of governments to implement their laws on compulsory education varies, as do enforcement measures. Many target parents by fines for their failure to secure enrolment or school attendance by their children. Some target children, however.

Enforcement of compulsory education thus raises important human rights issues. The Convention on the Rights of the Child goes no further than obligating States to encourage school attendance; enforcement is not mentioned. Older human rights treaties, such as the European Convention on Human Rights, provided for detention of a minor by lawful order for the purpose of educational supervision, which mandated compulsory schooling in the narrowest sense of this term.

The specific offence of truancy was created to punish the child for breaching the duty to attend school. The explicit wording of international human rights treaties requires primary education to be compulsory and free of charge. Categorizations of education and the terms used to describe the first stage of formal schooling (elementary, primary, fundamental, or basic) have changed during the past decades.

A division of schooling into primary and secondary was challenged by UNESCO as early as 1961. It held that primary and secondary schooling should be deemed to constitute 'successive phases of a continuing process' rather than two different entities. With the lengthening of compulsory education, this division is no longer valid in many countries. Countries are categorized in two groups: those in which compulsory education equals the length of primary schooling, and those that have prolonged compulsory education beyond primary schooling.

In some countries, compulsory schooling has been lengthened beyond primary schooling. Countries in which the two remain equal in length have become a minority; in more than 40 compulsory education is six years long or less, while just below forty countries have lengthened compulsory education to ten or more years. The only countries where primary schooling is reportedly longer than compulsory schooling are Jordan, Rwanda, and Tuvalu. Countries in which compulsory schooling is the shortest (such as Bangladesh, Laos, Nepal or Viet Nam) share financial obstacles to lengthening education, while the tendency in Western Europe to extend compulsory education beyond ten years (in Belgium, Germany, and the Netherlands, for example) reflects the necessary merging of the willingness and the ability to do so.

Children may be excluded from schooling because they are female, indigenous, refugees, or because they do not have identity papers hence they legally do not exist. Asylum-seeing and refugee children may be difficult to reach, but some may be excluded because the right to education is confined to citizens. Children with disabilities may be in practice excluded from school, whatever the law may say, because the buildings and classrooms make their access impossible. Children who are institutionalized may be excluded from schooling because the mandate and funding of the institution housing children excepts education.

5

Gender Disparities in Education

Gender parity, which refers to the equal participation of both sexes in different levels of education, is a quantitative concept. Its indicators are static, measuring, for example, the relative proportions of girls and boys with access to, or participating in, primary schooling. However, viewed over time, they can serve as more dynamic indicators of change. To the extent that progress towards gender parity suggests a weakening of the factors that keep women and men in unequal positions, it represents the first steps towards achieving equality of outcomes for the sexes. However, gender parity indicators have some limitations, even when they are available over time. First, even if progress towards parity appears to be being made, this sometimes masks declines in male or female enrolment and participation, rather than indicating positive gains for both boys and girls. Second, a focus on quantitative balances reveals nothing about the processes by which they are being secured, nor about the qualitative changes that would be necessary if gender parity is to lead to full equality.

Gender equality requires the achievement of equal outcomes for women and men, notwithstanding that they are starting from different positions of advantage, and are constrained in different ways. Women differ from men both in terms of their biological capacities and in the socially constructed disadvantages they currently face. Inequalities arise from unequal power relations between women and men, and hence assessments of progress towards gender equality need to establish whether the changes that are being achieved are significantly altering these relations. The erasure of the social norms that see women and men as making unequal contributions to society and having unequal entitlements to its benefits is critical to achieving a society free from gender discrimination. Thus, whether women and men are being treated equally will depend on whether the fundamental freedoms and choices they confront are the same.

Education is in many ways a fulcrum for this process. It reflects contemporary norms and values, but it also helps to change them. Full gender equality in education would imply that girls and boys are offered the same chances to go to school and that they enjoy teaching methods and curricula free of stereotypes, and academic orientation and counselling unaffected by gender bias. Most fundamentally, it implies equality of outcomes in terms of length of schooling, learning achievement and academic qualifications and, more broadly, equal job opportunities and earnings for similar qualifications and experience. These objectives are demanding, and are far from being achieved in most societies. It is clear that the achievement of gender equality in education – in the sense of equal outcomes – will not be possible in the absence of wider social change in many societies. The question of whether and how this might occur over the coming decade requires an assessment not merely of the prospects for, and limits of, educational reform, but also of more fundamental changes that affect many other sectors and areas of life and work.

RIGHTS TO EDUCATION

Extreme inequality in enrolments between girls and boys is particularly associated with low overall enrolments and with the incidence of poverty. Inequality is not determined by povertv, because there are cases of poor countries where parity of enrolments has been achieved, but it appears to be part of the story. Why is this so? In general, inequality in educational participation and outcomes reflects broader inequalities in society. These embrace social norms and customs, which create powerful incentives that guide people's behaviour, and determine the roles that women and men can have in the family and community. Social norms are embedded in kinship and religious systems that are highly diverse across – and often within – societies. However, such norms can and do change – in response to environmental and economic change and to broader political and social developments.

Change can result from deliberate actions of state and civil society groups, leading to reforms in the legislative and institutional framework of society. In these ways, changes in the expectations and incentives that govern human behaviour – including those that affect educational participation and performance – can be achieved. The critically important locus for decisionmaking as regards participation in schooling is the family. It is here that notions of gender relations are transmitted from one generation to the next. This happens implicitly via the gender roles that members of the household themselves fulfil, and explicitly by consequence of the gender frameworks within which children of each sex are brought up.

Households allocate time for different activities among their members, and they also allocate resources – for consumption, savings and investment, including those associated with the formation of human capital – between each of them. Decisions made by households are influenced by the broad social and institutional framework of custom and opportunity in which they are located. Nevertheless, changing the factors that affect household constraints, opportunities and incentives is a critically important means of influencing their decision-making.

The main ways in which children spend their time, and the amount of resources to which they have access, are determined by the households in which they live. The broad parameters for household behaviour are set by the social and institutional framework of each society. However, within that context, a key question is whether households make decisions in ways which balance the relative needs and interests of each of their individual members, or whether they do not. Traditionally it was thought they did.

Economic and social policy proceeded as if households had a single set of preferences. The ways in which household resources, work obligations and opportunities for leisure were allocated among household members were not thought to be important. According to this 'unitary' model, it was taken as given, for example, that changes in the balance of expenditure would be consistent, not necessarily with an equal distribution of resources, but at least with maximizing household welfare, however defined. Yet concern about subgroups within households – such as women or children – invites the question of whether the distribution of power within the household results in some of its members having a less than equal share of its joint resources.

Recent theoretical and empirical work shows that this is so. It appears that resource allocation decisions within households are inconsistent with the 'unitary' household model. In particular, additional income accruing to different household members has different implications for household expenditure patterns. Women seem to spend more on education, health and household services than do men. Thus the evidence against income and labour pooling and against family altruism is strong and an approach premised on bargaining within households better captures the reality.

While households are not a collection of individuals co-operating in the interests of maximizing economic gains, neither are they a group of people acting as if they were single individuals. Households are, by and large, made up of families, and hence they are the sites of particular kinds of social relationships, which are very distinct from other relationships in any society. Institutional approaches that take account of this have been used to elucidate the process of household decision-making.

Within such an approach, 'households' and other domestic arrangements are seen as institutional responses to the need for long-term stable relationships. These are based on meeting the basic survival needs of members, bearing and raising children and coping with illness, disability and old age in a world characterized by uncertainty.

Powerful ideologies of family and kinship bind household members to each other through socially sanctioned 'implicit contracts'. These ideologies carry mutual claims and obligations in ways that are often highly unequal. They are not 'invented' by individual households; they are embedded in wider social norms and values and hence exercise an influence that goes beyond the authority of senior individuals within the household.

Households take diverse forms across the world. One important principle of difference relates to gender relations. Most societies observe some gender division of labour within the home, with women taking primary responsibility for caring for the family, whereas men tend to be associated with the work outside the home, often on a paid basis. This division of labour goes some way towards explaining the gender inequalities in human capabilities observed in many nations.

However, societies differ considerably in the extent to which women also participate in paid work outside the home: the most marked gender inequalities are generally found in societies where women are confined to the home and denied the possibility of participating in work outside it. These restrictions tend to be associated with other values and practices that further inhibit women's life chances, including patrilineal principles of inheritance and descent, where family line and property is transmitted through men; patriarchal structures of authority, where families are tightly knit and where most resources are under the control of the senior male; and patri-local systems of marriage requiring women to be absorbed into their husbands' families after marriage, distancing them from the support of their natal families. The restrictions on women's movements in the public domain in such societies reflect the importance attached to the biological paternity of children and the need to control women's sexuality. Denied access to resources of their own and restricted in their ability to provide for themselves, women tend to be regarded as economic dependents in such societies.

SOCIAL AND ECONOMIC FORCES

It is the complexity of interaction between social norms and values and broader economic change which explains the diversity of enrolment outcomes. The mechanisms that are capable of delivering greater equality are not necessarily put in place by economic growth – or by income growth at the household level – alone. Other social forces are of equal significance.

SON PREFERENCE

Many societies have been characterized by marked son-preference and by discrimination against daughters from the early years of life. This occurs to such an extent that such societies often have excess levels of female mortality and a higher proportion of men to women in the population than is considered 'standard' in the rest of the world.

Countries in which there is strong cultural preference for sons also tend to have the greatest levels of gender inequalities. These societies exhibit 'extreme' forms of patriarchy. They are to be found in countries of North Africa, the Middle East, South and East Asia. Gender inequalities in education in such societies are simply one apect of a generalized and systematic discrimination against women and girls. Although other parts of the world are also characterized by a gender division of domestic labour, they do not exercise the same restrictions on women's ability to participate in the wider economy – even though such participation may be onerous, given women's other domestic responsibilities.

Differences in gender relations within and outside the household reflect societywide norms, values and practices rather than privately determined choices. To that extent they change only slowly in response to changes in individual or household circumstances. At the same time, they are not immutable. Like other aspects of social behaviour, they have often shown evidence of change over time, with both positive and negative outcomes for women.

CHILD LABOUR

Whether all children will be sent to school depends on the extent to which households continue to see themselves as requiring the labour of their children in order to achieve tolerable levels of welfare. Owing to the importance of child labour as a major constraint on school participation – with a strongly differentiated impact on girls and boys – this factor needs prominent attention in policy design.

One of the commonest reasons for children not attending school is that their families need them to work. Sometimes this work is paid, but mostly it is unpaid and takes place within the household or on the family farm. Global estimates of the incidence of work performed by children are available – as for adults – only for work leading to a marketable output. This includes waged work, but also regular work done on a household farm or enterprise. People engaged in these economic activities are conventionally described as being economically active and, when they are children, as being child labourers. Most recent estimates suggest that about 18% of children aged 5–14 are economically active in those ways, amounting to some 211 million children in 2000, roughly half of whom were girls.

About 25 million of these children were estimated to be involved in work for their families which was consistent with their development. But some 186 million of them were involved in some form of child labour which was harmful to their development. Although many of these child labourers work for only a few hours per week, more than half of them are estimated to be working full time on the production of marketable output.

There are no reliable global estimates for the number of children engaged in domestic chores and other household work that does not lead to marketable output. It is safe to assume, however, that the number of such children is several times greater than those formally described as being 'economically active' – and thus as comprising 'child labour' – and that the girls who find themselves in this category considerably outnumber the boys.

There are dramatic differences in the incidence of child labour by region. Africa has the highest incidence (41%) while Asia and Latin America have 21% and 17%, respectively. Asia, being more population-dense, has the largest number of child labourers. Of children in work, it is estimated that 61% are in Asia (128 million), 32% in Africa (68 million) and 7% (15 million) in Latin America.

While the incidence of child labour in Asia and Latin America has witnessed a secular decline in the post-war era, this is not the case in sub-Saharan Africa. There, fertility remains high and per capita resources for education have often been in decline. Slow or negative economic growth, famine and disease, war and conflict and the spread of HIV/AIDS in Africa have all contributed further to keeping the incidence of child labour high.

The vast majority of working children – i.e. those helping to produce marketable output – in developing countries are engaged in agricultural work, typically on family-run farms. Accordingly, the work participation rates of children tend to be higher in rural than in urban areas. Child work in export-sector factories, many of which are in urban locations, is thus by no means the general case of child labour.

Although in Latin America and Asia, a small but significant fraction of children work outside the household for a wage, this is much less common in Africa, where wage labour markets are more incipient. Parents are, therefore, the main employers of children, and affecting their circumstances and attitudes is the major challenge in reducing child labour.

Second, and contrary to what is often assumed, child labour is not the inverse of school attendance. Many children from all developing regions, but especially African children, combine working on family-run farms and enterprises with attending school. Inevitably, however, there is a trade-off between work participation and school attendance in such circumstances. Achievement is also affected: the quality of the school experience for working children is undermined not only by their more irregular attendance, but also by their ability to apply themselves while at school being reduced by their responsibilities outside it.

Third, most countries exhibit large gender differentials in child labour-force participation. In Africa and Asia, the educational participation and attainment of girls tends to be less than that of boys. However, the data on child labour do not always show girls as being more heavily engaged in work than boys because they are often more likely than boys to be classed as 'inactive'. This probably corresponds to their having a greater engagement in household chores, which is not conventionally counted as economic activity.

Often the poverty of households is a distinguishing characteristic – with those supplying boy labourers being on average poorer than those supplying girl labourers. In rural Pakistan, for example, it appears that boys take wage work only when their income contribution is necessary to household subsistence, whereas girls take wage work even when the household could survive without the money.

A broad interpretation of the empirical literature suggests that the proportions in work and out of school are larger for girls than for boys in Asia, the proportion in work but not necessarily the proportion out of school is larger for boys than for girls in Latin America, and the proportions of boys and girls in work are roughly similar in most parts of Africa, although the girls who are out of school comprise a significant majority.

GIRLS AND DOMESTIC WORK

Even where their labour participation rates are similar, boys and girls often specialize in different sorts of work. For example, in Ethiopia, Guinea and the United Republic of Tanzania, girls specialize in domestic work, such as looking after siblings, preparing and cooking food, cleaning the house and fetching water and firewood. Boys, on the other hand, are mainly involved in working on the family farm, looking after livestock and engaging in income-earning activities. In terms of the range and frequency of work activities practised in these three countries, including domestic chores, girls help their families more than boys.

In rural Pakistan, girls in waged work are mainly engaged in seasonal agricultural work, whereas boys in waged work are primarily engaged in the non-agricultural sector. Proxy evidence also exists from household surveys for many developing countries, which find that a substantial fraction of children are neither in work nor in school. This fraction is typically larger for girls than for boys – an indication that 'doing nothing', as reported by such surveys will, in many cases, correspond to doing housework. Other school-based surveys for a large number of countries show that household and domestic work is a significant reason for non-attendance, and more so for girls than for boys.

In Ethiopia and Guinea, between onequarter and one-third of school drop-outs surveyed indicated that their need to earn money or to work at home on the family farm were the main reasons for leaving school early. In both countries the girls who dropped out for these reasons did so mainly in order to help the family in the home, whereas the boys who did so cited work on the family farm, or earning money as having been their main intent.

The history and geography of child labour show that its incidence falls as economic development proceeds. Its existence is undoubtedly partly a result of poverty. However, the beneficial impact of increased wealth or income may often be rather indirect.

In many cases those at school are on average from richer households than school drop-outs who, in turn, are from better-off backgrounds than those children who have never been enrolled. On the other hand, household surveys often suggest that the relationship between income and child labour at the household level is weak and, related to this, surveys often reveal a considerable prevalence of child labour among households that are not subsistence poor.

Furthermore, the ownership of productive assets such as land sometimes increases child labour, owing to the increased need for household labour for those with larger land holdings. This needs further investigation in a broader range of contexts, because the effectiveness of income transfer programmes aimed at reducing child labour is dependent on parents being altruistic – in the sense that those having the choice would not want their children to work.

One of the explanations for the indirect relationship between income and child labour may be that women and men have different preferences and power within households. A growing literature argues that the relative power of women in deciding how to spend household resources increases with their earning power. Recent work has shown that the incidence of child labour can be expected to be lowest where power is equally divided between husbands and wives.

Data from Indonesia suggest that children work less and study more in households where the mother has more influence in decision-making. Other studies allow for the possibility that child workers are independent bargainers who influence the allocation of resources within the household. In rural Pakistan, for example, ignoring work status, no gender differential is apparent in the allocation of resources.

However, once work status is allowed for, it is found that working boys acquire a larger share of household resources such as food and child-specific goods than do non-working boys. In contrast, working does not bestow any benefit on girls. Although this may reflect differential preferences, it may rather be that dependent girls are as heavily engaged in domestic chores as working girls are in more explicit forms of work. This is in contrast to working boys who may in fact be more active than dependent boys.

Social norms play a significant role in explaining why and how gender differentiation occurs, how it becomes legitimized through divisions of labour between men and women, and how this division of labour results in the contributions of girls and boys being valued differently. Norms of female dependence on males are institutionalized through a range of social mechanisms so that they come to appear natural and immutable. These norms are usually stubborn, but they can be challenged through pro-active measures.

Contrary to the assumptions of many parents, girls will go to great lengths to attend school. Once there, they work hard and often outperform boys in their studies. However, many parents recognize that existing social conditions are often unsupportive of those girls and women who offend social norms.

Some Ethiopian fathers, for example, noted that more educated girls face problems because they cannot find a husband or employment opportunities; they will get older, have to stay with their parents and bring shame upon the family; thus the only options are for educated girls to migrate to bigger towns, often to lead a miserable life working as house servants or even prostitutes.

EARLY MARRIAGE

Where female autonomy is considered unstable or risky, early marriage is used as a means of securing daughters' futures. This massively impedes the educational progress of girls in many countries. Data from India for 1996 show that 38% of girls aged 15–19 were married. In rural areas of Albania and Tajikistan it is not uncommon for poor families to endorse the early marriage of girls to lighten the family's economic burden. In these circumstances, early marriage (at age 15 or 16) becomes a reason to leave school.

Although it is well known that marriage of children and adolescents before the age of 18 is very common in some parts of the world, its overall prevalence is difficult to assess. Many such marriages are not registered. Small-scale studies suggest, however, that national data significantly underestimate its prevalence. For example, in 1998, in the Indian state of Madhya Pradesh, 14% of girls between the ages of 10 and 14 were already married. In Nepal, 40% of girls are married by the time they are 15. In Ethiopia and in some countries in West Africa, marriage at 7 or 8 is not uncommon, although in some cases girls are reported to be able to carry on their education even after moving to their inlaws' household. Even boys marry under pressure from parents, earlier than they would wish although not as early as girls.

In themselves, changes to the legal age of marriage are unlikely to alter local practices if underlying conditions are not changed. For example, despite a recent policy change in Ethiopia, whereby the minimum official age of marriage for girls became 18, in some parts of the country girls are still married before the age of 10. Moreover, in some areas girls are not infrequently 'kidnapped' on their way to school, or even from within the school compound itself, by the parents of boys, for marriage to their sons.

Cognisant of this risk, some parents refuse to send their daughters to school. Promoting the importance of girls' education through campaigns, role models, improving conditions of safety and security for girls and working directly with adolescent girls to strengthen their voice are all important measures to help communities to allow girls to complete their education.

Cultural practices and rites of passage more complex set of issues affecting girls' education are traditional practices that mark adolescence and the rites of passage. Some cultural practices inadvertently affect the incentives to educate girls. For example, the practice of bride price or lobola in many parts of southern Africa, whereby educated girls may attract a higher bride price, can serve as a powerful incentive for some parents to educate their daughters. In contrast, the practice of dowry in India often acts as a depressant on investments in a daughter, be it their education or health, by emphasizing the importance of girls' eligibility for marriage to the exclusion of all other considerations of personhood.

However, where education is seen as improving the prospects for girls in the marriage market, it may be used purely as a means to that end.

Adolescent Sexuality

Social pressures on girls and boys are particularly strong during their puberty and the development of adolescent sexuality. In many countries, adolescent pregnancy, either within or outside marriage, almost always results in the discontinuation of a girl's schooling. In both Malawi and Chile, pregnancy was often mentioned as the most important reason for girls leaving school early, although statistical evidence is sparse.

In the United Republic of Tanzania, the strong enforcing of compulsory education has meant that early marriage is not an important factor affecting girls, but pregnancy was cited as an important reason for girls dropping out of school. In addition, the high costs of schooling and the inability of poorer girls to buy school uniforms also may encourage them to seek sexual relationships with older men who can provide them with money.

Data compiled by the Forum for African Women Educationalists in eastern and southern Africa indicate that the school careers of many girls are cut short because they are expelled from school on becoming pregnant. Pre-marital pregnancy among girls is stigmatized in African communities even though its determining factors remain unaddressed.

In Guinea and Malawi, where girls are now encouraged to return to school after pregnancy, few girls do so, partly because of parental fears that they would become pregnant again, and partly because girls are afraid of ridicule.

A recent series of studies about management of puberty in primary schools in Uganda, Kenya and Zimbabwe concluded that the current management of sexual maturation within the primary system fails to meet the needs of children, but especially those of girls. In particular, children were denied:

— accessible and accurate information about the process of sexual maturation;

— essential facilities to ensure that children, especially girls, are not excluded from participation because of their maturing bodies;

— an appropriate value system through which boys and girls can be guided into safe and healthy adulthood.

The studies document the ways in which poor management of sexual maturation has had a detrimental impact on children's acquisition of basic learning competencies, and how girls who experienced menstruation without adequate preparation, or facilities, were regularly absent or even dropped out of primary school.

CHILDREN IN SPECIAL CIRCUMSTANCES

Much of the preceding discussion has focused on families and the operation of gender inequalities within them. However, increasing numbers of children do not always fall within the conventional boundary of the 'family', and for them educational decision-making may be affected by a range of other factors. Households suffering from the strain of crises such as those unleashed by conflict and civil war and by the HIV/AIDS pandemic may no longer be able to send their children to school.

It may seem obvious to observe that whether or not children are brought up by their parents significantly affects their life chances. This, however, is an important factor in many developing countries, where households are large and complex. Nephews, nieces and sisters-in-law may often be counted among children along with sons and daughters of the head of household.

In sub-Saharan Africa there is, further, a high prevalence of the practice of fostering children and of taking in orphans. In principle, it might be expected that parental altruism towards their own children would lead to non-biological children of household heads being more prone to involvement in child labour and less likely to be enrolled in school than biological children. This is confirmed by evidence from African countries.

Evidence of the biological-child effect, however, appears to be less apparent for child labour than it is for schooling. For example, an analysis of Peruvian data finds no effect. On the other hand, in rural Pakistan, sons and daughters of the household head are more likely to be in work than other children in the household.

In rural Ghana, sons of the head of household are less likely to be in work but for daughters there are no differences, compared with other 10–14-year-old girls in the household. These differences may partly exist because – as in the case of several West African countries – education features prominently in the reasons for fostering, particularly in the case of boys.

HIV/AIDS PANDEMIC

In 2002, an estimated 42 million people worldwide lived with HIV/AIDS. The 5 million new infections and the 3.1 million HIV/AIDS-related deaths accounted for a rise of 2 million compared with the year before. Behind these cold figures hides the immeasurable detrimental impact of HIV/AIDS on development in general and on education in particular, described in the EFA Report 2002. The global proportion of women among the infected adults is estimated to be equal to, or somewhat higher than, the proportion of men.

But there are striking differences among regions, and there is a tendency for the proportion of women to be higher in less developed regions. In sub-Saharan Africa, women make up as much as 58% of those living with HIV/AIDS, against 20% in North America. The picture is especially bleak for adolescent girls, aged 15–19; in some of the worst-affected countries in southern Africa and the Caribbean, girls in this age group are infected at rates four to seven times higher than boys, a disparity linked to widespread exploitation, sexual abuse and discriminatory practices.

A primary factor in girls' vulnerability to HIV infection involves sexual violence and coercion. A Human Rights Watch report on Zambia stated: 'An alarming and apparently increasing number of abuses against girls come from members of their own families.

Given the high HIV prevalence in the Zambian population, sexual abuse carries a high risk of HIV transmission. Nevertheless, the family, the broader community, and the law enforcement agencies are often complicit in attempting to hide the abuse. Effective protection mechanisms targeted at abuse against girls in the family are virtually nonexistent.'

Not even schools are safe places for girls. A South African Demographic and Health Survey asked women about rape in childhood, and found that schoolteachers were those most commonly responsible. The data show that approximately 1 in 200 South African women aged 15–49 was raped by a school teacher before the age of 15.

For schoolgirls, more particularly, the South African Medical Research Council reported that half of those surveyed in 2000 had been forced to have sex against their will, one-third of them by teachers. If both these figures are accurate, they imply that the incidence of rape has increased very substantially over recent decades. Given that South Africa has the largest number of people living with HIV/AIDS in the world, the implications of these levels of sexual violence are particularly disturbing.

In many high-prevalence countries, poverty conspires with HIV/AIDS to affect the lives of girls very seriously. When HIV/AIDS hits a family, girls are often the first to be taken out of school to care for an ailing parent or family member, or to take on responsibility for their siblings, sometimes as head of household. The direct costs of schooling may also soon become unbearable for such affected families, where in the worst cases girls may even be forced to provide for themselves and their families by engaging in relationships that might heighten, for themselves, the risk of HIV infection.

Girls' education is an important means of breaking such patterns of economic deprivation and dependence. It is however, sadly ironic that although education is an effective means of addressing the HIV/AIDS crisis, the epidemic puts new barriers in the way of girls' abilities to access education, whilst also undermining the education system itself. Nevertheless, there are indications that HIV infection may be declining more markedly among young, educated women than among those with less education.

Studies point to the example of Zambia, where prevalence for young women aged between 15 and 19 dropped from 27% in 1993 to 15% in 1998. The decline was greatest among those with secondary and higher levels of education. Some have concluded that, if this apparent relationship between more education and less HIV is robust, in the absence of a physiological vaccine against HIV infection, society has at its disposal a 'social vaccine' in the form of education. In addition, there is some recent evidence of decline, or levelling off, of HIV prevalence in some urban areas of sub-Saharan Africa, which, for those between 15 and 19 years, may indicate some impact of prevention efforts.

However, it does not follow that 'health literacy' is a natural product of general literacy, as the experience of South Africa and Botswana demonstrates. Both countries have relatively high levels of literacy and high HIV prevalence rates. This underscores the need to invest both in general literacy and health literacy specific to HIV/AIDS. This requires attention not only to basic facts about HIV/AIDS but also to enabling girls and young women negotiate their social and sexual lives more independently, armed with a better understanding of the implications of sexual activity.

ARMED CONFLICT

Armed conflict is a major barrier to development in general and to gender equality in education in particular.

Armed conflict is estimated to affect some thirty countries in the world, mostly those who can least afford it; 80% of the world's wars are in Africa and Asia; most conflicts during 2001 were internal. In such internal struggle for control over territory and populations, civilians are increasingly placed at the heart of the conflict.

Militias multiply and small arms proliferate. Civilians not only make up the majority of victims, they are increasingly the targets of conflict. Far from being unfortunate collateral damage of war, the destruction of civilian populations has been the very aim of some of the wars of the 1990s, as in Rwanda and Bosnia. Civilian casualties in wartime have climbed from 5% of the total in the early twentieth century to up to 90% during the wars of the 1990s.

The effects of armed conflict are different for men, women, boys and girls. In Bosnia and Herzegovina in 1995, Muslim men and older boys were rounded up and detained or executed, whereas women and girls were forced to leave. Women and girls, on the other hand, are continually threatened by rape and sexual exploitation during armed conflict.

During the conflict in the former Yugoslavia there were an estimated 20,000 victims of sexual assault, and in the 1994 genocide in Rwanda, many adolescent girls who survived militia attacks were raped. In times of war, in addition to the dangers of gunfire, bombings, landmines and sexual assault, women and girls also face the risk of increased domestic violence.

Domestic violence is common during peacetime, but it increases during and after conflict. Many things contribute to the increase in domestic violence: the availability of weapons, the violence that male family members have experienced or caused, the lack of jobs, shelter and basic services. Girls and women are therefore doubly vulnerable in times of war.

The destruction of educational infrastructure represents one of the greatest developmental setbacks for countries affected by conflict. In Mozambique, some 45% of primary-school networks were destroyed, and during the crisis in Rwanda more than two-thirds of teachers either fled or were killed. The lost years of education make the recovery after war even more difficult. Once the fighting stops, the lack of schools and teachers, the inability of authorities to rebuild the education system and to train, retrain and deploy new or returning teachers, is a difficult challenge that can take many years to overcome.

Providing education in situations of emergency and crisis is critical, both as a way to resist the enemy and to provide some sense of normalcy in disrupted lives. It is also the foundation on which to rebuild societies. Because schools are often targeted, alternative sites for classrooms have to be found, alternating the venues regularly.

In Eritrea in the late 1980s, classes were often held under trees, in caves or in camouflaged huts built from sticks and foliage. Similar arrangements were made during the fighting in the former Yugoslavia, where classes were held in cellars of private homes, often by candlelight, witnessing the importance of maintaining education no matter how difficult the circumstances.

In interviews with the Women's Commission for Refugee Women and Children in 2000, Burundian women expressed concern about children's and adolescents' lack of access to school, where the situation had further deteriorated due to insecurity. They reiterated the need to raise levels of school attendance and literacy, and again offer children and adolescents alternatives to violence and prostitution.

Half of the 104 million out-of-school children, two-thirds of whom are girls, live in countries in the midst of or recovering from conflict. Of the seventeen sub-Saharan countries in which enrolment rates declined in the 1990s, six are states that are affected by or are recovering from major armed conflict and of the fourteen countries with a very low enrolment GPI of between 0.6 and 0.84, three are currently in conflict and two are recovering from it.

Of the twenty-five countries with the lowest levels of female adult literacy, ten are either experiencing armed conflict or recovering from it. It is also significant that of the twentyfive countries targeted recently by UNICEF for accelerated action to improve girls' participation in education, eight have experienced recent conflict within their borders.

There is ample evidence from the Machel report and from other sources that armed conflict particularly disrupts the education of girls.

During conflict girls may not be allowed to go to school because parents fear attacks on the way. The HIV/AIDs threat makes this of even greater concern. Of the seventeen countries with over 100,000 children orphaned by AIDS, thirteen are in conflict or on the brink of conflict. In the Democratic Republic of the Congo, it is thought that adult HIV/AIDS prevalence has risen steeply to 20%, and that in 2001, 930,000 children under 15 had lost either their mother or both parents to the epidemic.

The vulnerability of women and girls to sexual violence in situations of conflict makes them also especially vulnerable to HIV/AIDS infection. This was indicated in a recent study in the highly affected region of North Kivu (Democratic Republic of the Congo), where estimated infection rates are 54% among adult women, 32% among adult men, and 26% among children. Infection rates of military forces can be far higher than those of the local population.

Traditional chores such as collecting firewood and water represent a real danger during wartime. All these factors impact negatively on education. In southern Sudan, the demand that girls care for younger siblings and children has considerably increased during civil war, as adults and particularly women have become more engaged in livelihood activities than during pre-war periods.

In the case of the Aboke girls in northern Uganda, 139 girls were specifically targeted, removed from a girls' boarding school, and forced into the rebel forces. In northern Uganda, families have married their daughters to militia members in order to protect themselves and their girls. The same also happened in Somalia. In post-conflict periods, sexual violence and exploitation of women does not necessarily abate. In Rwanda, for example, during and after the conflict, girls tended to stay close to their homes, remaining for the most part with their mothers; education was the first of their activities to be sacrificed.

Recent conflicts have resulted in huge refugee populations, making demands on an already overstretched education system. The United Nations High Commissioner for Refugees (UNHCR) cares for 20 million 'persons of concern', mainly refugees and asylum seekers but also internally displaced persons. These have been uprooted because of internal warfare but have not reached a neighbouring country, and are therefore not protected by international law.

The United Nations Special Representative for Internally Displaced Persons estimates there are 25 million IDPs worldwide, with major concentrations in Afghanistan, Angola, Bosnia and Herzegovina, Colombia, the Democratic Republic of the Congo, Sri Lanka, the Sudan, and countries of the former Soviet Union.

The majority are women and children. In nearly half of these countries, IDPs faced sexual violence. A 2002 study in Guinea, Liberia and Sierra Leone found that displaced women and girls in camps were constrained to exchange sex for scarce food and other basics – even for humanitarian aid. Twelve million children aged 5–17 are without access to education due to conflict.

One of the most neglected but significant education-related outcomes of conflict is disability, particularly that caused by landmines. In Africa, an estimated 37 million mines are embedded in the soil of at least nineteen countries. Since May 1995, children have comprised about half the victims of the 50,000–100,000 anti-personnel mines laid in Rwanda. Angola alone has an estimated 10 million landmines and an amputee population of 70,000, of whom 8,000 are children. For every child killed in armed conflict, three are injured and permanently disabled. About two-fifths of the 26,000 persons killed and injured by landmines each year are children. Over 10 million children have been psychologically traumatized by armed conflicts.

Notwithstanding its many horrific outcomes, the general destruction caused by armed conflict may open up some avenues for women that challenge their traditional roles and responsibilities. Women may find themselves working outside the home for the first time, becoming the income-earners and living in a more public sphere. Male involvement in fighting often leaves women – and even young girls – heading households.

After the genocide in Rwanda, females for a time accounted for 70% of the population. In southern Sudan only one-third of the population is male. Thus, conflict tends to result in women taking on additional responsibilities. In post-conflict Somalia, in the absence of men, women have become increasingly involved in income-generating activities and in household decision-making. This is also true in El Salvador.

The role of women in the 1979 Iranian revolution led to their recognition of their own power and rights. In spite of the influence of religious fundamentalism and the rule of religiopolitical leaders, Iranian women have had significant achievements in the realm of education. In Eritrea, those fighting for national independence designed a school curriculum which reflected a commitment to socialist equality and the rights of women.

Classes were co-educational and girls were encouraged to participate fully in all fields, particularly the technical ones. Education is a political asset, and can be used as a stabilizing factor on which to build a new postconflict society, but education systems can also be used to alienate groups from each other.

One recent study notes that in many conflicts around the world, such as the Balkans and Rwanda, education systems can be used negatively, as a weapon of cultural repression and to promote intolerance. Segregated education, as in apartheid South Africa, can be used as a means of reinforcing inequality and promoting stereotypes, including gender stereotypes. Post-conflict reconstruction opens up the opportunity to transform conventional education systems and to renew both teaching methods and curricula.

Risks of Girls with Disabilities

Girls with disabilities are a large and diverse group whose educational needs have gone largely unnoticed by those committed to promoting either gender equity or disability equity. Evidence is scarce, but it seems clear that these girls are not faring well. Widespread cultural biases based on both gender and on disability greatly limit the educational opportunities of such girls.

Disabled children are at severe risk of exclusion from school and other social activities. Especially in the case of girls, the victims may be seen as a burden on the family because marriage prospects may be hampered. It is quite usual for a disabled woman to be hidden by her family. In the Palestinian Autonomous Territories, for example, because of the symbolic importance of female beauty and health and the pivotal role of women in the family, a disabled woman is seen as a failure on several counts.

Although available data are limited, they indicate that women and girls with disabilities fare less well in the educational arena than either their disabled male or non-disabled female counterparts. For example, UNESCO, the World Blind Union and others estimate the literacy rate for disabled women at only 1%, compared with an estimate of about 3% for people with disabilities as a whole. Statistics from individual countries and regions, while often higher, nonetheless confirm the gender inequalities. In terms of school enrolment, UNESCO suggests that more than 90% of children with disabilities in developing countries do not attend school.

There are many definitions of disability, not only across but also within countries. These varied definitions demonstrate that disability is a social construct, as much rooted in cultural, social, political, legal and economic factors as in biology.

While the World Health Organization (WHO) is currently leading an effort to achieve a new international definition that considers many of these factors, no consensus has yet been reached. Here, girls with disabilities are defined as those with physical, sensory, emotional, intellectual, learning, health or other disabilities that may be visible or invisible, stable or progressive, occurring at birth or during childhood. Their access to education is affected by their gender, their type of disability, the socioeconomic status of their family, their ethnicity, whether they live in an urban or rural area, and a host of other factors.

Given the diversity of definitions, no clear global statistics are available. WHO has estimated that between 7% and 10% of the world population have some type of disability and that 80% of these people live in developing countries. UNESCO and others estimate that the number of children with disabilities under the age of 18 around the world varies from 120 million to 150 million. Even assuming that girls make up somewhat less than half of all children with disabilities, as some research suggests, the number of girls with disabilities worldwide is very substantial.

There is a circular relationship between poverty and disability which also accentuates gender bias. On the one hand, insufficient nutrition causes disability, as is the case for 500,000 children every year who lose some part of their vision due to vitamin A deficiency, and for over 40 million babies who risk mental impairment due to insufficient iodine in their mothers' diets.

Child labour and maltreatment can lead to mental illness, physical and psychological disabilities. Women and girls, in the face of limited resources, are more likely than their male counterparts to be deprived of basic necessities, such as food and medicine. On the other hand, disability can also contribute to poverty, because of the additional expenses that it entails and because of the difficulties facing disabled income-earners. Thus, disabled girls are more likely to grow up in poor families, a reality that places them at further educational disadvantage.

Just as there is little available information, so there is a dearth of programmes specifically aimed at addressing the educational needs of disabled girls. In the United States, while there is a range of initiatives to promote educational equity for girls, these have largely overlooked disabled girls. Similarly, strong disability rights legislation has produced a range of efforts to promote educational equity for disabled children, but few initiatives have included gender-specific components to address the unique barriers facing disabled girls. Other countries have similar experience.

National statistics often conceal strong regional patterns of inequality. In Ethiopia, for example, under-enrolment is very much a rural phenomenon, and a gender gap is largely absent in urban areas, where primary GERs are over 100% for both boys and girls. In rural areas, on the other hand, only 25% of school-age girls are enrolled in primary school compared with 31% of boys, and it is estimated that a mere 1% of girls and 1.6% of boys in rural Ethiopia completed the eight-year primary cycle in 2000. The two predominantly pastoralist regions exhibit the lowest primary enrolment rates, whereas the rate for pastoralist girls is estimated to be below 1%. The achievement of enrolment and gender equity targets is therefore to a large extent dependent on improvements occurring particularly in the two pastoralist regions, and in rural areas more generally.

In Chile, data disaggregated by geographical location shows widening gender and rural–urban gaps in educational participation for teenage children. Household wealth also intervenes, with rural non-poor girls having marginal advantage over boys, but rural poor boys having an advantage over girls. Both poor and non-poor households have higher participation rates in urban compared with rural areas. The pattern is intensified in the 20–24 age group.

Contexts of poverty and marginalization are, of course, not static. In China, for example, access to education of disadvantaged groups – minorities, migrant populations and the urban and rural poor – has worsened as the transition to a market economy, the collapse of previous social support systems and increased rural–urban migration pose severe challenges for educational provision.

In Bangladesh, too, there has been a significant decline during the 1990s in the number of urban students achieving the basic competencies. This suggests an inability of the school system to cope with the large additional migrant population. Their destination is often the urban slum communities, which become educationally disadvantaged, particularly where these semi-permanent settlements are not legally recognized by urban authorities.

Indigenous peoples fare poorly in education relative to non-indigenous children. In Chile, indigenous children and young people perform less well than children of non-indigenous groups, especially at secondary and higher education levels, and with marked gender disparities. A high proportion of girls leave school early, as a consequence of 'behaviour problems.'

In Romania, indigenous girls' access to education tends to be limited by their communities' traditional attitudes to women's status. These Roma girls tend to drop out of school earlier than boys, because of their substantial household and family responsibilities. They may also be married early or bear children before the age of 15.

Data disaggregated by gender alone hides other inequalities. In the United Kingdom, attention paid to male disadvantage in education, masks both the educational disadvantages faced by some girls and the particular success of boys from elite and professional classes. Although gender differences have recently been eliminated in terms of performance, neither social class inequality nor ethnic differences have been transformed in such a way.

Recent research suggests that these other social divisions have become more extensive. Statistics that focus only on the national gender gap can therefore distort the picture. Thus, gender disadvantage in education is particularly concentrated among marginalized groups, and intensifies with poverty and social disadvantage.

Household decisions to send children to school are strongly influenced by the economic, social and cultural contexts in which they find themselves. They are also, however, affected by the terms on which schooling is made available to them, and by its quality. These 'supply-side' issues – which include matters of costs, distance to school, the school facilities available, and broader matters of school quality and content –can have a significant impact upon whether or not girls attend.

The direct costs of schooling to households are made up of tuition or other fees, and the costs of purchasing books, materials, school uniforms and transport to school. Household decisions to educate the children respond to changes in the cost of these items.

Although many empirical studies, based on household data, suggest that demand reductions are comparatively small in response to small increases in costs, some evidence indicates – as would be expected – that enrolments among the poor are much more sensitive to cost increases than is the case with richer households.

Evidence on the gendered impact of such charges is available from micro studies, although this is mainly from studies modelling the impact of lower travel costs, showing a strong and positive gendered impact: girls enrolments rise, and do so more strongly than those of boys, in response to reductions in travel costs to school. Similarly, clothing costs may differ for boys and girls. Clothes for school in Ethiopia, and uniforms in Guinea and the United Republic of Tanzania, were the highest direct cost items facing parents in the mid-1990s.

More recent work in the United Republic of Tanzania showed that uniforms remained the most expensive cost item, and that girls' uniforms were perceived by parents to be slightly more expensive than those for boys. Taking all these items into account, the direct costs of schooling in the United Republic of Tanzania were estimated to be 14% more for girls than for boys at primary level. There is strong evidence from more qualitative sources that direct costs are one of the most important causes of non-attendance and early drop-out from school. School costs are reported to be significant in this respect in China, Egypt, Ghana, Indonesia, Mexico, Pakistan and, for girls, in Bangladesh.

In Malawi, from over 1,000 primary-school dropouts interviewed, half of the boys from rural areas and 44% of the boys from urban areas cited the lack of money for school expenses as the main reason for their having left school prematurely. This was also the most important factor for girls, although a smaller proportion of girls than boys – about one-third in both rural and urban areas indicated this.

Children often also indicate their 'need to work' as the dominant reason for leaving school. If these two sets of causes are combined – i.e. costs and income – a majority of children are typically found to cite economic circumstances as the main reasons for their having left school. They accounted for 75% of the school drop-outs interviewed in Zambia, 70% in Uganda and Ethiopia, 57% in Ghana, 45% in Malawi and 40% in Guinea. In Tajikistan, in 2002, 68% of parents surveyed considered family poverty and the increased costs of education as the primary reason for girls' non-attendance.

Finally, separate evidence is available from a wide range of sources on the importance of household income as a determinant of school enrolments. In Senegal, the enrolment of children aged 6–14 from the poorest households is 52 percentage points lower than for those from the richest households. In Zambia there is a 36 percentage point gap.

Here too there are gender differences: in Ethiopia, increasing a household's wealth index by one unit increases a boy's chances of attending school by 16%, whereas a girl's chances are increased by 41%. In Guinea, whereas the effect is insignificant for boys, girls' chances are increased by 9%. These results indicate that poverty in a family will have a more detrimental effect on the decision to enrol a girl in school than a boy.

For all these reasons, measures to reduce the direct costs of schooling are one of the most potent ways of increasing school enrolments – particularly for poorer households, and particularly for girls. There is ample experience, now, of the potentially huge numbers of children who may enrol in school when costs are sharply reduced. For example, following the implementation of fee-free primary-education policies in Malawi and Uganda, primary enrolments increased in the mid-1990s by 52% and 200%, respectively. Despite this evidence and the many human rights instruments, ratified by the vast majority of nations, which commit states to the provision of 'free and compulsory' education at primary level, school fees continue to be levied in at least one hundred and one countries around the world.

The level and type of fees imposed vary between countries. A recent study undertaken across seventy-nine countries showed that seventyseven of them had at least one kind of fee at primary level. The most prevalent fee is PTA or community contributions – charged in over 70% of cases. The costs of textbooks and uniforms are also commonly assigned to parents, as are fees for sports and other activities. Tuition fees are charged in only about 40% of cases –somewhat less than the incidence of the other charges mentioned above. It is noteworthy, once again, that these charges are levied in a substantial proportion of countries where it is formally illegal to do so.

Fixing school costs, as part of UPE policy, may not work in practice. Schools often operate discretionary and ad hoc policies, and costs can often vary between schools. Treatment of poor children in such contexts tends to be highly arbitrary. Thus even where sanctions are not applied on non-payment of fees, the existence of fee policies obviously serves as a deterrent to their avoidance.

Unexpected costs such as funeral expenses for teachers, or farewell events, may be requested in an ad hoc fashion, as evidence from Zambia shows. In some cases, children may not be allowed to attend school if they are not able to afford books, pens or 'adequate' clothing. Finally, significant nonmonetary contributions are often made by parents in the form of preparation of food or cooking for school meetings, cleaning the playground and school buildings, maintenance of buildings and garden, and collecting water and firewood. In some countries, these activities are not voluntary but imposed.

At present, a substantial part of the costs of primary education are borne by households. It is estimated that this usually amounts to at least 20% and often as much as

90% of total annual unit costs. In Cambodia, for example, despite a constitutional commitment to provide free education for all, parents and the community together bear 75% of the real costs of education, with the state thereby contributing a minor amount. Furthermore, in six African least developed countries the average parental contribution represented slightly less than one-third of the total annual costs at primary level. None of these considerations imply that policies to institute 'free' schooling should not be pursued with urgency.

Even where direct costs do not serve as a barrier, it is well documented that the distance of the school from the home has an impact on enrolment. The average distance of schools from homes declines as the expansion of primary and secondary systems proceeds.

However, remote habitations and dispersed populations continue to suffer disadvantages based on the lack of physical access and this remains a problem, particularly at secondary level, in many countries. Where distance is a factor, girls feel the effects more severely. Focus group evidence from Africa indicates parents' reluctance to send girls to schools far from home. Reasons cited were sometimes that girls were considered to be weaker than boys and hence unable to expend the energy required to walk to and from school.

Where there are insufficient school places, enrolment is often staggered, resulting in children entering school later than they are meant to. Starting school late is likely to have greater negative impacts on girls' survival rates because, for reasons discussed above, they are more likely to be withdrawn from school at puberty than are boys.

Primary school availability may also be biased against girls where singlesex schooling is the norm, and where the priority of expanding enrolment is biased towards schools for boys. In Pakistan, despite a doubling in the number of single-sex public primary schools between 1988 and 1998, the percentage of girls' schools among all public primary schools has remained roughly unchanged, at about 30%. This proportion reflects the earlier government practice of building approximately one girls' school for every two boys' schools. Villages in rural Pakistan are hence more likely to have boys' than girls' schools. Little is known about the extent to which investments have been made to upgrade and improve conditions in existing public primary-school facilities nor about how these resources might have been distributed between schools for boys and girls.

Narrowing this gap is, therefore, a vital step in countries where single-sex schools are important for girls' schooling. A study of household demand and gender differences in primary-school access in Pakistan concluded that the decision by parents to enrol their daughters is most influenced by the presence of a single-sex public school in their village, followed closely by their perceptions of the quality of the school.

Co-ordinating the expansion of school places at both lower and higher levels of schooling can also be important. In Mali, for example, despite recent school expansion there remains a serious lack of places in the second stage of basic education. Many children in the first stage of basic education are enrolled under a double-shift system, and there are not enough spaces to include all who graduate in the second stage. Where some children have to remain out of school, it is more often the girls who lose out.

The provision of gender-aware infrastructure can be extremely important for ensuring girls' full participation in schooling. The absence of latrines for girls can be decisive, particularly for menstruating girls. Fewer than half the schools visited during a recent Ethiopian study had latrines, and only one of these schools had a separate latrine for boys and girls. Only one-third of schools studied in Guinea had latrines, and in most cases these were not suitable for use. Where enrolments increase rapidly, pressure on school infrastructure can result in overcrowding, and in poor sanitation and hygiene if there are insufficient toilets.

As with reducing the distance between schools and homes, the case for investing in water, toilets and basic school infrastructure is most persuasively made by governments that, having done so, have experienced remarkable progress in closing gender gaps and universalizing education. In Bangladesh, drinking water is now available in or near over 90% of schools. Almost half of government schools have their own drinking-water facilities. Shortfalls still remain however – over 30% of coeducational schools had no toilet facilities, and only 19% had separate facilities for boys and girls.

RIGHTS THROUGH EDUCATION

Where education systems are well developed and where girls enjoy equal participation in schooling, the boys often find themselves outperformed by them. Results from learning outcomes surveys and others show the following:

Girls achieve much better reading scores than boys in all the countries surveyed in the latest PISA survey;

boys do somewhat better than girls in mathematics in most countries; the performance of boys and girls is roughly equal in science. These results are drawn from countries which all have primary NERs higher than 95. Thus they each have a well-developed education system.

Data for developing countries show that the over-performance of girls is weaker than in the OECD group, and sometimes does not occur. These findings, however, cannot be generalized to other countries. For many, where gender parity is still far from being achieved, and where education systems are poor, both boys and girls fare badly.

Improvements in performance or variations in performance gaps may reflect socio-economic advantages. In Mali, where overall repetition rates are high, the gender gap in repetition is narrow for the first stage of basic education, but increases to about 5 percentage points by the second stage of basic education, with more girls repeating years and dropping out than boys. However, at secondary level, the opposite happens, with – over the period 1967–94 almost always a smaller proportion of girls repeating than boys. This probably reflects the low access of girls to secondary schooling in Mali, where those who do attend are usually from more privileged backgrounds.

Ethiopia, some subjects reveal wider gender gaps in performance than others, notably mathematics, in an education system where aggregate achievement for boys is slightly higher than for girls, though with some regional variations. Gaps between boys and girls do widen through the system – in 2000/01 only 20% of girls passed the Grade 10 examinations compared with 53% of boys, and 46% and 67% respectively passed the Grade 12 examinations. In Togo, both boys and girls fare badly in schools, but the impact of girls' failure has more serious implications in that parents are less tolerant of repetition on the part of their daughters than of their sons. Hence poor performance by girls more frequently leads their withdrawal from school.

Evidence that girls are outperforming boys has created a stir in many countries, not least because it appears to confound typical assumptions about the nature of gender inequality. Careful interpretation of the evidence is required to establish which girls are outperforming which boys, in what institutional context this occurs, and whether there are wider socio-cultural factors that affect these outcomes. Some of these issues are discussed below.

Evidence that girls are outperforming boys does not always indicate a reversal of gender inequality; it rather suggests changes in patterns of gender differentiation.The United Kingdom and France are both countries where the relative underperformance of boys has received much attention. Recent reports from the United Kingdom Government's Department for Education and Skills reflect this concern. The Caribbean region is also well known for girls' better performance, having closed the gender gap before the 1990s and having maintained a female enrolment advantage over the decade.

In Caribbean states, on average, girls start schooling earlier, attend school more regularly, drop out of school less frequently, stay in school longer, and achieve higher levels of functional education at the end of schooling than boys. This pattern also holds true for adult literacy. In these countries, women are more literate than men. For example, the National Literacy Survey in Jamaica in

1994 reported that the literacy rate among the population aged 15 and older was 81.3% for women and 69.4% for men. Thus, the gender gap in the Caribbean is the reverse of what it is in most other parts of the developing world.

In both France and the United Kingdom, policy reform has contributed greatly to closing gender gaps and to fostering a stronger culture of equality between male and female. The improved performance of girls relative to boys in the United Kingdom may partly reflect adjustments in the curriculum and examinations. Girls tend to master reading skills at an earlier age. Thus, the introduction of a National Curriculum requiring boys to engage more in language-based studies tends to improve girls' relative performance.

Similarly, assigning greater assessment weight to course work may also have benefited girls. Research suggests that girls tend to do better than boys on sustained tasks that are openended, process-based, related to realistic situations and that require pupils to think for themselves; boys, on the other hand, show greater adaptability to more traditional learning approaches with a strong emphasis on memorization.

Education policy reforms do not in all cases result in closing of gender gaps in learning and performance. The 'tremendous paradox' of Jamaican education revealed by one recent study is that, despite strongly positive investments in the education sector and high enrolment rates throughout lower-secondary school, students demonstrate low learning interest and participation. Special concerns arise about examination performance and reading ability, which in particular reflect socio-economic disadvantage.

Poor reading ability starts in the lower grades, and is particularly concentrated among boys. By the time students reach Grade 6, one-third of them read below their expected level. By Grade 9 a huge divide is in place, where large numbers of students, especially boys, are not able to read or write. Some are functionally illiterate. Because their reading deficiency, they are at a huge disadvantage.

Despite boys and girls entering Grade 1 in equal numbers, and with roughly the same kinds of experiences and skills, major distinctions are observable in their attitude to and interest in their studies. This leads to large differences in the quality of work produced and in their academic performance by the time they reach Grades 5 and 6. However, the evidence suggests that male performance tends to be mainly a reflection of lower attendance, rather than lower performance per se. The interconnections between schooling performance and gender identities provide indicative explanations for some of these trends.

As education systems move towards gender parity and improved quality, girls are likely to perform better than boys. However, what does this mean in terms of greater gender equality? Many examples exist of the ways in which girls are unable to convert their academic edge over boys into greater equality in other spheres of life. In these circumstances their 'rights through education' remain blighted. In Chile, for example, despite girls achieving better results than boys in secondary school, they perform less well in the university selection test.

A comparison of a cohort of students taking the System of Measurement of Educational Quality (SIMCE) test in 1998 and the university selection test in 2002 found that the poorer results of women in the latter were not reflected by their earlier schooling achievement. One explanation suggested was that men were more concerned to ensure that they achieved the scores needed to enter prestigious university programmes and hence took crash courses to prepare for the entrance tests.

6

Achieving Gender Parity

Girls are often treated as inferior and are socialized to put themselves last, thus undermining their self-esteem. Discrimination and neglect in childhood can initiate a lifelong downward spiral of deprivation and exclusion from the social mainstream. Initiatives should be taken to prepare girls to participate actively, effectively and equally with boys at all levels of social, economic, political and cultural leadership. Gender-biased educational processes, including curricula, educational materials and practices, teachers' attitudes and classroom interaction, reinforce existing gender inequalities.

Girls and adolescents may receive a variety of conflicting and confusing messages on their gender roles from their parents, teachers, peers and the media. Women and men need to work together with children and youth to break down persistent gender stereotypes, taking into account the rights of the child and the responsibilities, rights and duties of parents. Although the number of educated children has grown in the past 20 years in some countries, boys have proportionately fared much better than girls. In 1990, 130 million children had no access to primary school; of these, 81 million were girls.

This can be attributed to such factors as customary attitudes, child labour, early marriages, lack of funds and lack of adequate schooling facilities, teenage pregnancies and gender inequalities in society at large as well as in the family. In some countries the shortage of women teachers can inhibit the enrolment of girls. In many cases, girls start to undertake heavy domestic chores at a very early age and are expected to manage both educational and domestic responsibilities, often resulting in poor scholastic performance and an early dropout from schooling. The percentage of girls enrolled in secondary school remains significantly low in many countries.

Girls are often not encouraged or given the opportunity to pursue scientific and technological training and education, which limits the knowledge they require for their daily lives and their employment opportunities. Girls are less encouraged than boys to participate in and learn about the social, economic and political functioning of society, with the result that they are not offered the same opportunities as boys to take part in decision-making processes.

Existing discrimination against the girl child in her access to nutrition and physical and mental health services endangers her current and future health. An estimated 450 million adult women in developing countries are stunted as a result of childhood protein-energy malnutrition. In all actions concerning children, the best interests of the child shall be a primary consideration. Support should be given to integral sexual education for young people with parental support and guidance that stresses the responsibility of males for their own sexuality and fertility and that help them exercise their responsibilities. More than 15 million girls aged 15 to 19 give birth each year.

Motherhood at a very young age entails complications during pregnancy and delivery and a risk of maternal death that is much greater than average. The children of young mothers have higher levels of morbidity and mortality. Early child-bearing continues to be an impediment to improvements in the educational, economic and social status of women in all parts of the world.

Overall, early marriage and early motherhood can severely curtail educational and employment opportunities and are likely to have a long-term adverse impact on their and their children's quality of life. Sexual violence and sexually transmitted diseases, including HIV/AIDS, have a devastating effect on children's health, and girls are more vulnerable than boys to the consequences of unprotected and premature sexual relations.

Girls often face pressures to engage in sexual activity. Due to such factors as their youth, social pressures, lack of protective laws, or failure to enforce laws, girls are more vulnerable to all kinds of violence, particularly sexual violence, including rape, sexual abuse, sexual exploitation, trafficking, possibly the sale of their organs and tissues, and forced labour. The girl child with disabilities faces additional barriers and needs to be ensured nondiscrimination and equal enjoyment of all human rights and fundamental freedoms in accordance with the Standard Rules on the Equalization of Opportunities for Persons with Disabilities. Some children are particularly vulnerable, especially the abandoned, homeless and displaced, street children, children in areas in conflict, and children who are discriminated against because they belong to an ethnic or racial minority group.

All barriers must therefore be eliminated to enable girls without exception to develop their full potential and skills through equal access to education and training, nutrition, physical and mental health care and related information. In addressing issues concerning children and youth, Governments should promote an active and visible policy of mainstreaming a gender perspective into all policies and programmes so that before decisions are taken, an analysis is made of the effects on girls and boys, respectively.

The Governments should take the following actions to eliminate all forms of discrimination against the girl child. By States that have not signed or ratified the Convention on the Rights of the Child, take urgent measures towards signing and ratifying the Convention, bearing in mind the strong exhortation made at the World Conference on Human Rights to sign it before the end of 1995, and by States that have signed and ratified the Convention, ensure its full implementation through the adoption of all necessary legislative, administrative and other measures and by fostering an enabling environment that encourages full respect for the rights of children;

Consistent with article 7 of the Convention on the Rights of the Child, take measures to ensure that a child is registered immediately after birth and has the right from birth to a name, the right to acquire a nationality and, as far as possible, the right to know and be cared for by his or her parents.

Take steps to ensure that children receive appropriate financial support from their parents, by, among other measures, enforcing child-support laws. Eliminate the injustice and obstacles in relation to inheritance faced by the girl child so that all children may enjoy their rights without discrimination, by, *inter alia*, enacting, as appropriate, and enforcing legislation that guarantees equal right to succession and ensures equal right to inherit, regardless of the sex of the child.

Enact and strictly enforce laws to ensure that marriage is only entered into with the free and full consent of the intending spouses; in addition, enact and strictly enforce laws concerning the minimum legal age of consent and the minimum age for marriage and raise the minimum age for marriage where necessary. Develop and implement comprehensive policies, plans of action and programmes for the survival, protection, development and advancement of the girl child to promote and protect the full enjoyment of her human rights and to ensure equal opportunities for girls; these plans should form an integral part of the total development process.

Ensure the disaggregation by sex and age of all data related to children in the health, education and other sectors in order to include a gender perspective in planning, implementation and monitoring of such programmes. Disaggregate information and data on children by sex and age, undertake research on the situation of girls and integrate, as appropriate, the results in the formulation of policies, programmes and decision-making for the advancement of the girl child.

Generate social support for the enforcement of laws on the minimum legal age for marriage, in particular by providing educational opportunities for girls. The Governments should take the following actions to eliminate negative cultural attitudes and practices against girls. Encourage and support, as appropriate, non-governmental organizations and community-based organizations in their efforts to promote changes in negative attitudes and practices towards girls.

Set up educational programmes and develop teaching materials and textbooks that will sensitize and inform adults about the harmful effects of certain traditional or customary practices on girl children. Develop and adopt curricula, teaching materials and textbooks to improve the self-image, lives and work opportunities of girls, particularly in areas where women have traditionally been underrepresented, such as mathematics, science and technology.

Promote an educational setting that eliminates all barriers that impede the schooling of married and/or pregnant girls and young mothers, including, as appropriate, affordable and physically accessible child-care facilities and parental education to encourage those who have responsibilities for the care of their children and siblings during their school years to return to, or continue with, and complete schooling. Encourage educational institutions and the media to adopt and project balanced and non-stereotyped images of girls and boys, and work to eliminate child pornography and degrading and violent portrayals of the girl child.

Eliminate all forms of discrimination against the girl child and the root causes of son preference, which result in harmful and unethical practices such as prenatal sex selection and female infanticide; this is often compounded by the increasing use of technologies to determine foetal sex, resulting in abortion of female foetuses. Develop policies and programmes, giving priority to formal and informal education programmes that support girls and enable them to acquire knowledge, develop self-esteem and take responsibility for their own lives; and place special focus on programmes to educate women and men, especially parents, on the importance of girls' physical and mental health and well-being, including the elimination of discrimination against girls in food allocation, early marriage, violence against girls, female genital mutilation, child prostitution, sexual abuse, rape and incest.

The Governments should take the following actions to strengthen the role of the family in improving the status of the girl child

i) Formulate policies and programmes to help the family in its supporting, educating and nurturing roles, with particular emphasis on the elimination of intra-family discrimination against the girl child;

ii) Provide an environment conducive to the strengthening of the family with a view to providing supportive and preventive measures which protect, respect and promote the potential of the girl child;

iii) Educate and encourage parents and caregivers to treat girls and boys equally and to ensure shared responsibilities between girls and boys in the family.

In North Korea, primary education is being given to 73 per cent of the total pupil population, and it is at this level that the proportion of girls is the highest. There has, moreover, been no improvement in the situation in recent years. Despite the extraordinary increases in the world school-going population between 1960/61 and 1966/67-

an increase of 32 per cent in six years- the disproportion between the number of girls and the number of boys remained more or less unchanged instead of lessening, for the increase in the number of girl pupils was comparable to the overall increase, and not higher.

The educational opportunities for girls and women therefore remain distinctly below those open to boys and men. And this is true only in quantitative terms, but also in qualitative terms. On 7 November 1967 the United Nations adopted the 'Declaration of the Elimination of discrimination against Women'. Article 3 stipulates: 'All appropriate measures shall be taken to educate public opinion and to direct national aspirations towards the eradication of prejudice and the abolition of customary and all other practices which are based on the idea of the inferiority of women.' Yet this idea still has currency.

Women do not enjoy all the educational opportunities they should have, and often do not have any at all. Nearly everywhere in the world they are given less education than men, and, over vast areas of the globe, the majority of illiterates are women. The continuation of this state of affairs lends support to the traditional view which, in turn, contributes to the perpetuation of the *status quo* Education contributes in large measure not only to the elimination of the idea that women are inferior but also to the elimination of the inferiority of their actual status.

Over the past çenturies this fact has been realized by a great many women, in Europe and in the United States. To give but one example among many: about a hundred years ago, an American woman journalist, Mrs. Hale, writing in the magazine *Jodey's Lady's Book,* pointed out that little had been said about the rights of women, the first of which was the right to education in its widest sense, an education that would enable women to develop fully their individual, intellectual and moral qualities.

One women had access to education there would be no problems in regard to their rights, and those same rights could become harmful if women were incapable of exercising them. The inferior status of women is linked to their traditional role. This is an 'inside' role, within the limits of the family home. Evelyne Sullerot quotes a remark made by Xenophon twenty-four centuries ago: 'The gods created women for the discharge of duties inside the home, and men for all the others.. If behaves women to remain within the home and it ill becomes them to "hang about" outside'.

And the French sociologist shows that this 'outside-inside' contrast is in fact equivalent to a 'superior-inferior' distinction. It is fact that all over the world for thousands of years women have remained confined within more or less narrow limits. The women's role was dictated by the prime necessity: survival. Mothers did not have enough time to cope with all their 'inside' duties: agricultural work; tending animals; pounding millet; making candles, soap, preserves and clothing; carrying water and wood; and washing-all of which were exhausting tasks.

Until quire recently the performance of these duties called for no skills other than those that were handed down from generation to generation within the home, the concession or the tribe. Being confined 'inside', women were subject to men-not so much because they were more ignorant than men but because they were their chattels, body and soul. In many civilizations only one thing counted, namely the honour of the daughter or of the wife.

Even today there are many countries where the laws grant almost all rights to the husband over the wife and to the father over the children. And even in many of the countries where the law confers practically equal rights on both husband and wife, women do not feel really free. In 1956, Japanese sociologists conducted a survey among the population of Nagoya and the surrounding districts, asking them the following two questions: 'Are you glad to be a man/a woman? If so, why?' Six out of ten men said they were glad 'because men are free'.

Indeed, whereas the number of girls and women who want to improve not only their won lot but also that of others and of society is constantly increasing, the number of those who fear change is still distinctly greater. Such intertia is a matter requiring the greatest attention, for it constitutes a force of resistance to progress-and not only directly through the attitude of women, but also indirectly through the attitude of men, to whom it offers a most convenient excuse for neglecting the fate of women. In this respect, too, education is indispensable.

Through education, men as well as women must be convinced of the need for change. However, though education is necessary, it alone is not enough to change people's attitudes and to shake off the dead hand of the past. The future prospects of women depend also on far-reaching economic, social and legal changes being made that will promote the access of women to education. If reference has been made to the past in speaking of the inferior status of women, although that status has often continued to be a reality, it is merely to show that the roots lie in a social system that us doomed to disappear. Wherever it still survives as a coherent whole, its foundations are already cracking.

Everywhere indeed women have the right to education. But to what kind of an education? Just as education was originally often the preserve of boys, so modern technological and scientific know-how remains in many cases the privilege of men. The force of habit and prejudice, the lack of information, the innumerable difficulties that women encounter in the exercise of some occupations and in the discharge of their domestic duties-all these things tend to limit the opportunities of girls and women.

In so socially advanced a country as Sweden it has been observed that if the whole working potential of the female population were exploited there would be a 25 per cent increase in the national income, and if discrimination against women and all other barriers were completely eliminated there would be an increase of approximately 50 per cent in the national income. In the industrialized countries a great many women give up work in order to look after their young children.

However, by the time they are about 35, their youngest children are going to school and their domestic tasks are considerably eased by the aids and appliances they have in the home. Before reaching middle age they find themselves with time on their hands, and if they had the possibility of re-training in their former occupation, or of learning a new one, they could still play their part in the life of their country for another thirty years or so.

In theory, a political life is open to women since, with the exception of a few countries, all women have the right to vote and to stand for election. Instead of taking the path followed by the industrialized countries, the developing countries have fortunately taken a short cut. On gaining independence many of them rejected at the very outset any form of legal discrimination against women-at all events in regard to education and participation in the political life of the country.

Yet, in these parts of the world, the number of girls attending schools is nearly everywhere below that boys. One is bound to feel concerned at the consequences of this disparity. If care is not taken they will lead to a manysided social disequiliburium. It is not unusual, for example, for educated men to refuse to marry uneducated women, and it is this reluctance that has often been conducive to a movement in favour of education for girls.

On the other hand, men are sometimes afraid of marrying women who are too well educated, and it is this fear that often impedes the access of girls to higher education and scientific studies. According to one American survey, the more educated the mother the easier it will be for her children to win higher the easier it will be for her children to win higher education diplomas.

Among Muslim families, women of the elite receive much or all of their schooling at home. Nor have girls everywhere been excluded from monastery and temple schools. Thus the significances of any single index of girls' participation in schools can be appreciated only in the context of the whole array of educational agencies. The availability of educational options does not ensure their utilization. This distinction between provision and utilization is basic for policy, especially in the LDCs.

Reluctance or refusal of families to make use of available schools can be illustrated by the Masai in Kenya, by district variations within India, and also by the history of education in Appalachia. Many societies have their counterparts to those British working-class mothers who discouraged postcompulsory schooling as "not for the likes of us". More often today the injunction is "not for girls." Children have little to say about whether they avail themselves of opportunities for education; it is not the child but parent, kinfolk, or neighbours who decide about primary schools. For whom, then, do we measure accessibility?

From a collective or public policy viewpoint, primary schooling is available to the family for daughters as well as for sons. But for a girl whose parents dread the classroom give-and-take with boys, the free school across the road can be inaccessible. Such barriers against accessibility are deeper than "social disadvantage." There are also outlays for fees and "incidentals," and there are forgone economic contributions to the household or in other work that could yield cash.

If schools are to be costless to families there must be complete subsidization. Why girls' participation in primary schools differs from that of boys cannot be answered without looking at ensuing participation and the sequels to education in the postschool years. Whether schooling of a daughter is deemed worthwhile will be influenced by perceptions of the effects of schooling on jobs, on acquisition of a "better" husband, on quality of domestic life, on the daughter's personality development, and on the well-being of her children.

Parental perceptions very on many dimensions, requiring complex sets of data to disentangle their major determinants. How girls perform in school compared with boys is affected by the same factors that determine initial access and by other factors as well. If girls more often are kept at home to help with chores, and if they must do housework after school while brothers are allowed time for homework, girls actually have less access to education.

Repetition of a grade or becoming an 'early leaver' are crude indices to these more subtle components of access. Another question is, How do changes in the provision of schooling affect girls compared with boys? The availability of schools may reflect community demand for schools, even though to each family the availability of places is a supply or cost factor in its decision about schooling. Finally, we should point out the usefulness of studying educational patterns for understanding social change.

The link between educational participation and prospective effects of schooling means that sex differences in educational participation can be used as indicators of changing attitudes and expectations about life patterns of each sex, often signalling deep societal changes. Despite herculean efforts by UNESCO statisticians for 30 years, the data about enroilments for most of the Third World provide direct information only on short-term trends.

However, literacy rates for age categories serve as useful proxies for time series. For each country the literacy rates by age of females are compared with those of males within rural and urban populations. Many of the patterns of sex differences in primary school utilization that have been found by demographers and social scientists are reflected in these four national histories. We make two broad generalizations based on these and similar data for other countries. First, males are more often literate than females, irrespective of place of residence.

Literacy is higher among urban residents, whether males or females. However, societies differ in the relative literacy of urban females and rural males, and in any given society these relative positions may alter over time. Second, literacy rates for women tend to converge with those for men. However, the timing and speed of convergence depend on cultural heritage and on stages in the spread of schooling. How much convergence we estimate to have occurred will depend on how we measure disparities or changes in them. In rural Morocco the absolute difference in literacy between men and women increased substantially from the older adults to present-day children.

Rural women remained almost wholly illiterate until recently, rural males made slow but marked progress. Even today, however, only a minority of young rural men can read and write. The male/female differential cannot be explained by social patterns associated with Islam, for literacy has been spreading rapidly among urban females in Morocco. Urban women do, however, continue to lag behind urban men, and the gap has scarcely narrowed. In some countries sex differentials in literacy are small at all ages and in both rural and urban communities.

In Chile a majority of even the oldest rural females are literates, and younger females have overtaken the males-just the opposite of Morocco. A relatively common pattern that appears primary schooling has spread rapidly is a shift from marked disparity between males and females to virtual parity in urban places, but with a continuing large gap between urban and rural youth of each sex.

In parts of Latin America young adult women seem to be literate more often then their male contemporaries. Enrolment data entail more difficulties than those for literacy. Countries differ greatly, for example, in proportions of overage pupils and in whether overage is due mainly to late entry or to repetition of grades. These latter variations are associated in diverse ways with dropout rates by sex and level of school. Although societies display mush individuality in these patterns, we begin with comments on highly aggregated data, always with an eye to female representation.

The figures for Iran are hard to believe, though a pattern like this could occur where few children begin school and few drop out. Persistence in India is moderately high, and sex differentials are modest. Cambodia is similar to India for boys, prospects for continuation of girls are poorer. Since the population of potential pupils is almost evenly divided by sex, girls would be expected to comprise half of enrollments if there were no sex differences in use of schools. There is virtual parity at the primary level among the developed countries and in most of Latin America.

Shortfall of girls typically is largest at the tertiary level, but since 1960 there, have been remarkable gains in the female share of these enrollments everywhere including within the developing countries. A country can rank quite differently at each level of school for the proportion of girls, and countries vary greatly in female shares of pupils. For the rural sector alone in 1960, among countries girls ranged from 20 to 50 percent primary and from 6 to 63 percent of secondary pupils.

In some places, girls who are already married remain in school several years before their marriage is consummated. While more schooling usually improves fear of moral corruption of adolescent girls by school attendance is not directed solely to sexual matters. In all aspects of girls' schooling the availability of women teachers is salient as both an instrument and a product. Insistence that girls have women teachers can speed up formation of a cadre of female teachers, but until there is a generous flow of girls through postprimary grades, this supply of acceptable teachers will remain scanty.

In some countries it may be secondary rather than tertiary schooling that is critical; in these countries proportions of secondary teachers who are female parallel the proportions of females among secondary pupils. In muslim Africa, however, girls make up a larger proportions of secondary pupils than of teachers. This may reflect an early phase in a recent spread of secondary schooling among girls, but it means that adolescent girls are being taught by men nonetheless. Some Muslim societies do present a sort of ideal type of female seclusion with a large shortfall in girl pupils. Perhaps these societies are experiencing more severe strains arising from adaptation to new feminine roles.

Child care and household tasks do not exhaust girls' contributions to the family economy; they may work in garden or field, fetching and carrying, or help in trade and do home processing of products for sale. Time spent by girls in these activities can be especially important in poorer families where perceptions of benefits from the schooling of girls are dimmer. For instance, in some societies women have traditionally been independent and have encountered a high risk of divorce. Their means to independence is in subsistence farming and petty trade learned at the mother's side. The proportion of girls who are in school can vary more among provinces than among countries taken as wholes.

In Sierra Leone, primary rates for girls range from 11 percent in northern and 29 percent in southern to 77 percent in eastern provinces. In one hinterland province of Morocco, only 6 percent of primary pupils were girls, in contrast to over 40 percent in Rabat and Casablar.ca. Writers on education and development often observe that literacy is highest in coastal zones or along major waterways where the first contact with the Western world occurred. Even where competitions between Christian missions generated more attention to the hinterland, the diversities were similar. In Africa especially, localized evangelization produced almost helter-skelter spatial patterns, partly because missions held divergent views about the the importance of literacy, especially for girls. Location of secondary schools was more erratic than location of primary schools, and the influence of outside agencies, such as missions or colonial administrators, played an even larger part.

The catchment areas for girls' secondary schools were typically as large as for boys, but fewer girls than boys attended from the remoter areas. Schooled mothers everywhere are key influences on the spread of girls' schooling, and such mothers also are role models. But since schooled women are often few, the better-schooled fathers may have the greater influence in spurning traditional resistance to allowing girls to begin or continue in school.

Distance from a school handicaps lower-status individuals of either sex more than those from higher-placed homes. Rising aspirations for schooling normally diffuse down the status scale and along the networks of the ecological structure. On the other hand, families aspiring to a better status may tacitly reaffirm traditional practices such as female seclusion. Amid this complexity, we can mention only a few salient patterns of social selectivity in education of girls.

This must be done cautiously, for too often simpiistic generalization take on a life of their own. Perhaps the firmest generalization is that socioeconomic status of parents has more influence on the schooling of girls than of boys. Thus influence often is greater in rural localities or among disadvantaged ethnic groups than it is in favored segments of the population.

GENDER PARITY IN BASIC EDUCATION

Gender equity in education was one of the main goals established at the World Conference on Education for All, at Jomtien, Thailand, and was reiterated at the Beijing World Conference on Women, and at the Hamburg International Conference on Adult Education. On that occasion the UN Secretary General, launched the 10-year UN Girls' Education Initiative (UNGEI). Within its overall objective of eliminating 'gender discrimination and gender disparities in education systems.

The analysis of literacy is an appropriate departure point for examining overall gender disparity in education. It gives an idea of the current situation, and of the extent and direction of the work to be done in terms of providing formal and non-formal education. Compared with targets set at world conferences, it enables an assessment to be made whether these targets have been achieved, or been approached more closely.

The illiteracy rate for the developing countries as a whole has decreased by one quarter (from 33.4 per cent to 26.6 per cent), far from the Jomtien target of 50 per cent reduction. If drastic measures are not taken to change the trend, the illiteracy rate is projected to be still over 20 per cent in 2010 (the latest year for which projections are available), with persistent gender disparities (15 per cent for men, and 27 per cent for women).

The UIS estimates that there are still 875 million illiterates in the world in the year 2000, of whom women still constitute almost two thirds, a situation practically unchanged since 1990 (from 63 to 64 per cent).

Southern Asia, the region with the highest number of illiterates, males and females, has seen this number increase by about 8 per cent during the last decade while in Eastern Asia the number of illiterates has declined by about 20 per cent. In all developing regions the percentage of women has remained stable, with values ranging from 55 per cent in Latin America/the Caribbean to 72 per cent in Eastern Asia/Oceania. If literacy is considered in relation to the population the picture is slightly different.

As concerns gender disparities it should first be noted that while 81 per cent of the male population is literate, this percentage falls to 66 for the female population. The two measures of disparities, the Gender Parity Index (GPI), and the Gender Gap convey the following indications:

— The situation has improved between 1990 and 2000;

— GPI for all regions are closer to 1, i.e. nearer to parity, and the gender gap has narrowed in all regions;

— In the year 2000 there are still gender gaps, widest in the Arab States and Southern Asia (23 percentage points in both regions) while the relative disparity measured by the GPI is worse in Southern Asia (0.66) than in the Arab States (0.68);

— the former region has the lowest literacy rates for both men and women (67 per cent and 44 per cent respectively).

These regional values conceal significant inter-country variations. There are, first of all, variations in absolute terms relating to the population and the number of illiterates. It is clear that the values of certain populous countries in Southern Asia weigh markedly on the regional aggregates, which in turn affect the world total.

Thus an improvement in the literacy rate, or on the gender balance, in one of these countries has a visible impact on the world situation. It is, therefore, important to examine in more detail the national situation within each region and country, if effective measures are to be taken to reduce overall illiteracy, as well as gender and other types of disparity in this field.

Estimates of literacy levels are available by country for both the adult (age 15+), and youth (15-24 age group) population. A comparative analysis of literacy levels in the year 2000 for the two groups permits both the present state of literacy, and recent progress in literacy levels, to be determined. The youth population group reflects more precisely the results of recent efforts to increase literacy and enrolment levels.

As regards overall literacy levels:

— There are still 21 countries (13 in sub-Saharan Africa, 3 in the Arab States, and 5 in Asia) where adult literacy levels are below 50 per cent. Among these there are 6 countries, mostly in Western and Central Africa, where adult literacy rates are below 40 per cent;

— Among the youth group only two countries have literacy rates below 50 per cent: Burkina Faso (35 per cent) and Niger (23 per cent).

As regards gender disparities:

— The GPI for adult literacy rates is below 0.50 in eight countries, indicating that the female literacy rate is less than half the male rate. However, if the youth literacy rates are considered, only Guinea-Bissau, Niger and Benin show such high disparities;

— In 23 countries, female adult literacy rates are three thirds, or less than the male rates. For the youth group, the number of countries in this situation has fallen to 11.

CHANGES IN ADULT LITERACY

Adult literacy (age 15+) can be considered to assess progress in literacy levels, and gender parity, over the decade 1990-2000 for the whole adult population.

Adult literacy rates have increased everywhere, and progress towards parity has been consistent. As regards overall literacy rates (male and female), increases of 50 per cent or more have occurred in two cases only (Mali and Chad), between 1990 and 2000. If it is remembered that a target of 50 per cent increase in literacy rates particularly for women, has also been fixed at Dakar for the year 2015, it may be questioned whether this target is attainable; It is estimated, however, that as regards female literacy, increases exceeding 50 per cent have occurred in 12 countries in sub-Saharan Africa, and in 5 countries of Southern Asia, all with extremely low rates in 1990;

In two Arab States, Qatar and the United Arab Emirates, the disparity, which in 1990 was in favour of men, seems to be to the advantage of women in the year 2000.

Beyond these national values, significant variations exist within countries among social groups, and geographical or urban/rural areas, which it is necessary to analyse when designing national policy. It can be observed that differences between male and female literacy rates are more marked in rural than in urban areas (GPI = 0.41 in rural areas as compared with 0.77 in urban areas), and that with a rural/urban literacy ratio of 0.66, disparities between rural and urban areas are also to be addressed if equality is to be achieved. The impressive gap between rural women and urban men shows the compound effect of gender and rural/urban residence on the probability of becoming literate.

EARLY CHILDHOOD CARE AND EDUCATION

The Jomtien Declaration, recalling that education begins at birth, called 'for early childhood care and initial education (ECCE)', to 'be provided through arrangements involving families, communities, or institutional programmes, as appropriate'. The goal of 'expanding and improving comprehensive early childhood care and education, especially for the most vulnerable and disadvantaged children', was reaffirmed at Dakar.

There is some controversy about the desirability of exposing very young children to early childhood care and development programmes, and on the advisability of devoting limited educational resources (especially in the sub-Saharan African region), to these types of programme. Certainly their provision by public or other authorities is seen by many women as a welcome means of releasing mothers to find employment outside the home, and older children to be free to go to school. For this reason women's NGOs have endeavoured to provide day-care centres for children who are not yet of school age—the initiatives of the Council of Women and the YWCA in Botswana, are some of the examples of this commitment.

From the statistical point of view the scope of ECCE was too broad, and the UIS had to define it more precisely limiting the programmes surveyed to those catering for children from the age of three. Despite this effort to make the definition more operational, it still appears difficult to collect reliable and comparable data on ECD programmes. In its Survey 2000, the UIS requested data separately on pre-primary education, and on other ECD programmes, but most of the countries had difficulty in distinguishing between the two types of programmes, mostly organized in informal settings, the result being that only seven countries answered satisfactorily.

Pre-primary Education

Considering the evident difficulties in collecting realistic information on all ECD programmes. Levels of enrolment in this type of education vary from one region/country to another in relation to levels of socioeconomic development, and specific cultural and historical considerations. Pre-primary education is only marginally developed in sub-Saharan African countries, where, until recently, it did not figure among the priorities or concerns of the governments, striving to meet the demand for basic education. The issue is now prominent in most National Plans, but the development is still extremely weak, which makes it difficult to assess its progress. GER do not exceed 10 per cent in two thirds of the countries for which data are available. Among the reasons for the low enrolments in this type of programme, is the fact that in many countries they are provided mainly, or only, in urban areas. Besides, they are often privately organized and managed, implying the need to pay fees, that many families in poor countries and areas cannot afford. In most countries fees are also required in public pre-primary schools, although generally they are not so high as in private schools. The highest enrolment is in Mauritius, where all children are enrolled in pre-primary schools.

In Latin America/the Caribbean pre-primary schools are much more developed, the median GER being 56 per cent. In the Arab States GER range from 1 per cent in Yemen, to 73 per cent in the United Arab Emirates, with a median value of 14 per cent in Tunisia. In Yemen the high population growth rate, the insufficient provision of public pre-primary schools, only available in the capitals of certain districts, and non-existent in small cities or rural areas, and the high costs of private schools, are among the factors explaining the low enrolment. In Asia/Oceania the range goes from the low of Myanmar (3 per cent) to the high of Thailand (93 per cent).

Care should be taken in making comparisons with 1990, as the emphasis put since Jomtien on ECD programmes, may have led some countries to adopt a broader definition of pre-primary education as compared to 1990. Central Asian countries of the former USSR contrast sharply with this positive picture. UIS data, and those available from other sources, show that educational provision at this level has dramatically decreased since 1990, particularly in Kazakhs-tan, Kyrgyzstan, and Tajikistan, but also in Armenia, Azerbaijan, and Georgia, while Mongolia has also registered a decline. This decline in gross enrolment ratios indicates that the fall in enrolment is much more pronounced than the demographic decline, which has also occurred during this period. The UNICEF Report analyses the reasons for the decline, and warns about the implications for children and mothers:

It seems, however, that gender disparities in pre-primary education are in general less pronounced than at other levels of education, and are often negligible. Apart from the countries of West and Central Africa, where data are poor, and the development of pre-primary education still only marginal, for most countries the GPI is close to unity, and in favour of girls. Even if it is difficult to programme such observations to other levels of education, this may be seen as a sign of forthcoming progress in girls' participation at higher levels of education. At any rate enrolment in pre-primary education is a positive factor for further school participation, and often an opportunity for children to benefit from welfare, health and nutrition programmes associated with pre-school provisions.

There are exceptions to this positive picture: Pakistan, where the overall GER is below 10 per cent and the GPI below 0.50, i.e. girls account for about half the male enrolment, Morocco (GPI=0.52, up 6 points from the 0.46 of 1990), and Liberia (GPI=0.74).

ACCESS TO SCHOOLING

Disparities between girls and boys start with access to school. Inequality at this critical time in children's development continues to have an impact on girls' participation in primary and further levels of education. Poverty is an overall factor affecting school access and participation, particularly for girls. Even when education is declared free many families cannot afford the costs of transport (when available), uniforms, and textbooks.

Opportunity costs may have a strong incidence: they are related to the need for girls, in some cases for boys too, to help families with the household and agricultural chores, and to mind younger siblings, or care for the elderly and sick. The impact of HIV/ AIDS on the wealth of the poorest countries reinforces the existing barriers. Other factors affect girls' access to school: the distance from school, which in many countries is a hindrance for both boys and girls, the lack of adequate infrastructures, the low proportion of female teachers, and the lack of pedagogical training and sensitization in gender-issues, for both male and female teachers.

According to the UIS estimates, the number of new entrants increased by about 11 per cent in the less developed regions between 1990 and 1998. This is not as positive as would appear, as the population of normal school-entrance age (6 years), increased by more than 9 per cent during the same period. At the global level the increase in the number of new entrants seems to have benefited boys and girls alike, as the proportion of girls remained unchanged at 46 per cent, ranging from 44 per cent in Southern Asia to 49 per cent in Latin America/the Caribbean. Western and Central Africa register the lowest AIR, reflecting the limited availability of school places in countries like Burkina Faso, Congo, Niger, the Central African Republic, and the Democratic Republic of the Congo, where rates are still below 50 per cent. War, or postwar, situations in some of these countries certainly contribute to the deterioration of access to education.

Access to school for girls is lower than for boys. The majority of countries fall into this category. In countries of Western and Central Africa and in Yemen, the apparent admission rates for girls are three quarters, or less than, the male rates. It should be pointed out that most of these countries also have rather low overall values of access to school (for both boys and girls). With the exception of Djibouti and Liberia, for which data are not available, these countries also have the lowest GDP per capita (below US$400 per year) and decreasing over the last decade, except in Burkina and Mali, belong to the group of the least developed countries, are countries highly affected by HIV/AIDS (except Yemen), and figure among the highly indebted poor countries (except Djibouti). This points to the conclusion that while social and cultural factors need to be studied, and taken into account, in designing and implementing policy aimed at reducing gender disparities, poverty is the underlying barrier to education, for girls in particular. This means that unless national authorities, and international partners, take substantial measures, integrating the socio-economic, political and cultural approach, it will be impossible to reach the EFA goals set at Dakar: 'ensuring that by 2015 all children, particularly girls... have access to, and complete, free and compulsory primary education of good quality', and 'eliminating gender disparities in primary and secondary education by 2005'.

Disparities are in favour of girls: In sub-Saharan Africa slight disparities in favour of girls are noted in Namibia, Lesotho and the Democratic Republic of the Congo. While for the first two countries the phenomenon is an historical reality, explained mostly by the need for boys to mind livestock, in the latter case the situation seems recent, and may be due to an exceptional situation following the war, or even to the poor quality. Gender imbalances in favour of girls are also observed in some Latin American and Caribbean countries (e.g. Nicaragua, Guyana, and Uruguay) and in some Asian countries (Azerbaijan, Bahrain, Macau, and Vietnam) although they are not so pronounced as for other aspects or levels of education. As regards changes between 1990 and 1998 two major trends are observed:

For countries with available data for the two reference years, the overall apparent intake rates (male and female) have decreased in almost half of the countries, most of them in sub-Saharan Africa. Gender disparities have narrowed particularly where the situation was most inequitable for girls, e.g. Benin, Guinea, Mali, and Mauritania, proving that the measures taken during the last decade are bringing results, however moderate. In Benin for instance, where the GPI has improved from 0.56 to 0.72, and the gender gap has narrowed from 32 to 22 percentage points, policy measures included a significant work of sensitizing parents through the media, and the suppression of school fees for girls in public primary schools in rural areas.

Similarly, in Mauritania where the GPI has improved from 0.79 to 0.95, and the gender gap has narrowed from 13 to 4 percentage points, an overall strategy for improving girls' participation has been defined, which integrates socio-economic, cultural and institutional considerations. In this framework incentive measures included the facilitation of proximity school/families, increasing the number of female teachers, establishing fellowships in favour of girls, and increasing the number of school canteens.

Data on current levels of school participation in a country, enable an estimate to be made of the number of years that a boy or a girl of admission age to primary education is expected to remain at school. This summary measure of the expected overall participation in the whole education system is the School Life Expectancy (SLE). Based on the age-specific enrolment ratios, the SLE is subject to the same limitations associated with all net ratios: lack of, or incompleteness of data on enrolment by age reduces considerably the number of countries for which the indicator can be obtained.

For countries where data or estimates are available, the expected number of years a boy or a girl can expect to be enrolled at school, is extremely variable from one region to another, and within regions. In sub-Saharan Africa the median value is 7.1 years for boys and 5.6 for girls. This region is marked by wide variations, particularly for females: for a girl the expected number of years of schooling varies from a low of 1.8 in Niger, to a high of 13 years in Namibia.

In the Arab States the medians are lower for girls (9.7 years as against 10.7 for boys), and significant variations are observed (from 5.1 years for girls in Yemen, to 13.7

for girls in Lebanon). In Asia/Oceania and in Latin America and the Caribbean female medians are slightly higher than male. SLE vary greatly in the Asia/Oceania region, but reflect greater homogeneity in Latin America and the Caribbean. The values of male and female expected years of schooling, and the gaps between male and female SLE. The following observations can be made:

— In 60 per cent of the countries for which data are available girls entering school are expected to stay at school for less time than their male counterparts. Countries where the gender gaps are highest, mostly sub-Saharan African countries, but Yemen and some Southern Asian countries as well, are also those where SLE is lowest.

— Among countries where the gender gap is in favour of girls are some Southern African countries (Namibia, Lesotho, and Botswana), the majority of Latin American/ Caribbean countries, and increasingly more Arab States (the United Arab Emirates, Qatar, Lebanon, and Kuwait). SLE are also higher for girls in many Eastern Asian and Oceanian countries, e.g. Malaysia, Mongolia, the Philippines, Sri Lanka, Thailand, and Samoa. In these countries the SLE of both boys and girls are generally high.

PRIMARY EDUCATION

Despite the considerable increase in enrolments in less developed regions, the goal of universal primary education, set at Jomtien in 1990, is far from being achieved. Although it is well known that an additional number of children are enrolled in non-formal education programmes, the trend is nevertheless worrying, especially in sub-Saharan Africa, where gross enrolment ratios are still below 80 per cent in South/East Africa, and below 70 per cent in Central/West Africa. If the present trend continues it will not be possible to reach universal primary education by the year 2015. Gross enrolment ratios have increased in less developed regions, with the apparent exception of South/East Africa, where they are unchanged, and that of the East Asia/Oceania region. The high rise in the Caribbean, with GER exceeding 100 per cent, reflects the increase in the number of overage children, due to a high proportion of late-entrants and repeaters.

During the same period substantial progress towards gender parity has been registered in the Arab States, in South-West Asia and in the Caribbean, whilst in the other regions the situation has remained virtually unchanged. Before looking closer at enrolment, it may be worthwhile to examine briefly the trend in numbers of outof-school children.

OUT-OF-SCHOOL CHILDREN

Estimates of the number of out-of-school children seem to point to a global decrease during the last decade in the developing countries, falling from 123 in 1990, to 110 millions in 1998, with girls representing still 60 per cent of the total, an overall proportion practically unchanged since 1990. However the out-of-school population has increased in sub-Saharan Africa and the Arab States. In relation to the population the share of out-of-school children has decreased in all regions for both boys and girls, and the gender gap has narrowed everywhere with the exception of the two sub-Saharan African regions, where the gap in favour of boys has widened, particularly in Central and West Africa.

The case of the Arab States is worth mentioning, where the percentage of out-of-school boys seems to have increased, while the same percentage has decreased for girls, narrowing the gap considerably. Central Asia is the only region where the proportion of outof-school girls is lower than that of boys.

PARTICIPATION IN PRIMARY EDUCATION

It is not possible to compare systematically the 1990 and 1998 GER, due to the new approaches and methodology adopted by the UIS, particularly after the revision of the International Standard Classification of Education (ISCED), in 1997. Nevertheless certain trends in the overall value of the GER can be identified for a number of countries. On the whole the situation, for boys and girls, has improved in most of the countries.

In sub-Saharan Africa considerable progress has been registered for Benin, Chad, Mali, Mauritania, Burkina Faso, Guinea, Guinea Bissau, Chad, Gambia, and Morocco, where the 1998 GER have increased by 25 per cent, or more, in relation to those of 1990. Among postconflict countries Angola registered an increase of 50 per cent of its GER, Liberia and Sierra Leone reopened their school systems, and in Rwanda the values exceeding 100 per cent may indicate re-entry into the system of children and youth who were kept out of school by war.

In Asia, Pakistan experienced a steady increase in the GER during the decade, and Kuwait seems to be recovering from the dramatic fall of 1990, although enrolment does not appear to reach again the 100 per cent values registered before that date. A few countries, mostly in sub-Saharan Africa, where the levels of school participation were already critically low, have seen the situation deteriorate further. Among these are Congo, the Democratic Republic of the Congo, Burundi, and the Central African Republic, (all countries which have gone through conflict) and, to a lesser extent, Madagascar, Zambia, Cameroon and the United Republic of Tanzania.

Moderate declines are noted in a few Asian and Arab countries, like the Islamic Republic of Iran, Indonesia, Oman, the Republic of Korea, Thailand, and the United Arab Emirates. It should be pointed out that, since in many of these countries the GER exceeded 100 per cent in 1990, it is possible that these declines are, at least partly, due to a regularization of the age of the pupils, as confirmed by the fact that such declines are more limited in terms of NER.

The reduction of gender gaps featured highly in educational plans after Jomtien, and various initiatives were taken in many countries during the 1990s to promote girls' access and participation. The results have been positive in many cases, and examples of successful policy measures in certain countries, like Benin and Mauritania, have been described in the section concerning policy initiatives. Data and indicators often illustrate better than policy declarations to what extent these measures have been successful.

Disparities in favour of boys are still the general rule in Central and Western Africa and, to a lesser extent, in the Arab States as well as in certain Asian countries, especially from Southern Asia. Disparities are particularly high in Chad, Ethiopia, Guinea, Niger, Benin, Yemen and

Pakistan, where enrolment ratios for girls are still less than two thirds of those registered for boys. In these countries the absolute gender gap exceeds 30 percentage points, with values as high as 47 and 45 in Pakistan and Yemen respectively. It should be added that Afghanistan would also fall in this group. In fact, although this country does not appear in the relevant tables, due to the lack of recent data, the latest available data, referring to the school year 1995/96, give a GER of 64 per cent for boys, and 32 per cent for girls, i.e. a GPI of 0.50. The case of boys at a disadvantage should also be underscored:

— The pattern is to be observed particularly in Latin America and the Caribbean—although not as pronounced as will be seen for secondary education—where the problem is increasingly that of keeping boys in schools;

— In many Southern African countries girls profit from education more than boys, as already shown in literacy data, a feature that may be explained by the fact that boys are needed to mind livestock in these countries, resulting in low male attendance and early dropouts;

— Disparities in favour of girls appear in some Arab countries, which in certain cases may be explained by the strong number of immigrants, mostly males, in the population.

In comparing the 1998 levels of disparities of gross enrolment ratios with those of 1990, it will be noticed that progress towards gender parity has occurred in most countries:

— It is worth noting that progress has been registered in Guinea, Mauritania, Benin, Chad, and Mali, which were among the countries with the highest disparities in 1990, as well as in the Gambia, the Comoros and the Democratic Republic of the Congo. Substantial progress has also occurred in Sudan, Pakistan and Nepal;

— In some countries where the disparities were in favour of girls, the GPI came closer to gender parity. These are mostly Latin American/Caribbean countries such as Venezuela, Colombia, Honduras and Nicaragua, Southern African countries like Lesotho, Botswana and Namibia, or the countries of Oceania, such as Samoa;

— In other sub-Saharan African countries, like Mozambique, Cameroon and Angola, the situation has slightly worsened;

— Despite the considerable progress made towards gender parity in most countries, in Chad and Yemen the GPI are still the world's lowest, making the Dakar goal elusive; the Yemen national education plan itself implicitly acknowledges the difficulty of reaching parity by the year 2005.

Thus, while noting the considerable progress made in many countries, especially in those with the highest disparities in 1990, it can be concluded that if the trend continues at the same rate, it is unrealistic to expect that the Dakar objectives for 2005 'eliminating gender disparities in primary and secondary education', will be achieved in all countries.

The situation is slightly better if, instead of the GER, the net enrolment ratios are considered, indicating that when taking into account only children of regular school age, the proportion of girls enrolled compares slightly better with that of boys. In other words boys are more numerous than the girls to be enrolled, but the proportion of over-age pupils is also higher among them. It should be recalled that the phenomenon of over age is due, not only to the high proportions of late entrants, but also to the high percentage of repeaters. Thus the higher GER for boys are at least partly explained by the fact that boys remain in school longer than girls they repeat more often than girls do.

REPETITION IN PRIMARY EDUCATION

In developing countries the challenge is not only to facilitate access to school, but also to ensure that pupils receive an education of quality, and one which is in harmony with their social and cultural environment. It is also necessary for the system to work as efficiently as possible, to avoid a wastage of the limited resources available to meet the demand for education. Repetition is considered an important aspect of both the quality of education and, along with school survival, of the internal efficiency of the education system.

A high proportion of repeaters in a class is likely to lower the quality of the education provided. While in many developed countries there is a tendency to apply an automatic promotion policy, the levels of repetition are still rather high in certain developing countries, especially from sub-Saharan Africa and the Latin American/Caribbean region. It should be mentioned that some countries apply a policy of automatic promotion, at least in theory, or allow one repetition only. In other countries government regulations do not allow repeaters to exceed a certain proportion. In certain African countries this means in practice that repeaters are still admitted at school at the request of their parents, concerned that their children are definitely excluded from school. From the statistical point of view this leads to inconsistent school cohort data, and to distorted results in the analysis of the internal efficiency. This also means that pupils carry on from one grade to another, without acquiring the necessary knowledge, and drop out during, or shortly after, the primary cycle.

The percentage of repeaters is fairly high in certain developing countries:

— In over half of the countries in sub-Saharan Africa more than 10 per cent of their primary pupils repeat some grade of primary education. Repeaters make up over one quarter of total enrolments in Angola, Burundi, the Central African Republic, Chad, Comoros, Congo, Guinea, Madagascar, Mozambique, Rwanda, Sao Tome and Principe and Togo;

— The situation is most critical in Congo, Gabon, Angola, the Central African Republic, and Madagascar, where repeaters represent one third of primary enrolments, or more;

— No other region of the world registers such high values, the highest percentages being in Brazil (24 per cent), Lao PDR (21 per cent) and Nepal (23 per cent); nevertheless values of 10 per cent and over are found in some Arab States and Latin American/Caribbean countries;

— Most of the countries with the highest proportion of repeaters also had high values in 1990, indicating that the situation has not changed substantially since then.

In designing policy aimed at facilitating girls' participation in education, it may be interesting to examine patterns of school participation for boys and girls, and to assess who repeats, and who drops out more.

— In the majority of countries under study boys repeat more than girls;

— The countries where girls repeat more than boys are almost all in Central and West Africa, where overall repetition levels above 15 per cent are common. Sudan, Belize and Nepal are also among the countries where girls repeat more.

Thus it is generally in the same countries where the lowest overall enrolment, and the highest disparities in favour of boys, are observed for access and enrolment, that girls found themselves at a disadvantage as regards repetition. The high levels of repetition registered in certain regions should push policy-makers to question the relevance of school curricula to the conditions, or needs, of learners. As regards boys and girls it is to be questioned whether the significant gender disparities in repetition in the diverse regions reflect a corresponding gender bias in curricula.

SCHOOL SURVIVAL

High repetition rates often point to high drop-out rates. Children who repeat a grade, one or more times during the primary cycle, are often discouraged from continuing their progress in school, and the majority of the school systems where this phenomenon is most pronounced, are generally not equipped to give them the necessary additional attention. However, some special programmes for children who repeat have been organized in certain countries, where high repetition rates are perceived as a critical step leading to dropout. In some Latin American/ Caribbean countries 'increasing attention is being given to over-age pupils, in particular to children and youth more than two years older than the official age for their grade, for example through the implementation of accelerated learning programmes'.

For 1998 the survival rate is based on data on enrolment and repeaters by grade for 1997 and 1998. Since consistent data for these two years were available for only a few countries. It conveys the following messages:

— Sub-Saharan Africa is once again the region where the situation is most critical, with the lowest survival rates, particularly in the Central and Western sub-regions;

— Compared with 1990, survival rates seem to have increased in the majority of the countries;

— A noticeable exception to this positive picture is Malawi, where the survival rate fell by 30 percentage points (from 64 per cent to 34 per cent) probably due to the policy of free education introduced in the early 1990s, which resulted in extremely high admission rates, followed by unprecedented dropouts;

— Substantial reductions in the rates of survival were also observed in Sudan (20 points), Mauritania, Sri Lanka and Botswana (11 points), South Africa and the Gambia (7 points). In several other countries (Ethiopia, Burkina Faso, Kiribati, Chad and Guyana) the fall was less significant (from 2 to 4 points);

— Girls stay in primary education longer than boys, as shown by the values of the GPI, often above the unity. Indeed in certain countries of Latin America and the Caribbean boys are more a concern than girls when it comes to dropout—the reverse of school survival.

Bibliography

Bach, Rebecca et al, "Mothers' Influence on Daughters' Orientations toward Education: An Egyptian Case Study." *Comparative Education Review* 29:3 (August): 375-384, 1985.

Bellew, Rosemary and E. King, "Educating Women: Lessons from Experience." In E. King and M.A. Hill eds., *Women's Education in Developing Countries*. Baltimore: Johns Hopkins University Press for the World Bank, 1993.

Bown, Lalage, "Preparing the Future, Women Literacy and Development: The Impact of Female Literacy on Human Development and the Participation of Literate Women in Change", Bristol: Action Aid, 1990.

Bustillo, Ines, "Latin America and the Caribbean", In E.M King and M.A. Hill, eds., *Women's Education in Developing Countries*, Baltimore: Johns Hopkins University Press for the World Bank, 1993.

Chowdhury, Kowsar P., "Women's Education: Barriers and Solutions", *Mimeo. Education and Social Policy Department*, World Bank, Washington, D.C., 1993.

Herz, Barbara et al, "Letting Girls Learn: Promising Approaches in Primary and Secondary Education", *World Bank Discussion Paper No.* 133. Washington, D.C.: The World Bank, 1991.

Kalia, N., "Images of Men and Women in Indian Textbooks", In G. Kelly and C. Elliott, eds., *Women's Education in the Third World*. Albany, NY: State University of New York Press, 1982.

King, Elizabeth M. and M. Ann Hill, "Women's Education In Developing Countries - Barriers, Benefits, and Policies", Baltimore: Johns Hopkins University Press for the World Bank, 1993.

Lockheed, Marlaine E. and Adriaan Verspoor, "Improving Primary Education in Developing Countries", New York: Oxford University Press, 1991.

UNESCO, "Compendium of Statistics and Indicators on the Situation of Women 1986", New York: Department of International Economic and Social Affairs, 1986.

UNICEF, "Equal Access of Women to Education Programmes in Nepal", Center for Educational Research, Innovation and Development, 1978.

World Bank, "Primary Education: A World Bank Policy Paper", Washington, DC, 1990.

Index